Studies in Public Choice

Founding Editor
Gordon Tullock

Volume 45

Series Editor
Randall G. Holcombe, Department of Economics, Florida State University, Tallahassee, USA

The Studies in Public Choice series is dedicated to publishing scholarship in the field of public choice and constitutional political economy. The series includes research monographs, edited volumes, textbooks, and reference works in all areas of public choice and constitutional political economy. Theoretical models of political processes, empirical studies, and case studies of political processes and events fall within the scope of the series, as do volumes analyzing the impacts of political decision-making on public policy. Public choice has been well-recognized as an interdisciplinary area of academic interest, but public choice analysis often has been absent in public policy studies. Applications of public choice to subfields such as macroeconomic policy, health policy, income security policy, and other public policy areas are welcome. The target audience of the series is broad, ranging from academics to policy practitioners.

Projects submitted to the series undergo evaluation from the series editor at the proposal and manuscript submission stages. Additional rounds of peer review may be required at the series editor's discretion.

Joshua Hall • Katherine Starr
Editors

Empirical Applications of the Median Voter Model

Editors
Joshua Hall
John Chambers College of Business and Economics
West Virginia University
Morgantown, WV, USA

Katherine Starr
John Chambers College of Business and Economics
West Virginia University
Morgantown, WV, USA

ISSN 0924-4700 ISSN 2731-5258 (electronic)
Studies in Public Choice
ISBN 978-3-031-87178-8 ISBN 978-3-031-87179-5 (eBook)
https://doi.org/10.1007/978-3-031-87179-5

© The Editor(s) (if applicable) and The Author(s), under exclusive license to Springer Nature Switzerland AG 2025

This work is subject to copyright. All rights are solely and exclusively licensed by the Publisher, whether the whole or part of the material is concerned, specifically the rights of translation, reprinting, reuse of illustrations, recitation, broadcasting, reproduction on microfilms or in any other physical way, and transmission or information storage and retrieval, electronic adaptation, computer software, or by similar or dissimilar methodology now known or hereafter developed.
The use of general descriptive names, registered names, trademarks, service marks, etc. in this publication does not imply, even in the absence of a specific statement, that such names are exempt from the relevant protective laws and regulations and therefore free for general use.
The publisher, the authors and the editors are safe to assume that the advice and information in this book are believed to be true and accurate at the date of publication. Neither the publisher nor the authors or the editors give a warranty, expressed or implied, with respect to the material contained herein or for any errors or omissions that may have been made. The publisher remains neutral with regard to jurisdictional claims in published maps and institutional affiliations.

This Springer imprint is published by the registered company Springer Nature Switzerland AG
The registered company address is: Gewerbestrasse 11, 6330 Cham, Switzerland

If disposing of this product, please recycle the paper.

Acknowledgments

We would like to thank the Center for Free Enterprise at West Virginia University for general research support.

Contents

1 **Introduction: Empirical Applications of the Median Voter Model** 1
Joshua Hall and Katherine Starr

2 **Do Voter Initiatives Affect the Interest Group Orientation of Government Spending?** 11
Gregory M. Randolph

3 **The Political Economy of Automobile Insurance: Elected vs. Appointed Regulators** 27
Ghanshyam Sharma

4 **Conflicting Objectives of Cartel Members: Analysis of Voting Behavior in the NCAA** 59
Kathleen A. Carroll, Dennis Coates, and Brad R. Humphreys

5 **Get Psyched! An Empirical Analysis of Colorado's Legalization of Psychedelic Drugs** 87
Adam Witham and Lillian Fitzgerald

6 **The Racial Political Economy of Bank Entry Restrictions** 105
James Dean

7 **The Political Economy of Public Pension Reform** 115
Dashle G. Kelley

8 **Determining If a State Will Adopt a Renewable Portfolio Standard** ... 137
Laura Lamontagne

9 **California Voters Reject the "Fair Pricing" for the Dialysis Act** 151
Tuyen Pham, Shishir Shakya, and Alexandre Scarcioffolo

Contributors

Kathleen A. Carroll University of Maryland Baltimore County, Baltimore, MD, USA

Dennis Coates University of Maryland Baltimore County, Baltimore, MD, USA

James Dean Western Carolina University, Cullowhee, NC, USA

Lillian Fitzgerald Salve Regina University, Newport, RI, USA

Joshua Hall John Chambers College of Business and Economics, West Virginia University, Morgantown, WV, USA

Brad R. Humphreys West Virginia University, Morgantown, WV, USA

Dashle G. Kelley Grand View University, Des Moines, IA, USA

Laura Lamontagne Framingham State University, Framingham, MA, USA

Tuyen Pham Ohio University, Athens, OH, USA

Gregory M. Randolph Southern New Hampshire University, Manchester, NH, USA

Alexandre Scarcioffolo Denison University, Granville, OH, USA

Shishir Shakya Appalachian State University, Boone, NC, USA

Ghanshyam Sharma RV University, Bangalore, India

Katherine Starr John Chambers College of Business and Economics, West Virginia University, Morgantown, WV, USA

Adam Witham Salve Regina University, Newport, RI, USA

Chapter 1
Introduction: Empirical Applications of the Median Voter Model

Joshua Hall and Katherine Starr

Abstract This book presents eight empirical papers utilizing the median voter model. Like the model of perfect competition, the median voter model is often the starting point for understanding public sector demand. As collective decision-making extends to even more areas of life, the median voter model is a useful starting point for understanding changes in government output. In addition, the median voter model provides the benchmark by which we evaluate the effect of different institutional regimes on outcomes. In this introduction, we provide a brief overview of the median voter model and discuss the papers in this book in the context of the larger literature.

1.1 Introduction

The median voter means many things to many scholars. Congleton (2004) and Holcombe (1989a) provide an excellent overview of the median voter model, its history, and different approaches to understanding the usefulness and saliency of the median voter model. The arguments of Congleton (2004) and Holcombe (1989a) deserve to be read on their own, and we encourage readers interested in learning more about median voter theory to read their work. We take as a starting point the view of Holcombe (1989a, p. 123) that "the median voter model is a good approximation of demand aggregation in the public sector for many issues." Or as (Congleton 2004, p. 712) notes, "... the median voter model appears to be quite robust as a model of public policy formation in areas where the median voter can credibly be thought to understand and care about public policy".

All of the chapters in our book implicitly or explicitly utilize the median voter model to better understand public policy. Our first two chapters use the median voter

J. Hall (✉) · K. Starr
John Chambers College of Business and Economics, West Virginia University, Morgantown, WV, USA
e-mail: joshua.hall@mail.wvu.edu; ks00066@mix.wvu.edu

as the benchmark to understand how different institutional structures affect public sector output. The remaining six chapters use the median voter model as a starting point of an analysis of public policy formation. While each of them differs in how they add onto the median voter model—for example, by allowing for special interest influence—they all employ the median voter model as their starting point.

1.2 Outcomes of Different Institutional Structures

The median voter model suggests that government decision-making will cater toward the preferences of the median voter. This conclusion, however, can be complicated by many factors, such as agenda control or the role of special interest groups. The first two chapters in this book use the median voter as a benchmark to explore how different institutional structures may move the political process away from the median voter.

In Chapter 2, Randolph (2025) uses the median voter model to examine whether the voter initiative process benefits the median voter or interest groups. The previous literature on voter initiative has found conflicting results. For instance, Matsusaka (2004) finds spending and taxes are lower in voter initiative states than nonvoter initiative states, suggesting the voter initiative process benefits the median voter. In contrast, Boehmke (2002) and Boehmke (2005) find more interest groups in voter initiative states, suggesting the voter initiative process benefits interest groups. Randolph uses an empirical median voter model to estimate whether state government spending is more of a private good or a public good in voter initiative states than nonvoter initiative states. Randolph finds voter initiative states have higher shares of government spending that is private, suggesting interest groups do not have less influence over government spending in voter initiative states than nonvoter initiative states.

In using a median voter model to estimate the degree of publicness of legislative activity or outcome, Randolph (2025) is following in a large literature. Bergstrom and Goodman (1973) use median voter characteristics to estimate demand for public goods provided by local government. Holcombe and Sobel (1995) examine state legislative activities and find legislation is primarily a private good, with the degree of publicness declining over time. Similarly, numerous other studies explore the public versus private nature of various legislative outcomes, such as fire protection (Brueckner 1981), education (King 2007), AIDS prevention (Mathers 2009), and foreign aid (Wiseman and Young 2015). Moreover, Portmann and Stadelmann (2017) highlight how the median voter model often fails to accurately predict legislative decisions, suggesting the need to incorporate interest groups when predicting legislative behavior.

In chapter 3, Sharma (2025) uses the median voter model as a benchmark to determine whether legislatures cater to the median voter regarding auto insurance. Specifically, Sharma examines the impact of the selection mechanism (elected vs.

appointed) of regulators on auto insurance policy outcomes. A defining contribution of this work is his collection of data by scraping the website of a major auto insurance provider to obtain specific data on auto insurance rates for the median voter across states. Sharma then uses this data to examine who elected regulators cater to. Existing literature and theory suggest elected regulators lead to pro-consumer outcomes, while appointed regulators lead to pro-industry outcomes (Crain and McCormick 1984; Besley and Coate 2003; Grace and Phillips 2008). In contrast, Sharma (2025) finds states with elected regulators have lower policy premiums, but only in more densely populated counties. Sharma also finds states with appointed regulators—and competition among firms—have higher payments on claims. Thus, elected regulators do not necessarily lead to pro-consumer outcomes, and appointed regulators do not guarantee pro-industry outcomes.

1.3 Policy Formation

The median voter model is typically used to better understand policy formation. Holcombe (1980) empirically tests the median voter model using school district data and finds education expenditures are consistent with the level of expenditures preferred by the median voter, suggesting the median voter model can appropriately explain decisions. Holcombe (1989b) emphasizes the usefulness of the median voter model in explaining decisions. The usefulness of the median voter model in empirical public choice literature is further discussed in Congleton (2004), and Turnbull and Mitias (1995) provide guidance on which variables to include in median voter models. Yandle (1983) discusses the role of special interest groups in regulatory decisions. Congleton and Bennett (1995) find the median voter models can substantially explain state road expenditures and special interests alone do not account for all variation in expenditures, further demonstrating the importance of the median voter model in explaining policy decisions. More recently, Hall and Pokharel (2017) also find the median voter model is able to explain state highway expenditures, as opposed to special interests.

Researchers typically use the median voter model to analyze determinants of voting behavior on a particular policy, either within the legislature or at the ballot box. The median voter model has been applied to a wide range of referenda, such as allowing the Ten Commandments to be displayed on government property (Wadsworth 2020), the Brexit vote (Matti and Zhou 2017), and tuition increases for public universities (Hall and Karadas 2018).

The median voter model has not only been applied to contemporary policy outcomes but has also been applied to better understand important policy changes in history. Some examples include women's suffrage (Wong et al. 2018), the Arbitration Act of 1888 (Gotkin 2018), lobotomy usage (March and Geloso 2020), and Rhode Island's vote to reject ratifying the constitution (Herndon and Murray 2019). Additionally, Hall et al. (2012) and Crowley (2012) incorporate the potential role of spatial dependence in constitutional and congressional decision-making. The remaining six chapters apply the median voter model to explain voting behavior on various policies. We discuss each of these chapters and other empirical median voter papers or books in each area.

1.3.1 Sports

The median voter model has been applied to various topics in sports economics. Given the wide-spread use of public financing for sports stadiums, it is not surprising that the median voter model has been used to analyze voter support for stadium subsidies (Coates and Humphreys 2006; Johnson and Hall 2019). In Chapter 4, Carroll et al. (2025) examine the voting behavior of members of the National Collegiate Athletic Association (NCAA). Their work builds on Fleisher et al. (1990) and Fleisher et al. (1992) who were the first to analyze voting behavior of members of the NCAA. They do so by examining heterogeneity in voting behavior between power (well-known, consistently successful) and non-power (lower profile) teams. Carroll et al. (2025) specifically study voting behavior of power and non-power teams for regulations on athletic recruitment and minimum academic quality standards. They find power and non-power teams are influenced differently by observable team and school characteristics, illustrating important dynamics of the NCAA cartel at the time.

1.3.2 Drug and Alcohol Policies

Another prominent area in which the median voter model has been applied is voting behavior on drug and alcohol policies. For instance, Hall and Schiefelbein (2011) explore the determinants of a state's legalization of medical marijuana. They find states with higher church attendance, republican voters, and economic freedom are less likely to pass medical marijuana laws. In Chapter 5, Witham and Fitzgerald (2025) study the role of county-level economic and demographic characteristics in explaining Colorado's 2022 legalization of psychedelic drugs. Notably, Frendreis and Tatalovich (2020) find those with college education are more likely to support legalization of marijuana. Witham and Fitzgerald (2025) extend this relationship to psychedelic drugs, finding a positive and statistically significant relationship between a county's population with a bachelor's degree and votes for legalization. Consistent with the findings of Hall and Schiefelbein (2011), they find counties with higher share of Democrats have a higher proportion of votes for legalization. Additionally, they find a statistically significant and negative relationship between a county's female population and votes for legalization, consistent with the findings of Galston and Dionne Jr (2013) that women are more likely to vote against drug freedom policies.

1.3.3 Monetary Policy

Given the importance of monetary policy, it is perhaps not surprising that public choice scholars have used the median voter model to understand the structure of the Federal Reserve, state-level banking policy, and monetary policy decisions. For example, Heckelman and Wood (2018) analyze the political factors determining the selection of Federal Reserve districts and banks. Eichler et al. (2018) examine voting behavior of Federal Open Market Committee (FOMC) members and find poor district bank health and members' career backgrounds influence FOMC votes on monetary policy. In contrast, Harris et al. (2011) study voting behavior of the Bank of England Monetary Policy Committee and find members' career backgrounds do not influence voting behavior. Additionally, Chappell Jr et al. (2004) explore voting behavior of the FOMC and find the chairman has a strong influence on policy decisions. Similarly, Smales and Apergis (2016) also find the chairman's influence is an important factor in monetary policy decisions of the FOMC.

Beyond the United States, Horvath et al. (2014) analyze the voting behavior of central bank boards in the Czech Republic, Hungary, Sweden, the United Kingdom, as well as the United States. They find macroeconomic uncertainty is not a strong predictor of dissent voting behavior in central bank boards.

A subtopic of monetary policy for which the median voter can also be applied is analyzing voting behavior on branching restrictions. Calomiris and Ramírez (2018) explore the political economy of branching restrictions and find bank clients, not just bankers, can influence policy adoptions. In Chapter 6, Dean (2025) focuses on the racial political economy of bank restrictions, specifically state-level branching restrictions in the 1920s. Since unit banks tend to favor the wealthy, black communities may prefer fewer branching restrictions. On the other hand, lighter branching restrictions can also benefit banks that are financially stronger, potentially harming black-owned banks. Dean (2025) tests those conflicting arguments and finds a state's share of black population is negatively associated with branching restrictions. Dean also finds that in restricted branching states, black residents experience lower banking quality and access.

1.3.4 Fiscal Policy

Some of the earliest empirical studies using the median voter model looked at the determinants of public spending (Bergstrom and Goodman 1973). A large variety of literature examines the determinants of numerous fiscal policies. For example, Duncan and Gerrish (2014) and Hall and Ross (2010) study whether a government's tax policies are influenced by neighboring areas' policies. Kenny and Winer (2006) provide a cross-country analysis of determinants of a country's tax system. Holcombe and Caudill (1985), Holcombe (1978), and Borcherding and Deacon (1972) analyze tax shares and/or government spending. Hoffer (2016) studies the role of special interest on tobacco taxation. Holcombe and Kenny (2007), Holcombe and Kenny (2008), and Barlow (1970) all study school financing and expenditures.

Regarding reforms on retirement benefits, Congleton and Shughart (1990) examine the influence of both the median voter and special interest groups in explaining the growth of social security. Congleton and Shughart (1990) find increases in retirement benefits are influenced by median voter factors and not special interest groups. In Chapter 7, Kelley (2025) expands upon this work by examining the role of the median voter and special interest groups in explaining public pension reforms. Furthermore, Kelley (2025) adds a third model, a benevolent government model, a new measure of the magnitude of public pension reform, and examines the role of information from media in explaining public pension reform. Kelley finds pension underfunding, a benevolent government factor, is one of the most influential factors for pension reform. Kelley also finds informational factors are significantly and positively related to pension reform.

1.3.5 *Energy and Environmental Policies*

Another popular application of the median voter model is to the determinants of energy and environmental policy adoption, such as carbon emissions taxes (Reed et al. 2019), diesel fuel excise tax rates (Decker and Wohar 2007), fracking restrictions (Walsh et al. 2015), and spending on environmental goods (Troyan and Hall 2019).

In chapter 8, Lamontagne (2025) examines the determinants of a state's renewable energy policy, specifically if a state adopts a Renewable Portfolio Standard (RPS). Lamontagne extends prior work of Huang et al. (2007) and Lyon and Yin (2010), who also examine determinants of RPS, by expanding the time period covered and adding electricity trade among states as an additional explanatory variable. Lamontagne's (2025) results are largely consistent with prior literature, finding that the percent of Democrats in a state's legislation has the biggest effect on a state adopting an RPS. Other factors that substantially increase the probability a state adopts an RPS include a restructured energy market and large amounts of electricity already being produced by renewable energy. Electricity trade is not a significant predictor.

1.3.6 *Healthcare*

Finally, the median voter can also be applied to healthcare policy. For example, Sobel (2014) studies determinants of a state not expanding Medicaid, and Costa (2018) analyzes the demand for health insurance in the early 1900s. Ghosh and Joshua (2015) analyze the forces explaining state-level taxes on soda, focusing on health-related determinants.

In Chapter 9, Pham et al. (2025) contribute to the literature, not only on healthcare policy adoption but also on the literature analyzing the role of advertising on voting behavior. Regarding the role of advertising on voting behavior, existing literature has conflicting results. For example, Lazarsfeld et al. (1944), Berelson et al. (1986), and Coppock et al. (2020) all find advertising only has a small effect on voting. In contrast, Ferraz and Finan (2008) find advertising does have a substantial impact on voting behavior. Pham et al. (2025) add to the literature on the impact of advertising on voting behavior by examining votes for Proposition 8, a California ballot initiative that would limit the profits of dialysis clinics and potentially improve the quality of care for patients. Their results suggest advertising by a dialysis clinic against the initiative did influence the behavior of voters. Higher obesity rates were also negatively associated with voting in favor of the initiative.

1.4 Conclusion

In our view, the usefulness of the median voter model has persisted for the reason outlined by Holcombe (1989a): It is a good approximation of demand aggregation. It therefore remains a useful starting point for those interested in understanding the outcomes of referenda, legislative votes, or changes in policies over space and over time. In addition, the median voter continues to be the benchmark for analyzing how the institutional structure and setting leads to outcomes not favored by the median voter.

References

Barlow R (1970) Efficiency aspects of local school finance. J Polit Econ 78(5):1028–1040
Berelson BR, Lazarsfeld PF, McPhee WN (1986) Voting: A Study of Opinion Formation in a Presidential Campaign. University of Chicago Press, Chicago
Bergstrom TC, Goodman RP (1973) Private demands for public goods. Am Econ Rev 63(3):280–296
Besley T, Coate S (2003) Elected versus appointed regulators: theory and evidence. J Eur Econ Assoc 1(5):1176–1206
Boehmke FJ (2002) The effect of direct democracy on the size and diversity of state interest group populations. J Polit 64(3):827–844
Boehmke FJ (2005) The Indirect Effect of Direct Legislation: How Institutions Shape Interest Group Systems. Ohio State University Press, Columbus
Borcherding TE, Deacon RT (1972) The demand for the services of non-federal governments. Am Econ Rev 62(5):891–901
Brueckner J (1981) Congested public goods: the case of fire protection. J Public Econ 15(1):45–58
Calomiris CW, Ramírez CD (2018) The political economy of bank entry restrictions: a theory of unit banking. In: Hall J, Witcher M (eds) Public Choice Analyses of American Economic History: Volume 2. Springer, New York, pp 99–119

Carroll KA, Coates D, Humphreys BR (2025) Conflicting objectives of cartel members: analysis of voting behavior in the NCAA. In: Hall JC, Starr K (eds) Empirical Applications of the Median Voter Model. Springer, New York, pp 51–74

Chappell Jr HW, McGregor RR, Vermilyea T (2004) Majority rule, consensus building, and the power of the chairman: Arthur Burns and the FOMC. J Money Credit Bank 36(3):407–422

Coates D, Humphreys BR (2006) Proximity benefits and voting on stadium and arena subsidies. J Urban Econ 59(2):285–299

Congleton RD (2004) The median voter model. In: Rowley CK, Schneider F (eds) The Encyclopedia of Public Choice. Springer, New York, pp 707–712

Congleton RD, Bennett RW (1995) On the political economy of state highway expenditures: some evidence of the relative performance of alternative public choice models. Public Choice 84(1–2):1–24

Congleton RD, Shughart IWF (1990) The growth of social security: electoral push or political pull? Econ Inq 28(1):109–132

Coppock A, Hill SJ, Vavreck L (2020) The small effects of political advertising are small regardless of context, message, sender, or receiver: evidence from 59 real-time randomized experiments. Sci Adv 6(36):eabc4046

Costa DL (2018) Demand for private and state-provided health insurance in the 1910s: evidence from California. In: Hall J, Witcher M (eds) Public Choice Analyses of American Economic History: Volume 1. Springer, New York, pp 155–179

Crain W, McCormick R (1984) In: Regulators as All-Interest Group, in Buchanan and Tollison (eds) The Theory of Public Choice-II. University of Michigan Press, Ann Arbor

Crowley GR (2012) Spatial dependence in constitutional constraints: the case of US states. Constitut Polit Econ 23(2):134–165

Dean J (2025) The racial political economy of bank entry restrictions. In: Hall JC, Starr K (eds) Empirical Applications of the Median Voter Model. Springer, New York, pp 93–102

Decker CS, Wohar ME (2007) Determinants of state diesel fuel excise tax rates: the political economy of fuel taxation in the United States. Ann Reg Sci 41(1):171–188

Duncan D, Gerrish E (2014) Personal income tax mimicry: evidence from international panel data. Int Tax Public Finance 21(1):119–152

Eichler S, Lähner T, Noth F (2018) Regional banking instability and FOMC voting. J Bank Finance 87:282–292

Ferraz C, Finan F (2008) Exposing corrupt politicians: the effects of Brazil's publicly released audits on electoral outcomes. Q J Econ 123(2):703–745

Fleisher AA, Goff BL, Tollison RD (1990) NCAA voting on academic requirements: public or private interest? In: Goff B, Tollison R (eds) Sportometrics. Texas A&M University Press, College Station

Fleisher AA, Goff BL, Tollison RD (1992) The National Collegiate Athletic Association: A Study In Cartel Behavior. The University of Chicago Press, Chicago

Frendreis J, Tatalovich R (2020) Postmaterialism and referenda voting to legalize marijuana. Int J Drug Policy 75:102595

Galston WA, Dionne Jr E (2013) The New Politics of Marijuana Legalization: Why Opinion is Changing. The Brookings Institution, Washington, DC

Ghosh S, Joshua C (2015) The political economy of soda taxation. Econ Bull 38(2):1045–1051

Gotkin J (2018) The political economy of the arbitration act of 1888. In: Hall J, Witcher M (eds) Public Choice Analyses of American Economic History: Volume 2. Springer, New York, pp 69–98

Grace MF, Phillips RD (2008) Regulator performance, regulatory environment and outcomes: an examination of insurance regulator career incentives on state insurance markets. J Bank Finance 32(1):116–133

Hall J, Pokharel SB (2017) Does the median voter or special interests determine state highway expenditures? Recent evidence. Atlantic Econ J 45(1):59–69

Hall JC, Karadas S (2018) Tuition increases Geaux away? Evidence from voting on Louisiana's Amendment 2. Appl Econ Lett 25(13):924–927

Hall JC, Ross JM (2010) Tiebout competition, yardstick competition, and tax instrument choice: evidence from Ohio school districts. Public Finance Rev 38(6):710–737

Hall JC, Schiefelbein J (2011) The political economy of medical marijuana laws. Atlantic Econ J 39(2):197–198

Hall JC, Nesbit T, Thorson R (2012) The determinants of congressional franking: Evidence from the 110th Congress. J Appl Econ Policy 31(1):25–34

Harris MN, Levine P, Spencer C (2011) A decade of dissent: explaining the dissent voting behavior of Bank of England MPC members. Public Choice 146:413–442

Heckelman JC, Wood JH (2018) Political selection of Federal Reserve Bank cities. In: Hall J, Witcher M (eds) Public Choice Analyses of American Economic History: Volume 1. Springer, New York, pp 135–153

Herndon RW, Murray JE (2019) An economic interpretation of Rhode Island's 1788 referendum on the constitution. In: Hall J, Witcher M (eds) Public Choice Analyses of American Economic History: Volume 3. Springer, New York, pp 117–135

Hoffer AJ (2016) Special-interest spillovers and tobacco taxation. Contemp Econ Policy 34(1):146–157

Holcombe RG (1978) Public choice and public spending. Natl Tax J 31(4):373–383

Holcombe RG (1980) An empirical test of the median voter model. Econ Inq 18(2):260–274

Holcombe RG (1989a) The median voter model in public choice theory. Public Choice 61(2):115–125

Holcombe RG (1989b) The median voter model in public choice theory. Public Choice 61(2):115–125

Holcombe RG, Caudill SB (1985) Tax shares and government spending in a median voter model. Public Choice 46:197–205

Holcombe RG, Kenny LW (2007) Evidence on voter preferences from unrestricted choice referendums. Public Choice 131:197–215

Holcombe RG, Kenny LW (2008) Does restricting choice in referenda enable governments to spend more? Public Choice 136:87–101

Holcombe R, Sobel R (1995) Empirical evidence on the publicness of state legislative activities. Public Choice 83(1):47–58

Horvath R, Rusnak M, Smidkova K, Zapal J (2014) The dissent voting behaviour of central bankers: what do we really know? Appl Econ 46(4):450–461

Huang MY, Alavalapati JRR, Carter D, Langholtz MH (2007) Is the choice of renewable portfolio standards random? Energy Policy 35(11):5571–5575

Johnson C, Hall J (2019) The public choice of public stadium financing: evidence from San Diego referenda. Economies 7(1):22

Kelley D (2025) The political economy of public pension reform. In: Hall JC, Starr K (eds) Empirical Applications of the Median Voter Model. Springer, New York, pp 103–122

Kenny LW, Winer SL (2006) Tax systems in the world: an empirical investigation into the importance of tax bases, administration costs, scale and political regime. Int Tax Public Finance 13(2–3):181–215

King K (2007) Do spillover benefits create a market inefficiency in K-12 public education. Cato J 27(1):447–458

Lamontagne L (2025) Determining if a state will adopt a renewable portfolio standard. In: Hall JC, Starr K (eds) Empirical Applications of the Median Voter Model. Springer, New York, pp 123–135

Lazarsfeld PF, Berelson B, Gaudet H (1944) The People's Choice. Duell, Sloan & Pearce, New York

Lyon TP, Yin H (2010) Why do states adopt renewable portfolio standards? Energy J 31(3):131–155

March RJ, Geloso V (2020) Gordon Tullock meets Phineas Gage: the political economy of lobotomies in the United States. Res Policy 49(1):103872

Mathers R (2009) The spillover benefits of AIDS prevention. J Public Finance Public Choice 27(1):45–61

Matsusaka JG (2004) For the Many or the Few: The Initiative, Public Policy, and American Democracy. University of Chicago Press, Chicago

Matti J, Zhou Y (2017) The political economy of Brexit: explaining the vote. Appl Econ Lett 24(16):1131–1134

Pham T, Shakya S, Scarcioffolo A (2025) California voters reject the fair pricing for dialysis act. In: Hall JC, Starr K (eds) Empirical Applications of the Median Voter Model. Springer, New York, pp 137–148

Portmann M, Stadelmann D (2017) Testing the median voter model and moving beyond its limits: do personal characteristics explain legislative shirking? Soc Sci Q 98(5):1264–1276

Randolph GM (2025) Do voter initiatives affect the interest group orientation of government spending? In: Hall JC, Starr K (eds) Empirical Applications of the Median Voter Model. Springer, New York, pp 11–23

Reed M, O'Reilly P, Hall J (2019) The economics and politics of carbon taxes and regulations: evidence from voting on Washington State's Initiative 732. Sustainability 11(13):3667

Sharma G (2025) The political economy of automobile insurance: elected vs appointed regulators. In: Hall JC, Starr K (eds) Empirical Applications of the Median Voter Model. Springer, New York, pp 25–50

Smales LA, Apergis N (2016) The influence of FOMC member characteristics on the monetary policy decision-making process. J Bank Finance 64:216–231

Sobel RS (2014) The elephant in the room: why some states are refusing to expand Medicaid. Appl Econ Lett 21(17):1226–1229

Troyan J, Hall J (2019) The political economy of abandoned mine land fund disbursements. Economies 7(1):3

Turnbull GK, Mitias PM (1995) Which median voter? Southern Econ J 62:183–191

Wadsworth AA (2020) Moore religious icons on state property? Alabamians pass bill to allow overlap of church and state. Appl Econ Lett 27:1430–1433

Walsh PJ, Bird S, Heintzelman MD (2015) Understanding local regulation of fracking: a spatial econometric approach. Agricult Res Econ Rev 44(2):138–163

Wiseman T, Young A (2015) Is foreign aid a pure public good for donor country citizens? Constitut Polit Econ 26:421–433

Witham A, Fitzgerald L (2025) Get psyched! an empirical analysis of Colorado's legalization of psychedelic drugs. In: Hall JC, Starr K (eds) Empirical Applications of the Median Voter Model. Springer, New York, pp 75–91

Wong HPC, Clark JR, Hall JC (2018) Immigrant ethnic composition and the adoption of women's suffrage in the United States. In: Hall J, Witcher M (eds) Public Choice Analyses of American Economic History: Volume 2. Springer, New York, pp 167–178

Yandle B (1983) Bootleggers and Baptists: the education of a regulatory economist. Regulation 7:12–16

Chapter 2
Do Voter Initiatives Affect the Interest Group Orientation of Government Spending?

Gregory M. Randolph

2.1 Introduction

The recently renewed interest in voter initiatives has rekindled a debate surrounding the primary beneficiaries of the voter initiative process. Matsusaka (2005a) outlines the primary arguments on both sides of the debate. Proponents of the voter initiative argue that the voter initiative generally shifts political power away from interest groups and toward the median voter. According to this theory, the voter initiative gives the public a method to check the activities of legislatures that would otherwise tend to cater to narrow special interest groups. The voter initiative also provides an indirect threat to any decisions made by the legislature. The legislators may make decisions that are more aligned with the views of the median voter in order to avoid a possible future voter initiative that might be less favorable to the legislature.

Opponents of the voter initiative, however, believe that well-organized and well-funded special interest groups may actually benefit from the voter initiative at the expense of the median voter. Supporters of this view often point to the massive amounts of money involved in the few voter initiatives that actually appear on the ballot each year. Over $400 million was spent on voter initiatives throughout the states in 1998 alone in comparison to $326 million that was spent by all parties in the 2000 presidential campaign, for example (Matsusaka, 2005a). In 2006, spending on California's Proposition 187 eclipsed $150 million. This hypothesis is based on several possible lines of reasoning. Special interest groups may be able to motivate their supporters to vote, while much of the general population does not vote. Individuals who do vote may lack the knowledge and information to vote in their own best interest, and instead vote in favor of a narrow special interest group

---

G. M. Randolph (✉)
Southern New Hampshire University, Manchester, NH, USA
e-mail: g.randolph@snhu.edu

due to misleading information. Finally, the behavior of legislators may be distorted by the threat of the voter initiative, leading to the passage of laws that harm the general public.

Another important contribution to the voter initiative literature involves the behavior of interest groups when the voter initiative process is available. The voter initiative affords another method by which interest groups can influence policy outcomes. In addition to targeting the votes of the legislature, interest groups may now also covet the direct support of voters. Interest group mobilization tends to increase when the voter initiative process is available as the increase in the expected benefits of mobilization outweighs the expected costs of mobilization (Boehmke, 2002, 2005). Additionally, due to the nature of the voter initiative process, broad-based citizen groups seem to benefit to a greater extent than narrow economic special interest groups. This results in an increase of broad-based citizen group representation relative to other economic special interest groups (Boehmke, 2002, 2005).

An interesting related issue is whether the voter initiative is able to change the composition of government spending. Total state government spending should be a quasi-public good because government spending is used for both public and private goods. It would be informative to see if the voter initiative can affect the degree to which government spending is public. A greater level of private spending would suggest that the spending was furthering the welfare of special interest groups. If less private spending were to be found in voter initiative states accounting for other variables, then the evidence would suggest that the voter initiative helps to restrict the influence of special interest groups. This chapter examines this issue using a median voter model to estimate the publicness of total state government spending.

2.2 Does the Voter Initiative Favor the Median Voter?

It is difficult to simply judge whether the voter initiative enhances the performance of government due to the subjective nature of the question. However, the general argument concerning the primary beneficiaries of the voter initiative has not changed since Nebraska became the first U.S. state to adopt the voter initiative process over a century ago. Does the voter initiative shift power into the hands of the voters or does it simply provide narrow special interest groups with more power to enact programs in their interests? Although well-organized and well-funded special interest groups probably exert more influence than voters on both the legislature and the voter initiative process (Lupia and Matsusaka, 2004), the true question involves the relative shift of power provided by the voter initiative process.

When solely examining the theory behind the voter initiative, the effect of the voter initiative on policy outcomes is ambiguous.[1] The voter initiative can help

---

[1] See Matsusaka (2004), Matsusaka (2005a,b) for a complete discussion of voter initiative theory.

overcome agency problems between legislators and constituents, logrolling, and issues involving information quality in some cases. However, the voter initiative can lead to outcomes that are unfavorable to the median voter under other conditions. Additionally, the issues of voter competence and the role of money in the voter initiative process have long been a point of discord between supporters and opponents of the voter initiative (Matsusaka, 2004, 2005a,b).

In order to evaluate the results of the voter initiative, it is important to note that the incentive structure for interest groups is altered when the voter initiative is available. Interest groups gain the advantage of the ability to directly propose a change in policy with the voter initiative, breaking the monopoly of the legislature. Additionally, the voter initiative can indirectly affect the decisions of legislators as they must consider the threat of a voter initiative when making policy decisions. Due to the possible increase in benefits to interest groups, the voter initiative tends to lead to an increase in the mobilization of interest groups in states that have the voter initiative process (Boehmke, 2002, 2005). Boehmke (2002, 2005) compares the number of interest groups in voter initiative states to non-initiative states. After controlling for other variables, he finds that the availability of the voter initiative tends to increase the quantity of interest groups.[2]

A key related issue involves the type of interest groups that receive the most benefit from the voter initiative process. Due to the nature of the voter initiative process, it seems reasonable that broad-based citizen groups would have an advantage over narrow economic special interest groups. For example, environmental activists may gain power relative to a concentrated manufacturing industry interest group. In order to successfully propose and possibly pass a voter initiative (or to achieve a policy change indirectly through the threat of a voter initiative), an interest group must be able to generate the support of the majority of the voters. This should be more feasible for citizen groups because they generally encompass a larger share of public support (Boehmke, 2005). This becomes especially important if the economic groups are more successful at achieving policy outcomes in the absence of the voter initiative process.[3] Boehmke (2002, 2005) finds that voter initiative states have a greater relative increase in citizen groups than economic groups. Furthermore, Gerber (1999) finds that citizen groups are more successful at achieving policy changes through the voter initiative process in comparison to narrow special interest groups.[4]

However the crucial determinant of the primary beneficiaries of the voter initiative rests in the policies that are the result of the voter initiative. Until recently, the policy outcomes of the voter initiative process were evaluated on a relatively

---

[2] Boehmke (2005) finds that states with the voter initiative tend to have about 28% more interest groups than non-initiative states.

[3] Many papers have noted the possible influence of special interest groups on the legislature, including Weingast et al. (1981), McCormick and Tollison (1981), and Holcombe (1983).

[4] Additionally, Donovan et al. (1998) find that a large majority of the voter initiatives proposed in California from 1986 to 1996 were supported by broad-based groups. Ernst (2001) found similar results on all state ballots from 1898 to 1995.

subjective basis through observations. Matsusaka (2004) provides a compelling empirical assessment of the voter initiative by examining state and local spending and taxation throughout the previous century. His study finds important differences between voter initiative states and non-initiative states. His primary result is that voter initiative states tend to have lower levels of spending and lower taxes. Furthermore, he finds that voter initiative states tend to rely more heavily on user fees as opposed to general taxes. Voter initiative states also tend to spend more at the local level and less at the state level. In order to evaluate the support for these differences in policies, Matsusaka (2004) examines results from opinion surveys. He finds that a large majority of the population favors all of these policy differences that can be found in voter initiative states. His study suggests that the voter initiative process does, in fact, benefit the median voter relative to interest groups.

Opinion surveys regarding term limits and social issues seem to further suggest that policies enacted in voter initiative states are favored by the median voter. A vast majority of voter initiative states have a type of legislative term limit, while most states that lack the voter initiative process do not.[5] Surveys suggest that voters strongly support the concept of term limits. This issue is especially important considering that term limits are one issue where legislators are placed directly at odds with the voters (Matsusaka, 2004). Gerber (1999) finds that voter initiative states are more likely to approve the death penalty and parental notification for abortions. Once again, opinion surveys suggest that these policies are preferred by the majority.

The initial empirical evaluations of the voter initiative imply that the voter initiative leads to the adoption of policies that are supported by the median voter. However critics remain skeptical and view the voter initiative simply as a method by which special interest groups can further their welfare at the expense of the median voter. In fact, Boehmke (2002, 2005) finds that a larger number of interest groups exist in states in which the voter initiative process is available. The question clearly merits further investigation as the debate over the primary beneficiary of the voter initiative continues.

2.3 The Model

This chapter uses an empirical median voter model to estimate the degree of publicness of total state government spending.[6] Turnbull and Mitias (1995) provide justification for the use of this empirical median voter model. The model has been used to examine the demand for public goods and services by Borcherding and Deacon (1972) and Gerber (1999). Deno and Mehay (1987) examine two different

---

[5] Only two out of states in which the voter initiative process is unavailable have some type of legislative term limits, while 22 out of 24 voter initiative states have some form of term limit.
[6] Bowen (1943) originally constructed the model. Downs (1957) and Black (1958) further contributed to the theory behind the model.

government forms and the related levels of expenditure with the model. A publicness measure of legislative activities is tested by Holcombe and Sobel (1995). Additional examples include Langbein's (2004) estimation of the publicness in public school music using the median voter model and King's (2007) examination of the spillover effects of public education. A higher degree of private spending suggests that interest groups exert a larger impact on spending. Special interest legislation is a private good as the benefits accrue to specific members of the population. The voter initiative would restrain the influence of interest groups if less private spending were to be found in states in which the voter initiative process is available.

When considering a pure public good, the optimal amount of the good provided in a state should not change when an additional individual relocates into the state. This is due to the fact that pure public goods are joint-in-consumption. An extra individual can share in the amount of the pure public good that is already provided in the state. For example, no further highway spending would be required for an additional individual to use an uncongested rural highway. On the other hand, the amount of spending for a pure private good will increase as additional individuals relocate to a state. Spending on a state farm subsidy program, for example, would expand if an additional farmer moved into the state. These goods are consumed by an individual and are not joint-in-consumption. When examining total state spending, it seems reasonable that a percentage of the spending will be private, while the rest will be public. The publicness estimate will measure the percentage of government spending that is public.

The estimation of publicness explains the summation of individual demand curves in the market for total government spending. Pure private goods are rival-in-consumption, and a horizontal summation of individual demand curves must be used in order to arrive at the social benefit curve. Total benefit is simply limited to the benefit that accrues to the individual consumer. Pure public goods are joint-in-consumption, and the corresponding individual demand curves are added vertically. Society shares the benefits provided by these goods. The degree to which the individual demand curves are added vertically or horizontally to create the social benefit curve is estimated by the publicness measure (King, 2007). A good with a greater degree of publicness would result in a larger angle with a more vertical summation of individual demand curves. A smaller angle would suggest a more horizontal summation of individual demand curves due to a good that is private to a larger degree. This relationship is displayed in Fig. 2.1.

Assuming that the total state government expenditure is determined in a political framework and voters have demands for the output generated by the expenditures, the median voter model can be used to estimate the demand for government-provided goods.[7] Voters will base their decision for the amount of desired government-provided goods on the comparison of the marginal benefits of government-provided goods with their marginal tax prices. The median voter will

---

[7] Inman (1978) and Holcombe (1980) provide empirical evidence suggesting that the median voter is decisive in majority rules politics.

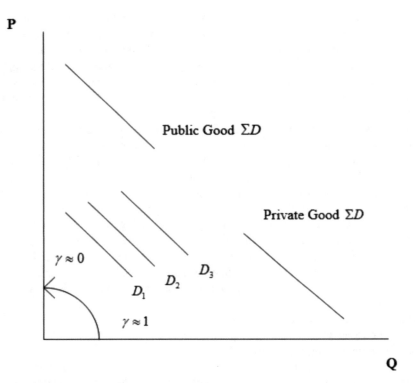

Fig. 2.1 Publicness measure. *Note*: Individual demand curves are represented by D_1, D_2, and D_3. γ is reflected in the angle that is the result of either a horizontal or vertical summation of the individual demands for a good. A measure of γ equal to zero implies a public good with a vertical demand summation. A measure of γ equal to one implies a private good with a horizontal demand summation. A value of γ between zero and one is the result of a quasi-public good

be decisive in the determination of the amount of government-provided goods. The utility function of the median voter is as follows:

$$U_i = U_i(X_i, s_i) \tag{2.1}$$

where s_i is the amount of government goods consumed by the median voter and X_i is the total amount of other goods consumed. The amount of government-provided goods consumed by the median voter (s_i) is related to the total amount of government-provided goods (S) through the function

$$s_i = N^{-\gamma} S \tag{2.2}$$

in which N represents the total state population.

A value of $\gamma = 0$ would imply that government-provided goods are pure public goods, while a value of $\gamma = 1$ would imply that government-provided goods are purely private. When $\gamma = 0$ and $s_i = S$, each individual consumes the total amount of the good available. When $\gamma = 1$ and $s_i = S/N$, each individual consumes an equal fraction of the good available. A quasi-public good would be the result of any value of γ between 0 and 1. A relatively more public good would be accompanied by a value of γ closer to zero.

In order to reveal the median voter's demand function for government-provided goods, Eq. 2.1 is maximized subject to the budget constraint

$$Y_i = P_X X_i + T_i P_S S \tag{2.3}$$

where Y_i is the median voter's disposable income, P_X is the price of other goods X, T_i is the tax share of the median voter, and P_s is the price per unit of government-provided goods.

The budget constraint can be rewritten after substituting from Eq. 2.2 as

$$Y_i = P_X X_i + T_i P_S s_i N^\gamma \tag{2.4}$$

which generates the demand equation through optimization

$$s_i = s_i(P_X, T_i, P_S, N, Y_i) \tag{2.5}$$

Following the previous literature, I assume that P_x and P_S are the same across states for empirical purposes. Including a vector A to represent differences in preferences across states and using a constant elasticity demand function, the following is obtained

$$s_i = A(T_i N^\gamma)^\alpha Y_i^\lambda \tag{2.6}$$

Substituting s_i from Eq. 2.2 into Eq. 2.6 represents the total demand for S as follows:

$$S = A T_i^\alpha N^{\gamma(1+\alpha)} Y_i^\lambda \tag{2.7}$$

or alternatively

$$S = A T_i^\alpha N^\delta Y_i^\lambda \tag{2.8}$$

where $\delta = \gamma(1+\alpha)$. The demand equation for the median voter in log form is

$$\ln S = \ln A + \alpha \ln T_i + \delta \ln N + \lambda \ln Y_i \tag{2.9}$$

The median voter's disposable income Y_i is calculated as

$$Y_i = Y_i^* + T_i G - F \tag{2.10}$$

where Y_i^* is gross state median income, G is the amount of federal grants to the median voter's state,[8] and F is the federal tax liability of the median voter.[9] $T_i G$ is used to represent the share of federal grants that accrue to the median voter. This requires the assumption that the voter's tax share is equivalent to the voter's share in the benefit of federal grants.[10] T_i is calculated by taking the effective average tax rate on sales and income taxes[11] and multiplying by the median income in order to obtain the median state sales and income tax liability, and then dividing the value by total state general sales and income tax revenue.[12]

Due to differences in voter preferences across states, other variables are included from parameter A in Eq. 2.9 to give us the following empirical specification:

$$\ln S = \beta_1 + \beta_2 \ln T_i + \beta_3 \ln N + \beta_4 \ln Y_i + \beta_5 \ln DEN \qquad (2.11)$$
$$+ \beta_6 \ln AGE + \beta_7 \ln NW + \beta_8 \ln LOCAL + \beta_9 CPOP + \epsilon$$

where DEN is state population density, AGE is median state age, NW is the state percentage of non-White population, $LOCAL$ is the state number of county and municipal governments per square mile, $CPOP$ is the state growth rate of population, and ϵ is the error term.[13]

In order to estimate the difference in the measure of publicness between voter initiative states and states in which the voter initiative process is unavailable, interaction terms are included to capture the marginal effect of the tax share and population variables in voter initiative states. Including I as a dummy variable for voter initiative states, the following empirical specification is obtained

$$\ln S = \beta_1 + \beta_2 \ln T_i + I * \beta_3 \ln T_i + \beta_4 \ln N + I * \beta_5 \ln N + \beta_6 \ln Y_i \qquad (2.12)$$
$$+ \beta_7 \ln DEN + \beta_8 \ln AGE + \beta_9 \ln NW$$
$$+ \beta_{10} ln LOCAL + \beta_{11} CPOP + \epsilon$$

---

[8] Borcherding and Deacon (1972) justify the inclusion of federal government grants in the calculation of state disposable income for voters.

[9] Federal tax liability was calculated by finding the relevant federal income tax for state median income. Inman (1978) provides evidence that median voter data is appropriate for voting models.

[10] Gramlich (1968) and Wilde (1968) indicate that federal grants are in theory a good substitute for state revenues.

[11] The effective average tax rate on sales and income tax was taken directly from Feenberg and Rosen (1986) for 1980. The 1990 and 2000 effective tax rates are obtained from the National Center for Higher Education Management Systems.

[12] The examples of papers employing the median voter model previously mentioned use this method to calculate disposable income.

[13] Wyoming is excluded as a voter initiative state due to its extremely large signature requirement (15%). Illinois is excluded because it is the only state that limits usage of the voter initiative to changes in the organization of the state's legislature. This follows the work of Matsusaka (2004). Including Wyoming or Illinois does not significantly alter the results.

The measure of publicness is calculated as

$$\gamma = \frac{\delta}{(1+\alpha)} \qquad (2.13)$$

The resulting value determines the percentage of private spending.[14] The measure of the publicness of government spending in non-initiative states (γ_N) is calculated from Eq. 2.12 as

$$\gamma_N = \frac{\beta_4}{(1+\beta_2)} \qquad (2.14)$$

where β_2 is the estimated elasticity of state government expenditure with respect to population and β_4 is the estimated elasticity of state government expenditure with respect to tax share. The measure of the publicness of government spending in voter initiative states (γ_I) is calculated from Eq. 2.12 as

$$\gamma_I = \frac{(\beta_4 + \beta_5)}{(1+\beta_2+\beta_3)} \qquad (2.15)$$

β_3 and β_5 add the marginal effect of the voter initiative to the elasticity of state government expenditure with respect to population and tax share, respectively. The calculated statistics γ_N and γ_I can be interpreted as the degree to which total state government spending is a private good. A value of 1 would suggest that total state spending is entirely private, while a value of 0 would suggest it to be purely public.

2.4 Empirical Results

The empirical specification 2.12 was estimated using state government expenditure data. The data sources are listed in Table 2.1. The first estimation was performed using cross-section data only for 1980. The second estimation uses pooled cross-section data from both 1990 and 2000. These were estimated separately due to

---

[14] As mentioned earlier, because they are joint-in-consumption, government spending on public goods will not directly change when population increases. Spending on private goods, however, will increase. However, one factor that complicates this distinction is that even with a pure public good, when another person shares in the consumption of the public good, it also results in a reduction in the tax share per person. Thus, for a pure public good, this increase in population would result in a reduction in the cost per person (the tax share) as individuals relocate to the state other things constant. As this price falls, the quantity demanded of government-provided goods will increase. Therefore, the optimal amount of total government spending will increase as individuals relocate to a state regardless of the relationship between total state spending and population. This is why the publicness parameter is a nonlinear combination of both the population and tax share elasticities.

Table 2.1 Data sources and variable definitions

Variable	Definition	Source
Total state government expenditures (S)	Total state expenditures in millions of dollars	A
Population (N)	State population in thousands	A
Income (Y_i^*)	Median state income in dollars	A
Population density (DEN)	State population per square mile	A
Median age (AGE)	State median age	B
% Non-White (NW)	State percentage of population non-White	A
# Local governments ($LOCAL$)	State number of municipal and county governments per square mile	A
Pop. growth rate ($CPOP$)	Percent change in population from previous year	A
Initiative (I)	= 1 for states with the voter initiative	E
Federal grants (F)	Federal grants to states in millions of dollars	A
	State general sales and income tax revenue in millions	A
	Average effective income and sales tax rate for 1980	C
	Average effective income and sales tax rate for 1990 (using estimates for 1992) and 2000	D

Notes: A = *Statistical Abstract of the United States*, various years, B = U.S. Census Bureau, *Census of Population*, various years, C = Feenberg and Rosen (1986), D = National Center for Higher Education Management Systems, E = Matsusaka (2004)

differences in the available measure of the effective average tax rate on sales and income for the different years.[15] A third estimation is performed using pooled cross-section data for the combination of all three years. The two pooled regressions include year fixed effects.[16]

The results of the regression are displayed in Table 2.2. Total state government spending was approximately 89% private for states without the voter initiative process and 97% private for initiative states in the 1980 regression. This indicates that spending was about 8% more interest group oriented in states in which the voter initiative process is available.

The pooled regression for 1990 and 2000 shows that total state government spending was about 91% private in states in which the voter initiative process is unavailable, while the spending in voter initiative states was almost purely private. Spending was again approximately 8% more private in voter initiative states. Finally, the pooled regression for 1980, 1990, and 2000 displays that about 89% of the total state government spending was private in states that lack the voter initiative process. Voter initiative state spending was around 99% private. Once again, a greater degree

---

[15] Feenberg and Rosen (1986) provided estimates of the effective average tax rate on sales and income for 1980. The National Center for Higher Education Management Systems estimates the effective average tax rate on sales and income tax for 1990 and 2000.

[16] Alaska is excluded in all years due to the significant revenues from severance taxes on oil and the lack of individual income and sales taxes. New Hampshire is excluded in 1980 and Nevada is excluded in 1990 due to missing data.

Table 2.2 Total state government expenditure estimates

Independent variable	1980		1990 and 2000 pooled		1980, 1990, and 2000 pooled	
Constant	−5.034	*	−11.253	***	−6.201	***
	(2.871)		(2.349)		(1.679)	
Tax share (T_i)	−0.183	***	−0.377	***	−0.276	***
	(0.055)		(0.050)		(0.034)	
Initiative*Tax share ($I * T_i$)	0.085	*	0.087	*	0.099	***
	(0.049)		(0.046)		(0.028)	
Population (N)	0.726	***	0.565	***	0.647	***
	(0.683)		(0.054)		(0.040)	
Initiative*Population ($I * N$)	0.149	*	0.142	*	0.166	***
	(0.087)		(0.078)		(0.048)	
Income (Y_i)	0.653	***	0.885	***	0.629	***
	(0.223)		(0.152)		(0.112)	
Population density (DEN)	0.034		−0.0169		0.013	***
	(0.034)		(0.021)		(0.017)	
Median age (AGE)	-0.547		0.536	*	0.036	
	(0.519)		(0.320)		(0.261)	
% Non-White (NW)	−0.009		0.017		0.008	
	−0.031		−0.026		−0.020	
# Local governments (sq. mile) ($LOCAL$)	−0.052		−0.027		−0.038	**
	(0.033)		(0.213)		(0.018)	
Pop. growth rate ($CPOP$)	−0.036		−0.042	*	−0.037	**
	(0.025)		(0.024)		(0.016)	
Year 1990 ($NINETY$)	–		−0.587	***	−0.682	***
			(0.052)		(0.042)	
Year 1980 ($EIGHTY$)	–		–		−0.819	***
					(0.014)	
(γ_N)—Non-initiative states	0.888		0.907		0.894	
(γ_I)—Initiative states	0.971		0.996		0.988	
Adjusted R-squared	0.976		0.984		0.983	
F-statistic	190.23		538.26		677.64	
Observations	48		97		145	

Note: Absolute standard errors in parentheses. *** = 1% level of significance, ** = 5% level of significance, and * = 10% level of significance

of private spending is found in the voter initiative states. Total state government spending is approximately 9% higher in voter initiative states.

The estimates for the publicness of total state government spending are calculated using nonlinear combinations of the parameters for tax share elasticity and population elasticity. Therefore a Monte Carlo simulation is performed to ensure that the calculated values are significantly different from one and that the

Table 2.3 Monte Carlo point estimates for γ_N and γ_I, estimated mean differences for $\gamma_N - \gamma_I$, and confidence intervals

Regression	Variable	Point estimate	Mean of empirical distribution	90% confidence interval	95% confidence interval
1980	γ_N	0.886**	0.888	0.813–0.955	0.797–0.970
	γ_I	0.970	0.971	0.891–1.045	0.873–1.060
	$\gamma_N - \gamma_I$	−0.084*	−0.082	−0.165 to −0.002	−0.185 to 0.013
1990 and 2000 Pooled	γ_N	0.908**	0.907	0.845–0.969	0.833–0.981
	γ_I	0.994	0.996	0.921–1.060	0.908–1.072
	$\gamma_N - \gamma_I$	−0.0857*	−0.0889	−0.1656 to −0.0006	−0.1816 to 0.0177
1980, 1990, and 2000 Pooled	γ_N	0.894**	0.894	0.850–0.937	0.843–0.947
	γ_I	0.988	0.988	0.943–1.032	0.933–1.040
	$\gamma_N - \gamma_I$	−0.094**	−0.094	−0.142 to −0.046	−0.150 to −0.037

Note: ** = 5% level of significance, and * = 10% level of significance

publicness estimates are significantly different between voter initiative states and states in which the voter initiative process is unavailable. A simulation of 3000 such calculations was generated using the parameter estimates in conjunction with the covariance matrix of the estimates. Table 2.3 shows the results from this Monte Carlo simulation. The point estimates differ slightly from the mean estimates from the empirical distribution because the covariance between the coefficient estimates makes the expected value of the ratio of the coefficient estimates different from the ratio of expected values of each individual coefficient.

The confidence intervals for the measure of publicness in states without the voter initiative process show that the value is significantly less than one. This signifies that the total state spending is not a pure private good. However, the confidence intervals for the voter initiative state measure of publicness show the value is not significantly different from one, suggesting that spending in voter initiative states may even be a pure private good. The confidence intervals for the mean difference show that the publicness of total state government spending is significantly different between voter initiative and non-initiative states at a 90% confidence level for both the 1980 regression and the 1980 and 2000 pooled regression. Total state government spending is significantly different at both the 90% and the 95% confidence levels for the 1980, 1990, and 2000 pooled regression.

These results indicate that total state government spending is private to a greater extent in voter initiative states in comparison to states in which the voter initiative process is unavailable. This suggests that interest groups may influence a larger percentage of state spending in states that have the voter initiative process. State government spending for legislation sponsored by interest groups will tend to be a private good, as the benefits of the legislation accrue in a rival fashion to the members of the group rather than in a non-rival fashion to society at large. However, this does not necessarily imply that *narrow* special interest groups have a larger influence in states with the voter initiative process. Voter initiative states have more broad-based citizen groups (Boehmke, 2002, 2005), and broad-based citizen groups are more effective at passing voter initiatives (Gerber, 1999).

Other interesting results are observable in Table 2.2. The tax share elasticity estimate, α or β_2 in the empirical model, is negative and very significant in all regressions. The estimate is less than one, suggesting that the demand for state government expenditures is price inelastic. The coefficient for the marginal effect of tax share elasticity in voter initiative states is positive and significant. This suggests that demand for state government spending is more price inelastic in voter initiative states. The estimate for population elasticity, δ or β_4 in the empirical model, is positive and significant for all regressions. The coefficient for the marginal effect of population elasticity for the voter initiative states is also positive and significant. The income elasticity estimate, λ or β_6 in the empirical model, is positive and significant in every regression. The coefficient suggests that the demand for state government spending is income inelastic as the value is less than one.

The remaining five independent variables were included because previous literature using the median voter demand model incorporated the variables. However, their exclusion does not significantly alter the results of the other estimates. Population density is negative in the 1990 and 2000 pooled estimate and positive otherwise. It is significant in the 1980, 1990, and 2000 pooled regression. Median age and the non-White percentage of the population are both negative in the 1980 cross-section regression and positive otherwise. They are insignificant with the exception of median age in the 1990 and 2000 pooled estimate. Negative estimates are found for the number of local governments per square mile and the population growth rate for all estimates. Both are significant in the 1980, 1990, and 2000 pooled regression, while the population growth estimate is significant in the 1990 and 2000 pooled estimate. The year variables are negative and significant in all cases.

2.5 Conclusion

Proponents of the voter initiative argue that political outcomes will be more aligned with the preferences of the median voter when the voter initiative is available. Opponents believe that the voter initiative is subject to abuse by special interest groups. This debate surrounding the primary beneficiaries of the voter initiative has been disputed for over a century. The results of this paper imply that the availability of the voter initiative does not reduce the interest group orientation of state government spending. Total state spending is found to be significantly more of a private good in states in which the voter initiative is available. Interest groups support policies that engage in spending that benefits the interest group. The resulting expenditures are a private good as the benefits accrue directly to the members of the group rather than to the population in general. At the very least, we can refute the idea that interest groups exert less influence over total state expenditures in states in which the voter initiative process is available.

This outcome seems to be consistent with the conclusion of (Boehmke, 2002, 2005). He finds that states with the voter initiative process have larger interest group populations. This occurs due to the increased benefit of interest group mobilization when the option of the voter initiative is available. The voter initiative affords interest groups the ability to directly propose changes in policy and to indirectly influence the legislature with the threat of a voter initiative. However we cannot assume that *narrow* special interest groups are the primary beneficiary of the voter initiative. Boehmke (2002, 2005) also finds that broad-based citizen groups increase in size relative to narrow special interest groups. This is primarily due to the nature of the voter initiative process. Broad-based support is necessary to successfully pass a voter initiative. Therefore, while the interest group orientation of state government spending might increase as a result of the presence of the voter initiative process in a state, it is unclear if it transfers power among different types of interest groups. Nonetheless, the evidence seems to clearly suggest that the voter initiative does not result in a reduction in the interest group orientation of government spending.

References

Black D (1958) The Theory of Committees and Elections. Cambridge University Press, Cambridge

Boehmke FJ (2002) The effect of direct democracy on the size and diversity of state interest group populations. J Polit 64(3):827–844

Boehmke FJ (2005) The Indirect Effect of Direct Legislation: How Institutions Shape Interest Group Systems. Ohio State University Press, Columbus

Borcherding TE, Deacon RT (1972) The demand for the services of non-federal governments. Am Econ Rev 62(5):891–901

Bowen HR (1943) The interpretation of voting in the allocation of economic resources. Q J Econ 58(1):27–48

Deno KT, Mehay SL (1987) Municipal management structure and fiscal performance: do city managers make a difference? Southern Econ J 53(3):627–642

Donovan T, Bowler S, McCuan D, Fernandez K, Tolbert CJ (1998) Contending players and strategies: opposition advantages in initiative campaigns. In: Bowler S, Donovan T, Tolbert C (eds) Citizens as Legislators: Direct Democracy in the United States. Ohio State University Press, Columbus, pp 80–108

Downs A (1957) An Economic Theory of Democracy. Harper and Row, New York

Ernst HR (2001) The historical role of narrow-minded interests. In: Sabato L, Larson BA, Ernst HR (eds) Dangerous Democracy? The Battle Over Ballot Initiatives in America. Rowman & Littlefield, Lanham, pp 1–25

Feenberg DR, Rosen HS (1986) State personal income and sales taxes, 1977–1983. In: Rosen H (ed) Studies in State and Local Public Finance. University of Chicago Press, Chicago

Gerber ER (1999) The Populist Paradox: Interest Group Influence and the Promise of Direct Legislation. Princeton University Press, Princeton

Gramlich EM (1968) Alternative federal policies for stimulating state and local expenditures: a comparison of their effects. Natl Tax J 21(2):119–129

Holcombe RG (1980) An empirical test of the median voter model. Econ Inq 18(2):260–274

Holcombe RG (1983) Public Finance and the Political Process. Southern Illinois University Press, Carbondale

Holcombe RG, Sobel RS (1995) Empirical evidence on the publicness of state legislative activities. Public Choice 83(1):47–58

Inman RP (1978) Testing political economy's 'as if' proposition: Is the median income voter really decisive? Public Choice 33(4):45–65
King KA (2007) Do spillover benefits create a market inefficiency in k-12 public education? Cato J 27(3):447–458
Langbein L (2004) Public school music: notes on the public provision of a quasi-private good. Public Choice 121(1):83–98
Lupia A, Matsusaka JG (2004) Direct democracy: new approaches to old questions. Ann Rev Polit Sci 7:463–482
Matsusaka JG (2004) For the Many or the Few: The Initiative, Public Policy, and American Democracy. University of Chicago Press, Chicago
Matsusaka JG (2005a) Direct democracy works. J Econ Perspect 19(2):185–206
Matsusaka JG (2005b) The eclipse of legislatures: direct democracy in the 21st century. Public Choice 124(1):157–177
McCormick RE, Tollison RD (1981) Politicians, Legislation and the Economy. Martinus Nijhoff, Boston
Turnbull GK, Mitias PM (1995) Which median voter? Southern Econ J 62(1):183–191
Weingast BR, Shepsle KA, Johnsen C (1981) The political economy of benefits and costs: a neoclassical approach to distributive politics. J Polit Econ 89(4):642–664
Wilde JA (1968) The expenditure effects of grant-in-aid programs. Natl Tax J 21(3):340–348

Chapter 3
The Political Economy of Automobile Insurance: Elected vs. Appointed Regulators

Ghanshyam Sharma

Abstract I examine how two selection systems for regulators, election and appointment, affect outcomes in a market with multiple firms. Traditional theory suggests that elected regulators are pro-consumers, while appointed regulators are pro-industry. I scrap the website of a major firm to collect individual-level data on premiums paid on auto insurance policies. I show that elected regulators choose policies salient for most consumers (lower premiums) in contrast to appointed regulators. This impact is larger and statistically significant in the counties where a majority of state's population is concentrated. This result is confirmed by the state-level data. I also show that competition between firms ensures that firms offer a better product (higher payments on claims filed by policyholders) in states with appointed commissioners. Hence, in a market with multiple firms, an elected regulator offers a bundle of lower prices and inferior product, while an appointed regulator does not ensure pro-industry outcomes.

3.1 Introduction

In 2013, about $1.8 trillion were paid in premiums on insurance policies sold across the United States (National Association of Insurance Commissioners 2016). This amounts to about 11.5% of the US GDP. The insurance industry employs about 2 million people which is about 1.3% of the US labor force.[1] A large fraction of the US population has exposure to different kinds of insurance like health, life, auto, etc.—underlying the importance of the sector. About 50 state regulators known as Insurance Commissioners[2] between themselves have significant influence over the sector which in monetary value is big enough to be the 11th largest economy in

---
[1] As per 2013 figures.
[2] Also known as Superintendents or Directors.

G. Sharma (✉)
RV University, Bangalore, India

the world. The role of these regulators is further strengthened by the McCarran-Ferguson Act (1945) which made the business of insurance exempt from most federal regulation, including federal antitrust laws.

Insurance commissioners are responsible for protecting the consumers, ensuring healthy competition within the industry and ensuring that insurance firms are financially solvent. However, Stigler (1971) and Peltzman (1976) have demonstrated that regulators often act in their own self-interest and respond to interest groups and electoral pressures. Crain and McCormick (1984) and Besley and Coate (2003) showed that the set of policies chosen by the regulators is motivated by their selection mechanism. Elected regulators have to face electoral pressures and hence tend to be pro-consumers. With appointed regulators, policy becomes bundled (and confused), and with other policy issues the appointing politicians oversee. However, as voters have only one vote and regulatory issues are not always salient for most voters, there are incentives on the part of the appointed regulator to respond to interest groups rather than voter interests.

In 11 states, the insurance commissioner is selected through a statewide simple majority election, while, in other states, the commissioner is appointed by the Governor (or the state government). A commissioner has a responsibility to regulate and monitor a large number of firms. According to National Association of Insurance Commissioners (NAIC), in 2013, Alaska had 733 domestic and licensed foreign insurers, while Wisconsin had about 2,102 domestic and foreign insurers. Hence, state insurance markets in the United States provide an excellent opportunity to extend the analysis of the theory of elected vs. appointed regulators to a market characterized by the presence of a large number of competing firms. Previous studies have looked at monopolistic environments like utilities (Crain and McCormick 1984; Besley and Coate 2003) or nonmarket environments like judiciary (Hanssen 1999; Lim 2013) and city treasurers (Whalley 2013; Makowsky and Sanders 2013).

I particularly focus on the automobile or "auto" insurance markets. Premiums on auto insurance is a salient issue for most voters when they vote to elect an insurance commissioner. This is because of the almost universal ownership of cars in the United States.[3] Automobile owners have to purchase auto insurance to cover the risks associated with owning and driving a car. Besides, most states (except New Hampshire) have made it mandatory for the drivers to purchase auto insurance for their vehicle. As a consequence, in 2014, the insurance industry was able to sell auto insurance policies worth $183 billion[4] in the United States.

To assess the impact of the selection mechanism of insurance commissioner on auto insurance premiums, I have collected individual-level data on premiums paid on several auto insurance policies by scrapping a website. This website is maintained by a major insurance firm to sell auto insurance. This website requires the individual buying a policy to provide a detailed information about himself (e.g., the driving history, age, and marital status), the car (e.g., model, make), and

---

[3] According to Federal Highway Administration, there were 84 registered vehicles per 100 people in the United States in 2013.

[4] Insurance Information Institute http://www.iii.org/table-archive/20967.

the preferred liability coverage. The website then uses this information to generate a monthly premium or a "quote" for the individual looking to purchase a policy. These "quotes" are competitive because various major and minor firms selling auto insurance maintain similar websites to attract a growing number of consumers who prefer to purchase products online. The company whose website I have scraped sells auto insurance in all the states in the United States. Hence, I was able to collect quotes on an insurance policy for a hypothetical driver living in 48 states and 3047 counties. I was not able to collect data for three states (Wyoming, Alaska, and Montana) because of the legal constraints imposed by the insurance company on data collection.

I have collected a variety of quotes. First, I have collected quotes for a policy purchased by an individual who represents the median voter. This is because traditional political models predict that politicians cater to the median voter. Second, I have collected quotes on the cheapest policy (providing minimum liability coverage) which an individual can purchase to insure his car. This is because for a driver looking to buy the cheapest available insurance cover, premiums on auto insurance will be a salient issue when electing an insurance commissioner. Hence, an elected commissioner is expected to pay attention to the pricing of policies providing minimum coverage. It is important to note that different states have different mandatory minimum liability coverage requirements for drivers purchasing policies in their state which affects premiums. Third, I have collected quotes on a policy which provides similar liability coverage to the individual as he moves across different states and counties. This is because the median voter would prefer a different insurance policy in different states and counties based on local conditions. Fourth, I have also collected quotes on a policy purchased by a rich voter. This allows us to observe whether the insurance commissioner caters only to the median voter.

I find evidence that the selection mechanism of an insurance commissioner has a causal impact on the determination of auto insurance premiums.[5] Auto insurance premium is a salient issue for most voters[6] when they vote to elect an insurance commissioner. Hence elected commissioners have an incentive to suppress the premiums on automobile insurance. This leads to lower auto insurance premiums in states with elected commissioners as opposed to states with appointed commissioners. However, this impact is substantially higher and statistically significant for drivers living in neighborhoods located in most populous counties (I call them urban counties[7]). In the sparsely populated or "rural" counties (other than the urban counties), this impact is smaller in magnitude and statistically insignificant. Even across rural counties, there is a negative bias on premiums in states with elected commissioners. These results are consistent for the quotes collected on a policy preferred by a median voter, a policy providing minimum coverage, a policy providing constant liability coverage, and the policy preferred by the rich voter.

---

[5] Discussions on causality later.

[6] This is because of the universal ownership of cars in the United States.

[7] Counties where 50% of a state's population is concentrated.

The differing impact of selection mechanism of an insurance commissioner in the urban and rural counties is explained by the fact that an insurance commissioner is elected through a simple majority rule in statewide elections. These elections are generally bipartisan in nature with two candidates in the fray affiliated to Republican and Democratic parties. The candidate who gets more than 50% of the votes polled across the state wins the election. About 50% of the US population (in my sample) is concentrated in 307 counties, while the other half of US population is disbursed in about 2700 counties. The marginal benefit of using resources to convince voters is potentially higher in counties where a significant proportion of the population lives. Alternatively, marginal cost of reaching out to a voter is substantially lower in counties where most of the population is located. Hence, it is in the interest of an insurance commissioner to pay greater attention to counties where a majority of state's population is concentrated.

The selection mechanism of an insurance commissioner is exogenous to changes in auto insurance premiums. This is because it is rare for a state to switch from an elected to appointed position or vice versa. I have collected historical information from state constitutions and state insurance offices to show that in the past 100 years, only three states have switched despite substantial variation in the economic and political environment.[8] I also provide a difference of means t-test (Table 3.6) to show that there is no substantial difference in the states having an elected commissioner and states having an appointed commissioner which might be driving the results. These states are also not different based on their political orientation.

The empirical results emerging from the individual-level data are confirmed by state-level aggregates based on data provided by the Auto Insurance Database Report.[9] Evidence suggests that auto insurance premium per registered vehicle is lower in states with elected commissioners. However, in states with appointed commissioners, higher premium per vehicle does not translate into additional profits for the industry (Grace and Phillips 2008) as suggested by the literature on elected vs. appointed regulators. The existing literature suggests that elected regulators are pro-industry. However, in a market with several competing firms where prices are regulated, individual firms can use the additional revenues to spend on unregulated domains (e.g., product quality, marketing) to attract consumers. Hence, competition would force the firms to operate on zero profits.

I provide evidence that in a competitive market where prices are regulated, firms compete with each other by altering the quality of the product. Payments made by the insurance firms on auto damage claims filed by the policyholders are substantially lower in states with elected commissioners. Since auto damage claims are not a salient issue for voters, this aspect of the insurance policy is left unregulated. As a matter of fact, no state has enacted a law to establish how insurance companies should process claims and payments. Hence, having an appointed regulator does not imply pro-industry outcomes.

---

[8] Please see Sect. 3.3 for a detailed discussion.

[9] Published by the National Association of Insurance Commissioners.

State-level data also makes it possible to examine the premiums written by the industry on the different components of an automobile insurance policy, namely liability coverage, collision coverage, and comprehensive coverage. Liability coverage is the coverage that protects other people and their properties if the policyholder causes an accident. Liability coverage is mandatory in most states. Collision coverage protects the car of the policyholder in case the policyholder hits other vehicles, people, or nonmoving objects like fences, poles, or kiosks. It covers the policyholder, regardless of who was at fault in an accident. Comprehensive coverage covers everything that collision coverage does not and is often referred to as "other than collision." It protects the policyholder from theft, fire, vandalism, and severe weather conditions.

In 2011, the value of the automobile insurance policies sold (or premiums written) in the United States was about $150 bn.[10] Liability coverage component of automobile policies alone amounted to about $ 100 bn accounting for about 65% of the total revenues. Premiums from collision coverage accounted for another 26%, while comprehensive coverage accounted for only 10% of the total revenues of the industry. Clearly, most people prefer to purchase liability coverage or collision coverage. I find evidence that premiums written on liability coverage per registered vehicle by the industry are substantially lower in states with elected commissioners. Similarly, I also find that premiums written on collision coverage per registered vehicle are lower in states with elected commissioners. However, I find no impact of the selection mechanism of the insurance commissioner on comprehensive coverage per registered vehicle. This is partly because few people prefer to buy comprehensive coverage. Hence, it ceases to be electorally salient for an elected commissioner to monitor.

State-level data also allows to examine the payments made by the industry on the claims made on liability coverage, collision coverage, and comprehensive coverage. Evidence suggests that payments per claim made by the auto insurance firms filed by the policyholders on liability coverage and collision coverage are significantly higher in states that have an appointed commissioner. Hence, this provides some evidence that firms wither away the extra revenue earned on account of higher premiums by making higher auto damage claims on liability and collision coverage components of the insurance policies to attract consumers. However, selection mechanism has no impact on payments made per claim on comprehensive coverage. This is consistent with the evidence of no impact of selection mechanism on premiums on comprehensive coverage.

Therefore, in this chapter, I extend the theory of elected vs. appointed regulators to a market characterized by the presence of several competing firms. I show that even though elected commissioners choose policies which are salient for most voters (lower premiums), competition between firms ensure that the outcomes are neither pro-consumer in states with elected commissioners nor pro-industry in states with appointed commissioners. In a state with an elected commissioner, consumers pay

---

[10] Auto Insurance Database Report 2011.

lower premiums but also get an inferior product (less payment per claim filed by a policyholder). The paper also provides critical evidence that elected commissioners do not make policies which are supportive of all consumers. As the evidence suggests, elected insurance commissioners tend to benefit the consumers in the urban counties and pay less attention to rural areas. Previous research has treated the elected regulator as pro-consumer and treated consumers as one homogeneous group (Besley and Coate 2003).

My paper contributes to the literature on the theory of elected vs. appointed regulators as well as insurance regulation. There have been various studies on the impact of elected vs. appointed regulators in nonmarket environments like judiciary (Lim 2013; Hanssen 1999), property assessors (Makowsky and Sanders 2013), treasurers (Whalley 2013), and public utility commissioners (Besley and Coate 2003; Crain and McCormick 1984). These studies have found a significant impact of selection system of regulators on their policy choices.

The relevant research in auto insurance regulation uses state-level aggregates[11] as proxies for auto insurance premiums paid by individuals. Grace and Phillips (2008) estimate that the unit price of insurance in regulated states when the commissioner is someone who desired higher elective office is approximately 8% higher than expected from a competitive state with similar characteristics. They argue that insurance commissioners use their position to gain favor with the industry presumably in return for political support during future campaigns. They also find that after taking into account the backgrounds and future employment choices of the regulators, states with rate regulation had higher average insurance prices.

The rest of this chapter is organized as follows. Section 3.2 provides background information on the role of state legislature and the regulatory powers of the insurance commissioners. Section 3.3 provides data sources and summary statistics. Section 3.4 gives econometric specification and deals with potential endogeneity issues with the selection of the Insurance Commissioner, and Sect. 3.5 provides a discussion on the results and the conclusion.

3.2 Background Information

Insurance sector has historically been and continues to be subject to state regulation with little intervention from the federal government.[12] McCarren-Fergusson Act

---

[11] For example, Grace and Phillips (2008) use "unit prices" as proxies for the prices faced by consumers. Unit prices for a given state are calculated as the total state premiums earned divided by the sum of total state direct losses and loss adjustment expenses plus policyholder dividend paid off private passenger auto insurance.

[12] In the Paul vs. Virginia case (1869) Supreme Court ruled that insurance would be subject to state regulation, beyond the legislative reach of US Congress. In 1944, the Supreme Court overturned the Paul vs. Virginia (1869) case. However, the Congress responded by enacting the McCarren-Fergusson Act in 1945 which exempted insurance industry from antitrust regulations and reinforced the authority of the states on insurance.

(1945) exempts insurance from antitrust federal regulation. This makes the state regulations and state regulators the key force driving policy outcomes.

State legislatures set broad policy for the regulation of insurance by enacting legislation providing regulatory framework under which insurance commissioners operate. They set tax rates and establish laws which grant regulatory authority to commissioners and oversee state insurance departments and approve regulatory budgets. Some of the key functions of the insurance commissioners as heads of insurance departments of their respective states are insurer licensing, producer licensing, product regulation, market conduct, financial regulation, and consumer services. There is interstate and inter-temporal heterogeneity in the regulatory powers and functions of an insurance commissioner. Some of these powers and functions are briefly discussed in the next subsection.

3.2.1 Functions and Regulatory Powers of an Insurance Commissioner

3.2.1.1 Product Regulation and Rate Regulation

All states equip an insurance commissioner with the power to regulate automobile insurance premiums. This regulatory power varies from state to state. This regulatory power is classified into five categories.

Prior Approval On one extreme is the prior approval system. In states with such a system, an insurance firm needs to take prior approval from the Office of Insurance Commissioner (OIC) before they can change the premiums they charge on different auto insurance policies. According to NAIC, there are 17 states which have a prior approval rate regulation system.

Flexible Rating In this system, insurance firms are allowed to change premiums charged on a policy within a range in a year and need approval from the OIC if they intend to change their premiums beyond those limits. According to NAIC, four states have a flexible rating system.

File and Use Some states have File and Use system, where an insurance firm needs to file an application with the OIC to change the premium it charges on a particular automobile insurance policy. After filing, the firm can switch to new premiums and continue to use them unless OIC objects to the change. According to NAIC, twenty states have file and use system.

Use and File Some states have Use and File system, where insurance firms can start using the new premiums they want to charge on a policy and inform the OIC of this change within a stipulated time period (usually three months). According to NAIC, nine states have a use and file system.

No File Only Wyoming has a no file system, where insurance firms are not required to seek any kind of approval from OIC to change premiums charged on a policy. However an insurance firm must supply evidence that necessitated a rate change if requested by the commissioner.

However, in a few states, there is a different rating system for different parts of the auto policy. The insurance firms have to seek approval to change the premium relating to only specific components of an insurance policy. Some of these parts could be bodily injury liability coverage, protection from uninsured motorists, changing rates in different geographical regions, etc. For example, in Connecticut, there is a Prior Approval rate regulation for body injury coverage and on coverage for protection from uninsured motorists. However, there is a File and Use system for property damage liability coverage for both comprehensive and collision parts of the policy. Besides, there is a flexible rating system of +/− 6% and not more than a 15% increase in any individual territory. Another state, New Hampshire, generally follows a File and Use system but switches to Prior Approval system for those sections of the market which the commissioner deems noncompetitive. For purposes of analysis in this chapter, I have used the generally prevalent rate regulation system as reported by NAIC.

In 2010, over 565,000 filings were processed through the System for Electronic Rate and Form Fillings across the country. National Association of Insurance Commissioners (NAIC) notes that even in states with competitive rating approach, regulators typically retain authority to disapprove rates if they think that competition is not working.[13] Commissioners can also make changes in the insurance policy provisions if they deem them to be unreasonable and unfair as per state law.

3.2.1.2 Insurer Licensing

State laws require insurers and insurance-related businesses to be licensed before selling their products. All US insurers are subject to regulation in their state of domicile and in the other states where they are licensed to sell insurance. Insurers who fail to comply with regulatory requirements are subject to license suspension or revocation, and states may exact fines for regulatory violations. In 2010, there were 342 companies that had their licenses suspended or revoked. Thus, commissioners can use insurer licensing as a potential threat to make companies fall in line.

3.2.1.3 Financial Regulation

State financial examiners investigate insurers' accounting methods, procedures, and financial statement presentation. These exams verify and validate what is presented

---

[13] Rates for life insurance and annuity products generally are not subject to regulatory approval, although Commissioners may seek to ensure that policy benefits are commensurate with the premiums charged.

in the insurers' annual statement to ascertain whether the insurer is in sound financial standing. When an examination of financial records shows the company to be financially impaired, the state insurance department takes control of the insurer.

3.2.1.4 Market Regulation

Traditional market conduct examinations review producer-licensing issues, complaints, types of products sold by insurers and producers, producer sales practices, compliance with filed rating plans, claims handling and other market-related aspects of an insurer's operation. When violations are found, the insurance department makes recommendations to improve the insurers operations and to bring the company into compliance with state law. In addition, an insurer or insurance producer may be subject to civil penalties or license suspension or revocation.

3.2.1.5 Producer Licensing

This refers to licensing of insurance agents and brokers. Currently 2 million individuals are licensed to provide insurance services in United States. Producers who fail to comply with regulatory requirements are subject to fines and license suspension or revocation. In 2010, roughly 5,000 agents and brokers had their licenses suspended or revoked. Fines exceeded $25 million and over $50 million was returned to rightful owners.

3.2.1.6 Insurance Premium Sales Tax Revenue

In about 35 states, Departments of Insurance are directly responsible for administration and collection of Insurance Premium Sales Tax Revenues. These tax rates are determined by the state legislatures and vary by lines of business. These taxes are levied on direct premiums written. These are in addition to other corporate taxes that the industry has to pay which are usually collected by other state/federal agencies.

3.2.2 Selection Mechanism of the Insurance Commissioner

In 11 states, insurance commissioners are selected through election (by ballot). These are California and Washington on the west; North Dakota and Montana in the north; Kansas and Oklahoma in the center; Louisiana and Mississippi in the south; Delaware, North Carolina, and Georgia in the east. In Virginia, the insurance commissioner is appointed by a three-member Virginia State Corporation

Commission[14] which in turn is elected by the General Assembly. In New Mexico, the commissioner is appointed by a five-member elected board.[15] In remaining states and Washington D.C, insurance commissioner is selected through appointment by Governor and serves at Governor's pleasure. Previous literature has treated Virginia and New Mexico as having an appointed commissioner, and I continue with this practice in this chapter.

3.2.2.1 Endogeneity Issues with Selection of Insurance Commissioners

This section explores whether the selection mechanism of insurance commissioners is endogenous. Does higher premiums on auto insurance premiums induce a switch from an appointed to elected position? I discuss historical occasions where states have made a switch from one selection method to another. I also discuss the political orientation of these states. In 2014, of the 11 insurance commissioners publicly elected to office, 6 were Republicans and 5 were Democrats. In the 37 states that authorized to appoint insurance commissioners, 17 were appointed by Democrats and 19 were appointed by Republicans.

I have collected information on when was the Office of Insurance Commissioner/Division of Insurance established in each state. Wherever possible, I have gathered information on who was regulating the insurance industry before such an office/division was established. I have also collected information on whether these states switched their selection mechanism (from elected to appointed position or vice versa). The source of this information is the state constitutions, state insurance offices, and general information available on the Internet.

In most of the states, by the turn of the twentieth century, an Office of Insurance Commissioner was in place. Since 1960, switches from an elected to appointed insurance commissioner have happened in only three states (Louisiana, California, and Florida). Louisiana and California switched in 1960 and 1989, respectively, from an appointed to an elected position. Florida has moved from an elected to appointed commissioner in 2003–04.

Other states have not switched since the regulatory body was established, despite changes in economic and political environment. Hunter et al (2013)[16] note that "Over the past quarter century, auto insurance expenditures in America have risen by more than 40%. Consumers in some states are paying 80%, 90%, and even 100% more for auto insurance than they paid in 1989." However we see none of the states switch from an appointed to elected position to force lower rates.

---

[14] The commission is responsible for handling all charters "of domestic corporations and all licenses of foreign corporations to do business" within the commonwealth.

[15] New Mexico Public Regulation Commission is responsible for regulation of public utilities, transportation companies, transmission and pipeline companies, insurance companies, and other public companies.

[16] What Works: A Review of Auto Insurance Rate Regulation in America and How Best Practices Save Billions of Dollars.

3 The Political Economy of Automobile Insurance: Elected vs. Appointed Regulators

Table 3.1 Statewide historical information on office of insurance commissioners

	Estd	Year	Note
Arizona	1969	None	Before 1969, Arizona State Commission regulated the industry
Arkansas	1917	None	
Colorado	1879	None	
Connecticut	1865	None	
Washington	1889	1907	Initially part of Secretary of State's office. Main function was to register insurers doing business
Rhode Island	1939	None	Department of Business Regulation established in 1939
Oregon	1887	None	
New Hampshire	1851	None	
Kansas	1871	1900	Switched from appointed to elected in year 1900
South Dakota	1897	None	
Wisconsin	1870	1881, 1911	Secretary of State was Commissioner of Insurance till 1878. Position of Commissioner was made elective in 1881 and made appointive again in 1911. It has since remained an appointive position
North Dakota	1889	None	
Pennsylvania	1873	None	
Texas	1876	None	
New Mexico	NA	None	
Maine	1870	None	
Alabama	1897	None	
Virginia	1906	None	
Florida	1848	1966, 2003	In 1966, Office switched to appointed position. In 2003, switched back to appointed
Maryland	1872	None	
North Carolina	1899	Yes	The first Commissioner of insurance was first elected by General Assembly and then appointed by Governor. In 1907, the position was made elected and has not changed since

Tables 3.1 and 3.2 provide information on when were these Office of Insurance Commissioners established, and in which year they switched (I have provided information on 35 states). The next section discusses the recent cases where states switched.

3.2.2.2 Cases Where Selection Mechanism was Changed

California switched from having an appointed insurance commissioner to having an elected insurance commissioner as a result of Proposition 103 in 1988. This proposition was narrowly passed with the approval of 51% of the voters. Proposition

Table 3.2 Statewide historical information on office of insurance commissioners Cont.

	Estd	Year	Note
Kentucky	1870	None	The department was established as a bureau in Auditor's office in 1870. In 1934, department was designated as a separate identity
Wyoming	1919	None	
Louisiana	1921	1960	State Constitution was amended in 1958 by Acts 1958, No. 125 to create Office of Insurance Commissioner. The position was appointed until 1960. It has been elected since then
Montana	1889	None	
Oklahoma	1907	None	
Missouri	1872	NA	
Vermont	1923	None	From 1923 to 1939, Office was part of the department of Insurance. In 1939, an independent Department of Banking and Finance was created. In 2012 the name was changed to Department of Finance Regulation
Nebraska	1913	None	First complete insurance code enacted in 1913, provided for an insurance board to administer the code. Before 1913, Territorial editor and later State Auditor issued certificates to insurance companies and exercise powers in an investigating and inspecting those companies. The duties of insurance board were given to the bureau of insurance in the Department of Trade and Commerce in 1919. In 1933, bureau became the Department of Insurance. In 1947, legislature passed laws that updated the 1913 code
New Jersey	At least 1895	None	
Indiana	1920	None	
New York	1859	None	
Illinois	1869	None	
Idaho	1901	None	
Massachusetts	1855	None	
California	1868	1988	Proposition 103 (discussed in detail in Section 5.1)

103 was a response to a 1984 law that required California drivers to have auto insurance. There were various provisions of Proposition 103. It required insurance companies to reduce rates for motor vehicle, fire and liability insurance by about 20% from 1987 levels and a rate freeze till 1989. It also required the commissioner to approve rate increases before they could take effect and change the Office of Insurance Commissioner from an appointed to an elected position. Characteristics such as the drivers' place of residence, age, sex, and marital status could no longer be used without the approval of the commissioner. These factors were frequently used by insurance companies prior to the passage of Proposition 103 (Jaffee and Russell 1998). Jaffee and Russell (1998) report a significant and positive relationship by county between higher insurance premiums and a yes vote on Proposition 103.

Florida switched from having an elected insurance commissioner to an appointed insurance commissioner with the passage of Florida Restructuring the State Cabinet Amendment approved on the ballot on November 3, 1998. Fifty-five percent of votes were polled in favor of the amendment. This amendment merged the cabinet offices of treasurer and comptroller into one chief financial officer; reduced cabinet membership to the chief financial officer, attorney general, agriculture commissioner; secretary of state and education commissioner eliminated from elected cabinet; changed the composition of State Board of Education comprising of the governor and the cabinet to a board appointed by the governor; this board would now appoint the education commissioner; defined the state board of administration, trustees of internal improvement trust fund, land acquisition trust fund. So in Florida, a switch from an elected to appointed position was not related to insurance premiums but a result of the restructuring of the state cabinet.

In the case of California, prices do seem to have motivated voters' decision to support Proposition 103. However, states with higher or similar average expenditures like New Jersey, Connecticut, or D.C. did not switch from an appointed to an elected position. In Florida, the switch was part of a large-scale restructuring of state cabinet. Other states have not switched despite dramatic changes in economic and political environments so I claim that selection mechanism of an insurance commissioner is exogenous.

3.3 Data and Summary Statistics

Urban and Rural Counties For electing an insurance commissioner, states follow a statewide simple majority electoral system. In such a system, a candidate who gets the most number of votes wins the election. The elections for the position of an insurance commissioner are generally bipartisan fights between Republican and Democratic candidates where the candidate with more than 50% of the votes polled is the winner. An elected commissioner will use his regulatory powers in those areas where most of the population is concentrated. About 50% of the US population is concentrated in 10% of its counties. Hence, for an insurance commissioner, such areas with heavy concentration of population become critical for electoral outcomes.

Therefore, I have classified counties as urban and rural based on the population living in those counties. I rank all the counties within a state in terms of population with the highest rank assigned to the county having the highest population. I then select those highest ranked counties which contain 50% of state's population. I label these counties as urban counties. All other counties are labeled as rural. Therefore, I classify 307 counties as urban and 2740 counties as rural. On an average, about 50% of a state's population is located in about 10% of its counties. For example, Georgia has 159 counties, but 50% of Georgia's population is concentrated in 16 counties. Hence, based on this classification, Georgia has 16 urban counties and 143 rural counties. Counties in most states are fairly similar in terms of their geographical areas.[17] Hence, most of the urban counties are also generally the most densely populated counties in a state.

Quotes on Auto Insurance Premiums Previous studies on automobile insurance regulation used unit price of insurance (the ratio of premium revenue received to losses incurred by the insurer) as a measure of average price paid by insureds per dollar of benefits (loss payments) received. These aggregates are usually at the state level. Data on insurance premiums is at the level of an individual. This is because insurance firms are vary of disclosing their pricing strategies to other insurance firms. However, recent innovations in website development have enabled insurance firms to reach out to potential consumers by providing them quotes on their desired insurance policy online. These websites allow consumers to get accurate quotes after taking into account various characteristics of the individual driver and car. Almost all major automobile insurance firms maintain such websites. A consumer can get a quote for his desired policy from various firms through their websites. Hence, firms use these websites to provide quotes which are competitively priced to attract consumers.

For this paper, I scrapped a website maintained by a major automobile insurance firm to get quotes on various insurance policies covering 48 counties and 3039 counties. Since it takes about 1.5 minutes to collect one quote, the entire data collection process took three months. I collected data from February 2015 to April 2015. In most states, automobile insurance premiums vary by zip codes. There are about 40,000 zip codes in the United States. It was not possible to collect quotes for all the zip codes because of time and legal constraints. Hence for this paper, I have selected one zip code from each county. This zip code has the highest resident population in comparison to other zip codes located in the county. All counties in 48 states are included in the study. For some counties, data on accident rates is not available. Hence, I have dropped these counties. The study does not include Montana, Wyoming, and Alaska because of legal constraints on data collection imposed by the firm whose website was being used to collect data.

The basic models in the existing literature suggest that politicians respond to the preferences of the median voter. Hence, for this paper, I collect quotes on automobile insurance policy preferred by a hypothetical individual who represents the median voter in the United States. The hypothetical individual is a 50-year-old male (primary driver) living with his wife who is 48 years old and registered as a secondary driver on the policy. Various sources in the industry suggest that for drivers in the age group of 25 years–65 years, age of the driver does not affect premiums. I also assume that the primary and the secondary drivers have a clean driving record[18] and they stay in a house they "own."[19]

---

[17] California is an exception.

[18] This is because drivers who care about premiums drive safely. Also it simplifies the data collection process.

[19] People who live in the houses they own are more likely to be the resident of the state and hence potential voters.

I also assume that the median voter drives Toyota Corolla. This is a realistic assumption because Toyota Corolla is a relatively inexpensive car (its market price is about $17,000). The cost of maintaining a Toyota Corolla is known to be lower in comparison to other cars. Besides, it can be used for a long period of time. Hence it is in the affordable range of the American middle class and ranks second among the best selling cars in the United States. I also assume that expected annual mileage of the car is about 12,000 miles which is in accordance with the average miles per vehicle reported by the Federal Highway Administration.[20] I have labeled this quote as the median voter quote. For a detailed questionnaire, please see the Appendix.

However, even a median voter in different parts of the country would choose a different insurance policy based on the local conditions. Hence, comparing quotes for a hypothetical individual as he moves to different counties would essentially mean comparing two different products. Hence, I have also collected quotes on a standard automobile insurance policy where I keep the liability coverage and deductibles constant. I have labeled these quotes as constant coverage quote. In other words, constant coverage quote represents the price of a similar product (automobile insurance policy) across different counties (for a hypothetical individual). In some states, state regulations make it mandatory for the firms to sell additional coverage like Personal Injury Protection, etc. However, attention has been paid to keep the coverage constant as much as possible.

Various drivers are only interested in getting the minimum liability coverage on their insurance policy to escape high automobile insurance premiums. For such drivers looking for cheapest possible options, auto insurance premiums are likely to be a salient issue when it comes to electing insurance commissioners. Hence, it is interesting to examine whether selection mechanism of an insurance commissioner will have an impact on the premiums on an auto insurance policy which offers minimum mandatory liability coverage as per state laws. This mandatory minimum coverage is different in different states. Hence, I have collected quotes on insurance policies which offer mandatory minimum coverage to the policyholder. I have labeled them as minimum quote.

It is also worth examining whether the elected insurance commissioner caters to the rich driver. This is because elected commissioners could theoretically subsidize median voters at the expense of the rich voters as suggested by Director's Law. Hence, I have collected quotes on auto insurance policies which are likely to be purchased by rich drivers. A rich driver is assumed to be a hypothetical individual (similar to the median voter) who drives Mercedes C Matic 350. This is an expensive car which sells for about $45,000 and is likely to be purchased by individuals with high disposable incomes. I have labeled these quotes as rich driver quotes.

Other Data Sources The data on zip code wise population is available from zipcodes.com. This website is also the source of data on average income per household,

---

[20] The exact estimate provided by the Federal Highway Administration is 11,244 average miles per vehicle in the year 2013.

proportion of Black people living in a zip code, and the elevation of the zip code from the sea level. Analysts working in auto insurance firms suggest that rich drivers tend to pay out of pocket in case of an accident. This helps them to avoid paying higher auto insurance premiums in the future. Poor people tend to have financial constraints and are more likely to file a claim in case of an accident. Hence, I have added average income per household in a zip code as a control. I also add proportion of Black people as a control because this measure is correlated with various neighborhood characteristics like crime rates, theft rates, etc. I have also added elevation from the sea level as a control because low-lying areas are prone to flooding risks and increase the premium on automobile insurance.

Motor vehicle crashes or accidents are an important factor that determines auto insurance premiums. Data on the number of motor vehicle accidents that happened in 2013 in a county is available from the National Highway Traffic Safety Administration (NHTSA). Most appropriate data should have been for the year 2014 which are not yet available. However, data from 2013 can be useful if we assume correlation in accidents in a city across years. This data is available at the level of the city. This is the most reliable data set on accident rates available for the purpose of this study. For 59 counties in the sample, the data on the number of accidents was not available, and hence those counties were dropped from the analysis. So, the study effectively covers 48 states and 2681 counties.

Information on whether the state has an elected or appointed insurance commissioner is available from National Association of Insurance Commissioners (NAIC). NAIC publishes an annual report, the Auto Insurance Database Report. This report also classifies the states in five categories depending on the status of rate regulation in the state. Auto Insurance Database Report also provides information on value of automobile insurance policies sold (or the auto insurance premiums written) providing liability coverage, collision coverage, and comprehensive coverage. The report provides information on the number of claims made on auto insurance policies written to provide liability coverage, collision coverage, and comprehensive coverage. The report also provides information on the payments made by the industry on the claims filed on policies providing liability coverage, collision coverage, and comprehensive coverage. This report also provides data on the number of motor vehicle accidents per 1000 registered vehicles and the number of motor vehicle thefts per 100,000 registered vehicles. This report also provides information on the number of registered vehicles in a state in a year. All this information is available at the state level for the years 2007–2011 for all states except Texas. Historical data on Gross Domestic Product (statewise) for all states and regions in the United States is available at Bureau of Economic Analysis (BEA).

Tables 3.3, 3.4, and 3.5 provide summary statistics for various variables used. Table 3.3 provides summary statistics of variables used in the analysis of premiums at the individual level. Table 3.4 provides summary statistics for variables used in examining the premium per vehicle at the state level. Table 3.5 provides summary statistics for variables used in the analysis of auto damage claims paid by the

Table 3.3 Summary statistics

Variable	Mean	Std. Dev.	Min	Max	N
Urban counties					
Quote (median voter)	159.9	84.4	47.5	652.5	307
Quote (rich voter)	163.2	84.3	53.2	516	307
Quote (min. coverage)	132.4	72.7	40.2	602.6	307
Quote (const. coverage)	155.9	79.3	49.7	467	307
Appointed	0.73	0.44	0	1	07
Prior approval	0.40	0.49	0	1	307
Flexible rating	0.12	0.33	0	1	307
Elevation	793.4	1064.2	0	6947	307
Income	54.7	17.2	24.5	123.0	307
No. of accidents	38.9	55.8	2	546	307
Prop. of Black population	0.16	0.19	0.01	0.9	307
Rural counties					
Quote (median voter)	135.2	54.6	47.8	412.9	2681
Quote (rich voter)	140.7	52.9	56.8	490	2681
Quote (min. coverage)	111.6	41.7	37.5	331.2	2681
Quote (const. coverage)	134.4	53.2	49.31	444	2681
Appointed	0.76	0.43	0	1	2681
Prior approval	0.34	0.47	0	1	2681
Flexible rating	0.09	0.29	0	1	2681
Elevation	1189.9	1400.3	0	10,190	2681
Income	43.9	12.6	13.9	126.9	2681
No. of accidents	6.6	8.9	0	121	2681
Prop. of Black population	0.10	0.16	0	0.97	2681

Appointed is a dummy variable which takes the value of 1 if the Insurance Commissioner is appointed, 0 otherwise; Prior approval is a dummy variable which takes the value of 1 if a state has a prior approval system of auto insurance regulation, 0 otherwise; Flex rating is a dummy variable which takes the value of 1 if a state has a Flexible Rating system of auto insurance regulation, 0 otherwise; Elevation is the geographical altitude of the zip code; Income (in thousands) is the average income of the households in the zip code; No. of accidents is the number of motor vehicle accidents as reported in a county in which the zip code is located; Proportion of Black population is the proportion of Black population living in the zip code

insurance industry. From Table 3.3, it is clear that premiums in urban counties are higher as compared to premiums in rural counties. Accidents and population density are much higher in urban counties than in rural counties. Also, standard deviation in premiums is much higher for urban counties as compared to rural counties providing some preliminary evidence of higher cross subsidization in urban counties as compared to rural counties in states with elected commissioners.

Table 3.6 provides a difference of means t-test for urban counties in states with elected commissioners vs. urban counties in states with appointed commissioners.

Table 3.4 Summary statistics: auto insurance premiums per registered vehicle written by the industry in a state

Variable	Mean	Std. Dev.	Min.	Max.	N
Liability premiums (LP) (in $ mn)	1,863	2,179	130	11,000	255
Collision premiums (CP) (in $ mn)	817	1,001	61	6,200	255
Comprehensive premiums (CmP) (in $mn)	394	397	42	2200	255
LP per vehicle	377	136	176	1149	255
CP per vehicle	164	53	78	479	255
CmP per vehicle	88	30	48	271	255
Appointed	0.78	0.41	0	1	255
Accident rate	0.16	0.07	0.06	0.43	255
Theft rate	0.3	0.3	0.01	0.3	255
Prior approval	0.31	0.46	0	1	255
Flex rating	0.078	0.269	0	1	255
GDP per capita ('000)	49.2	19.4	29.9	182.7	255
State GDP (in $ bn)	285	346	24	2,000	255
State population ('000)	5,978	6,665	534	37,000	255

Liability Premiums are the premiums (in $ mn) sold by the industry on the liability coverage component of auto insurance policies written in a state; Collision Premiums are the premiums (in $ mn) sold by the industry on the collision coverage component of auto insurance policies written in a state in a year; Comprehensive Coverage is the premiums (in $ mn) sold by the industry on the comprehensive coverage component of auto insurance policies written in a state; LP per vehicle is the liability premiums written by the insurance industry per registered vehicle in a state; CP per vehicle is the collision premiums written by the insurance industry per registered vehicle in a state; CmP per vehicle are the collision premiums written by the insurance industry per registered vehicle in a state; Appointed is a dummy variable which takes the value of 1 if the Insurance Commissioner is appointed, 0 otherwise; Accident rate is the number of motor vehicle accidents per 1000 registered vehicles; Theft rate is the number of motor vehicle thefts per 1000 registered vehicles; Prior approval is a dummy variable which takes the value of 1 if a state has a prior approval system, 0 otherwise; Flexible rating is a dummy variable which takes the value of 1 if a state has a prior approval system, 0 otherwise

The results show that premiums in urban counties are lower in states with an elected commissioner. These results are statistically significant. The no. of accidents and population (living in the zip code) for the urban counties are not significantly different in states with elected or appointed regulators. Urban counties in states with elected commissioners tend to have lower average income per household and are in low-lying areas (which increases the risks of flooding). Proportion of Black population too is significantly higher in urban counties located in states with elected commissioners. Low elevation levels and high proportion of Black population are associated with higher premiums. However, the table shows that the difference in premiums is significant even without controlling for these factors. Income levels are associated with lower premiums, but the difference in premiums is not large

Table 3.5 Summary statistics: payments by the industry on automobile damage claims (state aggregates)

Variable	Mean	Std. Dev.	Min.	Max.	N
Payments (liability)	1,261	1,483	5.4	7,722	250
Payments (collision)	505	579	41	3,750	250
Payments (comprehensive)	228	200	19	1,086	250
No. of claims (liability)	219	241	16	1,350	250
No. of claims (collision)	150	174	12	1,147	250
No. of claims (comprehensive)	227	199	23	907	250
Appointed	0.78	0.42	0	1	250
Prior approval	0.32	0.47	0	1	250
Flex rating	0.08	0.27	0	1	250

The payments are in $ mn; the No. of claims is in $ thousand; Payments (liability) are the aggregate payments by the insurance industry on claims related to liability coverage; Payments (Collision) are the aggregate payments by the insurance industry on claims related to collision coverage; Payments (Comprehensive) are the aggregate payments by the insurance industry on claims related to comprehensive coverage; No. of claims (Liability) is the number of claims made on liability coverage in a state in a year; No. of claims (Collision) is the number of claims made on collision coverage in a state in a year; No. of claims (Comprehensive) is the number of claims made on liability coverage in a state in a year; Appointed is a dummy variable which takes the value of 1 if the Insurance Commissioner is appointed, 0 otherwise; Prior approval is a dummy variable which takes the value of 1 if a state has a prior approval system, 0 otherwise; Flexible rating is a dummy variable which takes the value of 1 if a state has a prior approval system, 0 otherwise

Table 3.6 Difference of means (t-test): states with elected vs. appointed regulators

Variable	Mean	Difference	Std. Errors (Diff.)	N
Liability premiums per car	373	−9.3	39.51	51
Collision premiums per car	156	−2.27	13.30	51
Comprehensive premiums per car	85	8.6	7.17	51
Accident rate	0.14	0.04***	0.017	51
Theft rate	0.003	0.0004	0.0005	51
GDP per capita	51,780	−3,411	7,271	51
State GDP	302,202	78,412	1,25,455	51
State population	6,072,498	1,503,650	2,328,774	51

$*p < 0.1$, $**p < 0.05$, $***p < 0.01$

enough to warrant the difference in premiums. It should also be noted that income of an individual has already been taken into account while collecting the data. This is because a lot of variables which were used in collecting data (e.g., type of car owned, ownership of house, etc.) are correlated with the income of an individual.

3.4 Econometric Specification

The key variable of interest, the selection mechanism of the insurance commissioner, is a dummy variable. However, during the period of analysis, this variable does not change. Hence it is not possible to use a fixed effects model. I have presented my results on the individual-level data using a simple OLS estimation method. However, for the state-level analysis over a 5-year period, I have presented my results using a random effects model as well as a simple OLS model with errors being clustered at the state level. The random effects model allows for unobservable time-invariant heterogeneity at the state level which is uncorrelated with other variables.

3.4.1 Determinants of Auto Insurance Premiums: Individual-Level Data Set

I use OLS regression procedure to estimate the effect of mode of selection of an insurance commissioner on the monthly auto insurance premiums paid by the consumers. These results are clustered at the state level. The results are arrived at, after control for factors which might impact the car insurance premiums. Some of these are the accident rates in the county, elevation of the zip code from the sea level (low-lying areas pose increased risks to property because of flooding), average household incomes, and rate regulation. Various driver-specific and car-specific characteristics like driving history, age, income level, marital status, etc., have been controlled, while collecting data (Table 3.7).

I use the following econometric specification to estimate the determinants of quote for the policy preferred by the median voter, policy offering minimum

Table 3.7 Difference of means (t-test): Urban counties in states with elected vs. appointed regulators

Variable	Mean	Difference	Std. errors (Diff.)	N
Quote (median voter)	160.9	−20.5**	10.8	307
Quote (rich voter)	164.2	−23.5**	10.9	307
Quote (min. coverage)	133.3	−16.61*	9.4	307
Quote (const. coverage)	155.9	−14.8**	10.3	307
Income	54,650	−4,177**	2,214	307
No. of accidents	38.9	1.5	7.2	307
Elevation	793.4	−288.9*	137	307
Population	47,213	−822	2,260	307
Prop. of Black population	0.16	0.13***	0.02	307

$*p < 0.1$, $**p < 0.05$, $***p < 0.01$

coverage, policy offering constant coverage across states and counties, and the policies purchased by the rich voter.

$$Quote_i = \alpha_0 + \alpha_1 Appointed_i + \alpha_2 PriorApproval_i + \alpha_3 FlexibleRating_i + \quad (3.1)$$

$$\alpha_4 Elevation_i + \alpha_5 Income_i + \alpha_6 MotorVehicleAccidents_i +$$

$$\alpha_7 Prop.of BlackPopulation_i + y_i + \epsilon_i$$

where $Quote$ is the one-month car Insurance Premium in zip code i; $Appointed$ is a dummy variable which takes the value of 1 if the insurance commissioner is appointed in the state in which zip code i is located, 0 otherwise; $PriorApproval$ is the dummy variable which takes the value of 1 if the state has a prior approval rate regulation system, 0 otherwise; $FlexibleRating$ is the dummy variable which takes the value of 1 if the state has a flexible rating rate regulation system, 0 otherwise; $Elevation$ is the altitude of the zip code from the sea level measured in feet; $Income$ is the average income of the households living in zip code i; $MotorVehicleAccidents$ is the number of accidents in the county in which zip code i is located; $Prop.of BlackPopulation$ is the proportion of population who identify themselves as Black in zip code i; y represents year dummies; ϵ is the error term.

3.4.2 Determinants of Auto Insurance Premiums per Registered Vehicle: State-Level Data

To estimate the differential impact of appointed vs. elected regulators on the premiums paid per capita, I have used the random effects model and the following econometric specification. I have also shown results using the OLS specification. The results are clustered at the state level. The regression analysis uses data from the year 2007–2011.

$$Premium per vehicle_{st} = \alpha_0 + \alpha_1 Appointed_{st} + \alpha_2 PriorApproval_{st} \quad (3.2)$$

$$+ \alpha_3 FlexibleRating_{st} + \alpha_4 AccidentRate_{st}$$

$$+ \alpha_5 TheftRate_{st} + \alpha_6 GDPperCapita_{st}$$

$$+ \alpha_7 GDP_{st} + \alpha_8 Population_{st} + y_i + \epsilon_{st}$$

where $Premium per vehicle$ is the amount of auto insurance premiums per registered vehicle written in a state; $Appointed$ is the dummy variable which takes the value of 1 if the insurance commissioner is appointed in the state in which zip code i is located, 0 otherwise; $PriorApproval$ is the dummy variable which takes the value of 1 if the state has a prior approval rate regulation system, 0 otherwise; $FlexibleRating$ is the dummy variable which takes the value of 1 if the state has a flexible rating rate regulation system, 0 otherwise; $AccidentRate$ is the number of accidents per 1000 registered vehicles in the state as reported by Auto Insurance Database Report; $TheftRate$ is the number of motor vehicle thefts in the state per 100,000 registered vehicles; y is the year dummies; ϵ is the error term. s and t are state and year subscripts.

3.4.3 Determinants of Auto Damage Claims Paid Out on Auto Insurance Policies

To estimate the determinants of claims paid out on the auto insurance policies, I estimate the following equation using the random effects model. I also show the results using the OLS specification. The results are clustered at the state level and use data from the year 2007–2011.

$$Payments = \alpha_0 + \alpha_1(Premiums)_{st} + \alpha_2(No.of Claims)_{st} + \quad (3.3)$$
$$\alpha_3(Appointed) \times (No.of Claims)_{st} +$$
$$\alpha_4(Prior Approval) \times (No.of Claims)_{st} +$$
$$\alpha_5(Flexible Rating) \times (No.of Claims_{st} + \alpha_6(GDP)_{st} +$$
$$\alpha_7(Population)_{st} + y_i + \epsilon_{st}$$

where $Payments$ is the total amount of dollars paid out by the insurance industry on auto insurance policies; $Premiums$ have three components: Premiums on Liability Coverage, collision coverage, and comprehensive coverage, respectively. Liability Coverage Premiums are the premiums (in $) sold by the industry on the liability coverage component of auto insurance policies written in a state; Collision Coverage Premiums are the premiums (in $) sold by the industry on the collision coverage component of auto insurance policies written in a state in a year; Comprehensive Coverage Premium is the premium (in $) sold by the industry on the comprehensive coverage component of auto insurance policies written in a state; $No.of Claims$ is the number of claims filed by consumers on auto insurance policies in a state in a year; $Appointed$ is the dummy variable which takes the value of 1 if the insurance commissioner is appointed in the state in which zip code i is located, 0 otherwise; $Prior Approval$ is the dummy variable which takes the value of 1 if the state has a prior approval rate regulation system, 0 otherwise; $FlexibleRating$ is the dummy variable which takes the value of 1 if the state has a flexible rating rate regulation system, 0 otherwise; y represent year dummies; ϵ is the error term. s and t are state and year subscripts.

3.5 Results and Conclusion

In this chapter, I provide conclusive evidence that selection mechanism of an insurance commissioner has a causal impact on auto insurance premiums. Compared to states with an appointed commissioner, states with an elected commissioner have lower auto insurance premiums in the counties where a majority of state's population is concentrated. It is critical for an elected commissioner to offer policies which are salient for most voters as well as motivate the industry to make contributions for his electoral campaign. The insurance industry is the only major source of campaign contributions for an insurance commissioner. In a simple majority election, with generally two candidates in the electoral fray, the best strategy for an elected commissioner is to use the limited funds at his disposal to reach out to most voters. Therefore, a commissioner seems to pay greater attention to the counties where a majority of state's population is concentrated. On an average, in the United States, 50% population of a state is concentrated in only 10% of the counties. Hence, an elected commissioner prefers lower premiums in the most populous counties (as compared to appointed commissioners).

After controlling for a variety of factors like accident rates, theft rates, regulatory powers that a commissioner in a state has to control premiums, I find evidence that in the most populous counties (or urban counties), an elected commissioner leads to lower premiums. For urban counties, a median voter living in a state with an elected commissioner pays about $50 less on monthly automobile insurance premium as compared to a median voter living in a state with an appointed commissioner. A policy providing minimum coverage costs $42 less per month in an urban county in a state with an elected commissioner. Similarly, a policy providing similar coverage is about $42 less per month in a state with an elected commissioner. A comparison across urban counties reveals that even rich voters have to pay about $53 less per month on an auto insurance policy in a state with an elected commissioner.

The regulatory powers of insurance commissioners vary across states. For example, the power to regulate premiums on automobile insurance policies varies from state to state. Various states have a prior approval rate regulation system. In these states, an insurance firm needs to take prior approval from the Office of Insurance Commissioner (OIC) to change the premiums on auto insurance policies. Some states have a flexible rating system of rate regulation where an insurance firm does not need to get approval from OIC if they want to change premiums within a fixed range. On the other extreme is Wyoming where the commissioner has very limited power to regulate premiums.

Theoretically, the impact of rate regulation is ambiguous. The premiums charged by the firms on insurance policies in a state would be a function of the preferences of the regulator as well as his/her power to regulate premiums. Merely having greater regulatory powers does not imply that a regulator would favor lower premium levels. Before Proposition 103, the state insurance commissioner in California had the duty to ensure that insurance rates were neither excessive nor inadequate, but as noted by Sugarman (1990), this price control authority was rarely used. Besides, premiums would be sticky in an environment where it is costly to change premiums which might cause an upward bias on premiums. In this chapter, I find evidence which suggests that higher power to regulate premium is associated with higher premiums in urban counties. However, this association is generally not statistically significant. Empirically, rate regulation seems to have no impact on sparsely populated areas.

I have also added a variable to control for the elevation of the zip code from the sea level. This is because low-lying areas are prone to flooding and hence greater risks to properties in general. As expected, I found that there is a negative relationship between risks from flooding and auto insurance premiums. In the individual-level analysis, the no. of accidents seems to have no impact on auto insurance premiums. This is partly because while collecting the data, I have already taken into account the driving experiences of the policyholder. However, in the state-level analysis, higher accident rate does seem to be associated with higher premium per vehicle.

I have also added "proportion of black people" in a neighborhood to control for neighborhood characteristics. For example, a large number of Black people are poor, and hence they would be forced to live in neighborhoods which have higher crime rates and therefore drive down rental costs in that neighborhood. The results seem to suggest that neighborhoods with higher proportion of Black population are associated with higher premiums. Motor vehicle thefts too have a positive impact on auto insurance premiums. I was not able to use theft rates for the individual-level analysis because data on theft rates[21] is not available for a large number of counties. However, I do control for theft rates at the state level. I find evidence that higher theft rates are associated with higher premiums (Table 3.8).

State-level data throws some interesting observations. The bulk of revenue of the auto insurance industry comes from selling liability coverage which is mandatory in most states. About 65% of total premiums written by auto insurance industry comes from writing liability coverage, 23% comes from collision coverage, and only 12% comes from comprehensive coverage. I use both random effects model and simple ordinary least squares method to show that premium per vehicle is significantly lower in states with elected commissioners for liability and collision coverage. An elected commissioner makes a difference of about $90 per annum on premium per vehicle for liability coverage and $30 per annum on premium per vehicle for collision coverage (Table 3.9).

However, selection mechanism of the commissioner seems to have no impact on premium per vehicle for comprehensive coverage. This anomaly can be explained by the fact that most people do not care about comprehensive coverage. This is evident

---

[21] Available at Uniform Crime Reports, Federal Bureau of Investigation.

3 The Political Economy of Automobile Insurance: Elected vs. Appointed Regulators

Table 3.8 Monthly quote on automobile insurance policy (Urban)

	(1) Quote	(2) Quote	(3) Quote	(4) Quote
Appointed	53.48** (26.25)	42.75** (20.12)	42.39* (21.99)	53.46** (23.55)
Prior approval	30.58 (23.85)	17.66 (18.92)	29.28 (26.53)	26.52 (28.82)
Flexible rating	87.46* (47.26)	67.46* (44.67)	64.24* (34.01)	60.55* (30.30)
Elevation	−0.0125** (0.00607)	−0.0116** (0.00448)	−0.0107* (0.00621)	−0.0109* (0.00639)
Income	0.163 (0.349)	0.262 (0.276)	0.219 (0.467)	0.238 (0.518)
No. of accidents	0.166 (0.133)	0.154 (0.106)	0.0286 (0.102)	−0.00603 (0.0968)
Proportion of Black population	92.43* (54.86)	95.73** (46.24)	96.28 (76.81)	99.96 (87.33)
_cons	77.46* (41.85)	59.21* (33.39)	85.49** (41.63)	86.00* (45.51)
N	307	307	307	307
R^2	0.234	0.233	0.172	0.160

Column (1) refers to monthly quote on automobile insurance policy preferred by the Median Voter, (2) shows monthly quote providing Minimum Coverage as mandated by state laws, (3) shows Constant Liability Coverage, (4) shows policy bought by a Rich Voter. Appointed is a dummy variable which takes the value of 1 if the Insurance Commissioner is appointed, 0 otherwise; Prior approval is a dummy variable which takes the value of 1 if a state has a prior approval system of auto insurance regulation, 0 otherwise; Flexible rating is a dummy variable which takes the value of 1 if a state has a Flexible Rating system of auto insurance regulation, 0 otherwise; Elevation is the geographical altitude of the zip code; Income (in thousands) is the average income of the households in the zip code; No. of accidents is the number of motor vehicle accidents as reported in a county in which the zip code is located; Proportion of Black population is the proportion of Black population living in the zip code. Standard errors clustered at state level $*p < 0.1$, $**p < 0.05$, $***p < 0.01$

Table 3.9 Month quote on automobile insurance policy (Rural)

	(1) Quote	(2) Quote	(3) Quote	(4) Quote
Appointed	17.46 (16.83)	6.137 (10.17)	6.439 (16.84)	8.997 (16.38)
Prior approval	−5.876 (19.41)	−11.96 (15.08)	−0.986 (16.16)	−3.445 (17.14)
Flexible rating	53.74 (37.72)	22.05 (18.10)	69.40* (40.70)	64.45* (32.51)
Elevation	0.00442 (0.00279)	−0.00398* (0.00210)	−0.00327 (0.00312)	−0.00262 (0.00296)
Income	−0.234 (0.312)	−0.115 (0.243)	−0.558* (0.284)	−0.450 (0.284)
No. of accidents	0.904* (0.521)	0.729* (0.394)	0.455 (0.396)	0.390 (0.431)
Proportion of Black population	15.19 (32.28)	21.16 (20.21)	11.87 (33.10)	3.535 (33.49)
_cons	128.0*** (24.65)	112.4*** (19.61)	148.2*** (23.81)	149.9*** (24.15)
N	2681	2681	2681	2681
R^2	0.132	0.095	0.175	0.148

Column (1) refers to monthly quote on automobile insurance policy preferred by the Median Voter, (2) shows monthly quote providing Minimum Coverage as mandated by state laws, (3) shows Constant Liability Coverage, (4) shows policy bought by a Rich Voter. Appointed is a dummy variable which takes the value of 1 if the Insurance Commissioner is appointed, 0 otherwise; Prior approval is a dummy variable which takes the value of 1 if a state has a prior approval system of auto insurance regulation, 0 otherwise; Flexible rating is a dummy variable which takes the value of 1 if a state has a Flexible Rating system of auto insurance regulation, 0 otherwise; Elevation is the geographical altitude of the zip code; Income (in thousands) is the average income of the households in the zip code; No. of accidents is the number of motor vehicle accidents as reported in a county in which the zip code is located; Proportion of Black population is the proportion of Black population living in the zip code. Standard errors in parentheses; Standard errors clustered at state level *$p < 0.1$, **$p < 0.05$, ***$p < 0.01$

from the amount of revenue earned on account of comprehensive coverage by the industry. Hence, it is not electorally rewarding for the commissioner to regulate premiums on comprehensive coverage.

Standard economic theory apprises us that in competitive markets, firms operate on zero profits. However, using state-level data, Grace and Phillips (2008) found no evidence of impact of selection mechanism of an insurance commissioner on unit price which is an indicator of profits of the industry. I have provided evidence to explain this result. In states with appointed commissioners, firms wither away the extra revenues on account of higher premiums by making higher payments per claim. Since firms charge a higher premium per vehicle on liability and collision coverage in states with appointed commissioners, firms make higher payments on claims on liability coverage in such states. Since premium per vehicle on comprehensive does not seem to be related to the selection mechanism of the commissioner, payments on claims too are not associated to the selection mechanism of the commissioner. These results are robust to both random effects and clustering at the state level (Table 3.10).

Firms tend to make higher payments per claim in states with a higher degree of rate regulation. This result is in consonance with higher premiums associated with greater regulation. Hence, competition compels firms to offer a better product when they are able to charge higher premiums.

Hence, I provide evidence that firms respond to regulatory interventions by altering the quality of the product. Firms can alter the quality through payments because there are no laws in any state which gives the commissioner the power to regulate payments made by firms on claims filed by policyholders. Firms could also be spending extra revenues in other ways (e.g., marketing) to aggressively attract customers. However, data to test such claims is not available. Hence, I provide evidence that in a market with multiple competing firms, elected regulators offer pro-consumer policies to a select group of consumers. However, lower premiums result in a low-quality product. On the other hand, firms are able to charge higher premiums on auto insurance policies. But competition forces firms to use the extra revenue to offer a better quality product (e.g., higher payments per claim) (Table 3.11).

Interventions by the regulator may also have welfare effects for individuals. High-risk drivers would be worse off living in states with an elected commissioner, whereas low-risk drivers would be worse off living in states with an appointed commissioner. To conclude, elected regulators do choose policies which are salient for consumers. However, having an elected regulator does not lead to pro-consumer market outcomes. Similarly, having an appointed regulator does not lead to pro-industry outcomes.

Table 3.10 State-level results: Determinants of premiums written by the industry per registered vehicle

	(1) Liability RE	(2) Liability OLS	(3) Collision RE	(4) Collision OLS	(5) Comp. RE	(6) Comp. OLS
Appointed	92.47* (49.77)	77.35 (47.36)	32.22** (13.09)	25.97** (10.76)	2.7 (8.9)	3.29 (8.2)
Prior approval	70.51 (44.46)	75.9* (41.98)	11.23 (12.54)	13.23 (10.46)	−6.7 (7.0)	−6.9 (6.3)
Flexible rating	13.47 (30.75)	29.21 (25.44)	−14.51 (16.44)	−7.99 (11.98)	−3.2 (13.0)	−3.08 (12.4)
Accident rate	893.9 (564.2)	276.7 (333)	394.6* (221.2)	153.7 (125.4)	238* (136)	237*** (71)
Theft rate	12,427** (5,862)	23,892** (8,822)	7,794*** (2547)	11,050*** (2738)	4,499*** (815)	4,657*** (1327)
GDP per capita (in $ '000)	1.52** (0.7)	−1.5 (1.4)	0.6*** (0.2)	−0.39 (0.4)	0.3*** (0.1)	0.1 (0.2)
State GDP (in $ bn)	0.23 (0.26)	0.58 (0.40)	0.09 (0.06)	0.2** (0.08)	0.04 (0.02)	0.08** (0.03)
State population (in '000)	−0.006 (0.01)	−0.027 (0.02)	−0.003 (0.003)	−0.009** (0.004)	−0.002 (0.001)	−0.01** (0.002)
_Cons	−2.1 (132.2)	254.2*** (90.40)	8.14 (48.34)	95.26*** (26.87)	21.65 (29.98)	35.00** (16.08)
Year dummies	N	Y	N	Y	N	Y
N	255	255	255	255	255	255
R^2	0.29	0.367	0.49	0.55	0.55	0.560

Columns (1) and (2) show determinants of liability premiums; (3) and (4) show determinants of comprehensive premiums. The dependent variable is the premiums written per registered vehicle; Appointed is a dummy variable which takes the value of 1 if the Insurance Commissioner is appointed, 0 otherwise; Accident rate is the number of motor vehicle accidents per 1000 registered vehicles; Theft rate is the number of motor vehicle thefts per 1000 registered vehicles; Prior approval is a dummy variable which takes the value of 1 if a state has a prior approval system, 0 otherwise; Flexible rating is a dummy variable which takes the value of 1 if a state has a prior approval system, 0 otherwise Standard errors in parentheses; Standard errors clustered at state level *$p < 0.1$, **$p < 0.05$, ***$p < 0.01$. For specifications with Random Effects, R^2 is the Overall R^2

Table 3.11 State-level results: payments on coverage claims

	(1) Liability RE	(2) Liability OLS	(3) Collision RE	(4) Collision OLS	(5) Comp RE	(6) Comp OLS
Premiums	0.80*** (0.11)	0.80*** (0.11)	0.21*** (0.05)	0.35*** (0.06)	0.40*** (0.15)	0.58*** (0.11)
No. of claims (N)	111 (418)	127 (434)	1869*** (306)	865** (356)	419** (168)	164** (133)
Appointed*N	370* (203)	370* (205)	344*** (47)	305*** (52)	−80.8 (83)	−10.7 (69)
Prior approval*N	283 (241)	281 (242)	334*** (69)	156* (93)	−88.9 (77.6)	−88.9 (65.5)
Flexible rating*N	−274 (195)	−275 (196)	266*** (82)	154*** (76)	80.7 (65)	65.4 (43)
State GDP	−2331*** (494)	−2320*** (498)	204* (118)	94 (101)	136 (144)	86 (140)
State population	61 (37)	60 (37)	−11.6 (9.3)	4.86 (7.4)	−6.1 (9.6)	−7.27 (8.83)
_cons	266 (207)	266 (207)	163** (66)	89 (60)	61 (77)	68 (67)
Year dummies	N	Y	N	Y	N	Y
N	250	250	250	250	250	250
R^2	0.953	0.953	0.9962	0.9969	0.89	0.895

Columns (1) and (2) refer to payments on liability coverage claims; (3) and (4) refer to collision; (5) and (6) refer to comprehensive. The dependent variable is the aggregate payments made by the insurance industry on the respective coverage type on auto insurance in a state in a year; Premiums is the premiums sold by the industry on auto insurance policies for the respective coverage type written in a state in a year; No. of claims is the number of claims for the respective coverage type made in a state in a year; Appointed is a dummy variable which takes the value of 1 if the Insurance Commissioner is appointed, 0 otherwise; Prior approval is a dummy variable which takes the value of 1 if a state has a prior approval system, 0 otherwise; Flexible rating is a dummy variable which takes the value of 1 if a state has a prior approval system, 0 otherwise Standard errors in parentheses; Standard errors clustered at state level *$p < 0.1$, **$p < 0.05$, ***$p < 0.01$. For specifications with Random Effects, R^2 is the Overall R^2

Appendix

This annexure provides detailed web form that was filled to generate quotes for auto insurance premiums. There was a slight variation across states on the questions asked to generate a quote.

Car Information
- **Year** 2014
- **Make** Toyota \Mercedes
- **Model** Corolla \MATIC 350
- **Primary Use** Commuting to Work/School
- **What is your estimated annual mileage?** 10,000–15,000
- **What is the ownership status?** Financed (for Toyota) \Paid (for Mercedes)
- **Did you purchase the car when it was new?** Yes
- **How many years have you owned \leased this vehicle?** Less than one year
- **Do you want to add another vehicle?** No

Driver Information
- **Name** ....
- **Gender** Male
- **Date of Birth** 03-05-1964
- **When you got your first driver's license, how old were you?** 21
- **Email** fakeexmail@ex.com
- **Do you currently have car insurance** No
- **How long had it been since you had your car insurance** 30 days or less
- **Has this driver had any major violations in the last 5 years?** No
- **Accidents or minor violations in the last 3 years** No
- **Other auto damage claims in the last 3 years** No
- **Street Address** 385 Fake Circle 3
- **City** (the city in which the zip code is located)
- **State** (the state in which the zip code is located)
- **Primary Residence** Own Home
- **Education** Bachelor's Degree

Spouse Information
- **Name**.........
- **Would you like to include your spouse on this policy?** Yes, additional driver on policy
- **Gender** Female
- **Date of Birth** 04-02-1966
- **When you got your first driver's license, how old were you?**21
- **Has this driver had any major violations in the last 5 years?** No
- **Accidents or minor violations in the last 3 years** No
- **Other auto damage claims in the last 3 years** No

Car Insurance History

- **What was your most recent insurance company** Allstate Insurance
- **When did your policy end** Less than one month
- **When would you like your new policy to start** In a week
- **What were the body injury limits on your policy** $50,000–$100,000
- **What were the deductibles on your policy** $100

References

Besley T, Coate S (2003) Elected versus appointed regulators: theory and evidence. J Eur Econ Assoc 1(5):1176–1206

Crain W, McCormick R (1984) In Regulators as All-Interest Group, in Buchanan and Tollison (eds) The Theory of Public Choice-II. University of Michigan Press, Ann Arbor

Grace MF, Phillips RD (2008) Regulator performance, regulatory environment and outcomes: an examination of insurance regulator career incentives on state insurance markets. J Banking Finance 32(1):116–133

Hanssen FA (1999) The effect of judicial institutions on uncertainty and the rate of litigation: the election versus appointment of state judges. J Legal Stud 28(1):205–232

Hunter JR, Feltner T, Heller D (2013) What Works: A Review of Auto Insurance Rate Regulation in America and How Best Practices Save Billions of Dollars. Consumer Federation of America, Washington DC

Jaffee D, Russell T (1998) The causes and consequences of rate regulation in the auto insurance industry. In: Bradford DF (ed) The Economics of Property-Casualty Insurance. University of Chicago Press, Chicago, pp 81–112

Lim CS (2013) Preferences and incentives of appointed and elected public officials: evidence from state trial court judges. Am Econ Rev 103(4):1360–1397

Makowsky M, Sanders S (2013) Political costs and fiscal benefits: the political economy of residential property value assessment under Proposition 13. Econ Lett 120(3):359–363

National Association of Insurance Commissioners (2016) 2012–2013 Automobile Insurance Database Report. National Association of Insurance Commissioners, Washington DC

Peltzman S (1976) Toward a more general theory of regulation. J Law Econ 19(2):211–240

Stigler GJ (1971) The theory of economic regulation. Bell J Econ Manag Sci 2(1):3–21

Sugarman SD (1990) California's insurance regulation revolution: the first two years of Proposition 103. San Diego Law Rev 27:683

Whalley A (2013) Elected versus appointed policy makers: Evidence from city treasurers. J Law Econ 56(1):39–81

Chapter 4
Conflicting Objectives of Cartel Members: Analysis of Voting Behavior in the NCAA

Kathleen A. Carroll, Dennis Coates, and Brad R. Humphreys

Abstract This chapter models the behavior of universities and colleges as members of the NCAA with two different groups: power teams and non-power teams. The model develops behavioral predictions for voting decisions made by schools in the two groups with respect to regulations on entry barriers and academic quality. The predictions of the model are tested using voting data on regulations related to the maximum number of athletic scholarships as an entry barrier to Division I and to the eligibility requirements for athletes as an indicator of academic quality. The empirical results support the predictions of the theoretical model that power and non-power institutions will vote differently depending on observable determinants of voting behavior like school size and the intensity of fan commitment to teams. The work extends economists' understanding of how voter heterogeneity affects observed voting behavior.

4.1 Introduction

In the economics literature, the National Collegiate Athletic Association (NCAA) is most commonly considered to be a cartel (see, e.g., Koch 1978, 1986; Pacey 1985; Lawrence 1987; Fleisher et al 1992; Humphreys and Ruseski 2009). The NCAA cartel consists of a group of competing institutions of higher education held together through rules and regulations administered by the NCAA central organization.

In the cartel context, the NCAA central organization facilitates cartel behavior by coordinating and regulating athletic recruitment and competitions. Previous research formally modeled this behavior as a principal-agent relationship to investigate the effects of the NCAA's regulatory behavior in the situation of intercollegiate

---

K. A. Carroll · D. Coates
University of Maryland Baltimore County, Baltimore, MD, USA
e-mail: carroll@umbc.edu; coates@umbc.edu

B. R. Humphreys (✉)
West Virginia University, Morgantown, WV, USA
e-mail: brhumphreys@mail.wvu.edu

© The Author(s), under exclusive license to Springer Nature Switzerland AG 2025
J. Hall, K. Starr (eds.), *Empirical Applications of the Median Voter Model*, Studies in Public Choice 45, https://doi.org/10.1007/978-3-031-87179-5_4

football telecasts (Carroll and Humphreys 2016). That model explicitly assumes homogeneous member-team principals, although implications of some differences across principals are considered. Other research on the behavior of the NCAA and its member institutions, while not explicitly modeling the principal-agent relationship, implicitly assumes homogeneity among the member institutions in the NCAA (Fleisher et al 1990; DeBrock and Hendricks 1996).

We focus on heterogeneity in the member teams in the NCAA and examine its implications for NCAA policy. Koch (1978, p. 231) noted that the creation of Division IA represented "an open attempt to allow the big-time athletic powers to go their own way within the confines of the NCAA." The problem, he argued, was that the membership was too heterogeneous to stay as it had been, and the problems of this heterogeneity had risen to prominence in the contentiousness of proposals like that of Stephen Horn, the president of California State University at Long Beach, to share revenues from television contracts across all members of the NCAA. The differences in preferences and needs were "already apparent in NCAA convention voting patterns" (Koch 1978, p. 231).

Fleisher et al (1992) concurred with this sentiment, suggesting that NCAA members' behavior is consistent with attempts to maintain the power and status of athletically elite schools. More recently, issues raised by Sperber (2000), Shulman and Bowen (2001), and Bowen and Levin (2003) suggest that understanding the motivations of the different institutions, and how those motivations differ or are alike, is an important public policy concern.

In this chapter we formally model these differences.[1] We model the voting behavior of the NCAA Division I member institutions with two distinct groups of members, one comprising what we term "power" teams and the other "non-power" teams.[2] Power teams play Division IA (Football Bowl Division) football, frequently achieve ranking in postseason Top 20 or Top 25 polls, and appear frequently in postseason competitions, such as "March Madness" and bowl games. In addition, power basketball and/or football teams generate large revenues. All other NCAA members with Division I basketball teams, Division IA football teams, and members of Division I who do not play IA football or Division I basketball constitute the group of non-power schools. These other teams both outnumber the power teams and receive subsidies from revenues generated by the power teams and redistributed by the NCAA central organization.

We explicitly consider the heterogeneous interests or preferences of different members of the NCAA. The primary distinction across member institutions is that of power: the ability of some individual schools to generate revenue by fielding strong,

---

[1] Fleisher et al (1990, 1992) made the first attempt to analyze NCAA voting. Our approach adds a more formal theoretical structure into the analysis and derives testable implications from that theory.

[2] By assuming that the institutions are net benefit maximizers with respect to the levels of entry barriers and academic quality of the student athletes, this work is consistent with an existing literature on university-level decision-making. Work in this literature includes Garvin (1980), James (1990), Coates and Humphreys (2002), and Coates et al (2004).

nationally recognized, successful teams of athletes. Other NCAA members may be recognized for different attributes, such as academic reputation (Fleisher et al 1990). Academic prestige is not a source of revenue for athletic teams or a source of what may be termed athletic reputation. We focus on this dichotomy. We examine two types of regulations: the first related to athletic recruitment, which is important for power teams in achieving their objective of fielding nationally recognized teams that generate substantial revenues, and the second related to academic quality, which is important for the non-power teams and may be viewed in varying ways by power teams.

4.2 A Model of Voting in the NCAA

Each university or college team member of the NCAA faces voting on two areas of NCAA institutional regulations: regulations that relate to athletics and team quality (X) and regulations that relate to educational objectives and academic quality (Y). The two specific issues subject to regulation by vote in the NCAA members modeled here are x = level of scholarship-based entry barriers and y = level of academic quality.

Entry barriers relate to the number of basketball scholarships an institution can offer. More scholarships mean that schools with strong basketball programs that are interested in maintaining basketball supremacy can do so by stockpiling high-quality players, making it difficult for weaker programs to become competitive. The level of academic quality reflects the standards that student-athletes must meet to be eligible to play as freshmen.[3] The stricter the standards are, the greater the academic quality.

4.2.1 Voting Team Members

We define the following groups of NCAA members: n^i = total team members in group i, $i = P, NP$ = voting member in group consisting of Division I power teams, n^P = number of members in the power group, N = voting member in group consisting of non-power teams, and n^N = number of members in the non-power group.

---

[3] Chapter 6 of Fleisher et al (1992) which studies voting on Proposition 48, the eligibility requirements, is titled "NCAA Academic Requirements as Barriers to Entry." They do not make clear who is barred from what, though there is a discussion of higher academic requirements disproportionately harming black athletes. They seem to equate "barriers to entry" with pursuit of one's competitive interests. We emphasize a more explicit view of barriers to entry with the focus on the allowed number of scholarships; the fewer the scholarships required of Division I schools, the lower the cost of Division I status. While imposing greater academic standards for eligibility does, without a doubt, protect the status of the established power schools, it does not make it more difficult for schools to enter Division I.

4.2.2 Voting Behavior of Team Members

Each individual group member seeks to maximize net benefits from the proposed regulation up for vote. Institutions in both groups obtain benefits from regulations that increase their individual revenue and enhance their reputation. Members of group P (power teams) are interested primarily, although not exclusively, in their athletic reputation, as well as revenues generated by athletics. Members of group N (non-power teams) are interested primarily, although not exclusively, in their academic reputation. In addition, because of the subsidies they receive through redistribution of revenues from the high-earning, power athletic teams to the rest of the NCAA member teams, group N member institutions are also interested in revenues generated by athletics.

Consider the benefits to an institution from an additional athletic scholarship. These benefits include creating more prestige associated with Division I membership from a higher set of standards for teams to enter Division I, essentially increasing the Division I entry barrier; enhanced team quality due to the additional offer that can be made to a qualified student athlete; increased likelihood of team success, win-loss record, tournament game(s), and associated revenues; and increased likelihood of fan interest and associated revenues. The costs of an additional scholarship include the explicit cost to the institution of subsidizing the student-athlete's tuition and fees, the opportunity cost of the position taken by the athlete that is not available to an alternative player, and possible administrative costs spent researching, discussing, and lobbying for the regulation.

The benefits of increasing academic quality standards include a greater likelihood of student-athletes completing their degrees and an increase in the academic reputation and prestige of member institutions. The costs of increasing academic quality standards and promoting the regulation include lower team quality due to a more limited pool of potential number of athletic recruits, at least in the freshman year of eligibility, the cost of monitoring to ensure that the additional standards are met, the cost of imposing and enforcing penalties when the additional standards are not met, and possible staff time cost spent researching, discussing, and lobbying for the regulation.

We posit that group P members (1) have a preference for greater x because larger numbers of scholarships promote team quality and (2) have a preference for lower y because higher academic eligibility requirements reduce team quality by limiting the pool of potential athletic recruits and imposes monitoring costs. Group N members (1) have a preference for x because they expect that higher team quality may yield larger subsidies from group P teams and (2) have a strong preference for y because higher academic eligibility requirements promote academic quality and are consistent with enhancing their academic reputation even though there monitoring costs exist.

4.2.3 Net Benefit Functions

$b^i(x, y; I, D, S)$ = benefits to the voting members generated by levels of scholarship-based entry barriers x and academic quality y
$c^i(x, y; I, D, S)$ = opportunity costs of promoting and implementing x and y

where $i = P, N, b^i(x, y)$ is subject to the usual diminishing returns, and $c^i(x, y)$ increase with x and y.

Assumption 1: $b^i_x(x, y) > 0$, $b^i_y(x, y) > 0$, $b^i_{xx}(x, y) < 0$, $b^i_{yy}(x, y) < 0$.
Assumption 2: $c^i_x(x, y) > 0$, $c^i_y(x, y) > 0$, $c^i_{xx}(x, y) \geq 0$, $c^i_{yy}(x, y) \geq 0$.

The relationship between x and y for member teams in each group might not be symmetric. We consider the relationship between x and y by group below.

The objective of a member in either group is to maximize the net benefits to the institution by choosing a level of entry barriers and a level of academic quality.[4] The objective function is

$$\text{Maximize} \, b^i(x, y) - c^i(x, y) \tag{4.1}$$

First-order conditions are

$$b^i_x(x, y) - c^i_x(x, y) = 0 \tag{4.2}$$

$$b^i_x(x, y) - c^i_x(x, y) = 0 \tag{4.3}$$

Equations 4.2 and 4.3 must simultaneously hold, identifying the institution's ideal choice of x and y. Call these net benefit maximizing levels of x and y and $X*$ and $Y*$. Plotting equations 4.2 and 4.3 shows the combination of x and y that satisfy each condition as in Fig. 4.1. Voting on NCAA propositions regarding entry barriers and academic quality is based on the proximity of the proposals to the ideal point of the member institution. Member institutions will vote for a proposition that moves it toward their ideal position and against propositions that move them away from the ideal position.

Taking total derivatives of the first-order conditions and rearranging, one obtains

$$\left. \frac{dy}{dx} \right|_{x \text{ opt}} = -\frac{b^i_{xx} - c^i_{xx}}{b^i_{xy} - c^i_{xy}} \tag{4.4}$$

$$\left. \frac{dy}{dx} \right|_{y \text{ opt}} = -\frac{b^i_{yx} - c^i_{yx}}{b^i_{yy} - c^i_{yy}} \tag{4.5}$$

---

[4] The assumption that the institution maximizes net benefits ignores the process by which the colleges and universities select an optimizing strategy. Implicitly, the institution speaks with a single voice in this model. Coates and Humphreys (2002) and Coates et al (2004) present evidence that the voice may be that of the university president or provost.

Equation 4.4 is the slope along the locus of x, y combinations that satisfy Eq. 4.2, the first-order condition for the optimal choice of entry barriers, and Eq. 4.5 is the slope along the locus of x, y combinations that satisfy equation 4.3, the first-order condition for the optimal choice of academic quality. For a unique net benefit maximizing solution, 4.4 and 4.5 imply that

$$[-\frac{(b^i_{xx} - c^i_{xx})}{(b^i_{xy} - c^i_{xy})}] \times [-\frac{(b^i_{yx} - c^i_{yx})}{b^i_{yy} - c^i_{yy}}] < 1 \qquad (4.6)$$

and, given symmetry between b^i_{xy} and b^i_{yx} and c^i_{xy} and c^i_{yx},

$$\frac{b^i_{xx} - c^i_{xx}}{b^i_{yy} - c^i_{yy}} < 1 \qquad (4.7)$$

Equations 4.6 and 4.7 generate Fig. 4.1, which shows the relationship between regulation y (academic eligibility/quality) and x (scholarship limitations/entry barriers) for NCAA member teams for the optimal net benefit functions for y (y_{opt}) and (x_{opt}). Stability considerations do not rule out either of the left or right graphs in Fig. 4.1. An interesting question is, then, whether NCAA institutions of different types have net benefit functions that differ systematically. Moreover, are power schools like the graph on the left or the graph on the right? Are non-power schools better represented by either graph? Are there comparative static results that provide us with testable hypotheses about the voting behavior of the different types of institutions?

Suppose that the benefit and cost functions include variables I, D, and S which represent fan intensity, the type of degrees offered by the institution or the prestige of its mission, and the size of the student body, respectively. An increase in I indicates an increase in the avidness of the institution's sports fans. We assume that the marginal effect of each of these is nonnegative and generally positive: $b_I \geq 0$,

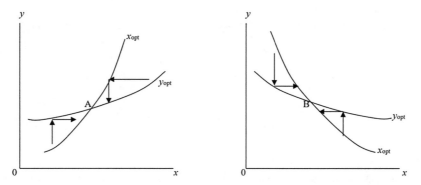

Fig. 4.1 The relationship between regulation of academic eligibility/quality (y) and scholarship limitations/entry barriers (x)

$b_D \geq 0, b_S \geq 0, c_I \geq 0, c_D \geq 0, c_S \geq 0$. Represent the cross partial derivatives of the benefit and cost functions with respect to I, D, and S as $b_{xD}, b_{yD}, b_{yI}, b_{xI}, b_{xS}, b_{yS}, c_{xD}, c_{yD}, c_{xI}, c_{yI}, c_{xS}$, and c_{yS}. Intuition about the signs of these second derivatives is ad hoc, so we proceed as far as possible without making any assumptions about the signs. Consider for simplicity the total derivative of Eq. 4.2 assuming that y, D, and S are held constant. That is,

$$(b_{ss} - c_{ss})ds + (b_{sI} - c_{sI})dI = 0 \quad (4.8)$$

or

$$ds = -\frac{b_{sI} - c_{sI}}{(b_{ss} - c_{ss})}dI \quad (4.9)$$

Equation 4.9 means that the optimal x curve shifts right ($X*$ is larger for given y, D, and S) with an increase in fan intensity I if $(b_{xI} - c_{xI})/(b_{xx} - c_{xx}) < 0$ but shifts left ($X*$ is smaller for given y, D, and S) if the inequality is reversed. Given normal assumptions about second derivatives of benefit and cost functions, $(b_{xx} - c_{xx}) < 0$, so with the minus sign in front of the right-hand side of Eq. 4.9, the sign of dx depends on the signs of dI and of $(b_{xI} - c_{xI})$. For what follows, we assume that dI is positive, that is, that fan intensity rises. Consequently, whether $X*$ rises or falls (holding constant y, D, and S) is determined by whether $(b_{xI} - c_{xI})$ is positive or negative. A similar result can be found for the effects of changes in D and S on the optimal x curve and for changes in each on the optimal y curve.

Several possibilities exist with respect to the comparative static implications of changes in fan intensity, prestige, or degrees offered and size of the institution depending on whether the optimal x and y curves are upward or downward sloping and whether the curves shift in the same or opposite directions. Precise implications require assumptions about the sizes and signs of the cross-partial derivatives. For example, in the case of an increase in fan intensity, I, the outcome for $X*$ and $Y*$ depends on Eq. 4.9 and on $dx = -[(b_{yI} - c_{yI})/(b_{yx} - c_{yx})]dI$ which indicates the movement of the optimal y curve in response to the increase in fan intensity, holding constant the levels of y, D, and S. We have no intuition about the relative sizes of these derivatives. For our purposes, however, we do not need precise information. We simply need to show that the implications differ depending on whether the curves are upward or downward sloping and argue that one set of curves represents power schools and the other represents non-power schools.

Suppose both curves are upward sloping, and the optimal x curve shifts right (down), while the optimal y curve shifts left (up) as fan intensity increases. In this case, both $X*$ and $Y*$ increase with the increase in fan intensity. However, if the optimal x and optimal y curves are downward sloping and an increase in fan intensity shifts the optimal x curve right (up), but the optimal y curve shifts left (down now), $Y*$ unambiguously falls, and $X*$ unambiguously rises. In other words, the implications of an increase in fan intensity depend upon and are clearly different, whether the curves are upward or downward sloping. In other circumstances, the

Table 4.1 Comparative static results—increase in fan intensity

	Upward sloping	X*	Y*
Case 1	Both move right (down)		
	Both shift left (up)		
X curve moves, y curve constant		+	+
		−	−
X curve constant, y curve moves		−	−
		+	+
Case 2	X moves right, y moves left		
	X shifts left, y shifts right		
X curve moves, y curve constant		+	+
		−	−
X curve constant, y curve moves		+	+
		−	−
	Downward sloping	X*	Y*
Case 3	Both move right (up)		
	Both shift left (down)		
X curve moves, y curve constant		+	−
		−	+
X curve constant, y curve moves		−	+
		+	−
Case 4	X moves right, y moves left		
	X shifts left, y shifts right		
X curve moves, y curve constant		+	−
		−	−
X curve constant, y curve moves		+	−
		−	+

effects of the increase in fan intensity depend on whether the optimal x or the optimal y curve shifts more, something about which we have no intuition and which is dependent on the sizes and signs of the cross-partial derivatives.

Table 4.1 helps clarify the comparative static effects of an increase in fan intensity on the net benefit maximizing levels $X*$ and $Y*$. The top portion of the table reports what happens if the optimal x and y curves are upward sloping, first (Case 1) if an increase in intensity shifts both curves right (down), and then (Case 2) if the x curve shifts right, but the y curve shifts left. The sign in the $X*$ and $Y*$ columns indicates an increase (+) or a decrease (−) in that quantity at the new intersection of the optimal x and optimal y curves. Under the hypothesis that both curves are affected by the increase in fan intensity, if the sign in two adjacent rows differs, then the effect on that variable is ambiguous, depending upon which of the curves moves more. If the sign in two adjacent rows is the same, then the effect of an increase in fan intensity is unambiguous for the variable in that column. The lower part of the table reports what happens if the optimal x and y curves are downward sloping. The first in this part (Case 3) shows the effects if an increase in fan intensity shifts both curves right (up) and the second (Case 4) if the x curve shifts right, but the y curve shifts left. Again, the reverse movements for Cases 3 and 4 are shown in bold. We use these now to illustrate the comparative statics.

The table shows eight separate circumstances identified as the four cases indicated above. Formally, the first line of a case assumes that $(b_{xI} - c_{xI}) > 0$, that is, that there are positive net benefits from scholarship-based entry barriers (x) with respect to fan intensity (I), and the second line (shown in bold) assumes the opposite. Each case also depends upon the equivalent expression from the optimal y curve (academic quality requirements); if the y curve moves right, the expression is positive, and if it moves left, the expression is negative. In Case 1, $X*$ and $Y*$ can both rise, both fall, move opposite, or even both be unchanged.

By contrast, in Case 2 $X*$ and $Y*$ move together, either both rising or both falling in response to the change in fan intensity. In Case 3, $X*$ and $Y*$ may rise together, they may move opposite to one another, or one may rise while the other is unchanged. In this circumstance they cannot both fall in response to the increase in fan intensity. Finally, in Case 4 the increase in fan intensity unambiguously raises $X*$ and lowers $Y*$. Note that for $X*$, in every line in which the optimal x curve shifts, but the optimal y curve does not, the pattern of $+$ and $-$ signs is the same. When the y curve shifts, but the x curve does not, then Cases 1 and 3 have the same pattern of $+$ and $-$ signs, and Cases 2 and 4 do. In other words, an increase in fan intensity effects $X*$ in the same direction, regardless of whether the curves slope up or down. That does not mean, of course, that the sizes of the effects are the same. On the other hand, the effects on $Y*$ from upward sloping optimal x and y curves are opposite to those of downward sloping curves.

If power and non-power institutions can be identified or associated with upward or downward sloping optimal x and y curves, these results provide testable implications for a model of voting on NCAA propositions. We hypothesize that non-power schools would face upward sloping optimal x and y curves. These institutions benefit from both greater academic quality and, indirectly, from the revenue sharing aspect of the financial success of entry barriers. Theory tells us, then, that in estimating the determinants of voting on scholarship based entry barriers (x) and academic quality requirements (y) that fan intensity should work in the same direction regardless of power or non-power school status in the case of the former, but in opposite directions in the case of the latter.

That is, the intensity of fan interest will affect voting of both power and non-power schools in the same direction on the scholarship-based entry barrier propositions and will affect the decisions in the opposite direction on the eligibility requirement proposition. These conclusions hold also for the impact of increased degrees offered or prestige and the size of the institution. Note however that if the effects were derived explicitly for degrees and size and the separate cases identified, there is no reason to suppose that the same case holds for each of the three exogenous determinants of voting, intensity, prestige, and size. For example, Case 1 might hold for fan intensity, Case 2 for prestige, and Case 4 for size. This means that the effects of power versus non-power schools for each of the three exogenous variables may have the same or different signs in the equations for voting on the different issues.

4.3 Empirical Analysis

We test the predictions of the model developed in the previous section using roll-call voting data from votes taken at the annual NCAA Convention. The NCAA Bylaws apply to the behavior of both the NCAA central organization and member institutions. At the annual NCAA Convention, delegates from all member institutions vote on legislative proposals to amend or alter the NCAA Bylaws brought to the floor. Since the mid-1980s, these votes have been made on a roll-call basis, so the vote of each institution can be observed.

Hundreds of different proposals are voted on at each convention, and the votes are sometimes limited to subsets of member institutions. For example, proposals that affect only Division I-A football (the largest of the four NCAA football divisions) are voted on by only those member institutions in Division I-A. Some proposals are deemed to be noncontroversial and are voted on as a bloc and typically approved by simple voice vote. The NCAA calls these "housekeeping" proposals; they include issues such as minor changes in syntax, definitions of basic elements like "a collegiate institution," and changes in the deadlines for fees and reports.

Other proposals are deemed more controversial by the NCAA central organization. These proposals are debated on the floor of the convention and voted on by roll-call vote. We analyze voting on a subset of related proposals brought before members of Division I—institutions that play basketball at the highest level and football at either the highest (Division I-A) or the second highest (I-AA) level—and decided by roll-call votes taken between 1986 and 1996.

4.3.1 Data Description

The NCAA publishes an annual volume, *Convention Proceedings*, containing a considerable amount of information on the deliberations and votes taken at each annual NCAA Convention. Since 1986, this volume has contained votes made by each member institution on a number of propositions that come to the floor for votes during the convention. The outcomes of these roll-call votes comprise the core of the data analyzed here. DeBrock and Hendricks (1996) supplied us with the voting data they used in their 1996 paper, which analyzed 275 roll-call votes taken between 1986 and 1994. We supplemented these data with a vote on the maximum number of NCAA Division I basketball scholarships taken at the 1996 NCAA Convention.

The NCAA Bylaws regulate every aspect of intercollegiate athletics. We focus on two types of proposals to alter the NCAA Bylaws: Regulations governing the academic quality of students who can receive athletic scholarships and participate in sanctioned NCAA athletic events and regulations specifying the maximum number of scholarships that can be awarded to Division I men's basketball players. We interpret the scholarship regulation as an entry barrier: As more basketball scholarships are offered, the more costly is the athletic program. Table 4.2—DI Men's Basketball Scholarship Roll-Call Votes—describes the five votes on scholarship requirements we focus on.

The maximum number of basketball scholarships allowed was reduced from 15 to 13—phased in over a 3-year period—by Proposition 40-C in 1991. The decision clearly did not sit well with some NCAA Division I members, as evidenced by the repeated attempts to stall and reverse this decision in the following 5 years.

The other type of regulation analyzed involves academic requirements placed on student-athletes. These requirements take the form of eligibility "indexes"—a sliding scale composed of combinations of high school grade point averages and scores on the SAT or ACT exam—that dictate whether or not a recruit can participate in intercollegiate athletics at an NCAA member institution. In the jargon of the NCAA, a student who meets or exceeds the criteria specified by the eligibility index is called a "qualifier" and may participate in practices and games immediately. A student who does not meet the criteria specified by the eligibility index is called a "partial qualifier" and may enroll in the university without an athletic scholarship but may not participate in games.

Table 4.3—D1 Academic Quality Roll-Call Votes—contains descriptions of the roll-call votes on academic requirements analyzed here. Roll-call voting on academic requirements began in 1986. At the 1986 convention, a series of three proposals on academic requirements were considered. The first two, Propositions 14 and 15, were attempts to head off the imposition of minimum academic requirements for freshmen eligibility. The third, listed as Proposition 16 in the NCAA Convention Proceedings (1986), is typically referred to as "Proposition 48"

Table 4.2 D1 men's basketball scholarship roll-call votes

Proposal number	Year	Intent	Outcome
40-C	1991	Reduce basketball scholarships from 15 to 13	Adopted 272–52
30	1992	Delay the effective date of the reduction until 1995–95	Defeated 134–178

Table 4.3 D1 academic quality roll-call votes

Proposal number	Year	Intent	Outcome
14	1986	Eliminate minimum SAT or ACT test score to determine initial eligibility in Division I	Defeated 47–249
15	1986	Utilize SAT or ACT scores only for institutional placement purposes	Defeated 66–233
16	1986	Define "qualifier" status using an eligibility index	Adopted 207–97

in the popular press, as well as in scholarly research, although the reasons for this nomenclature elude us.[5] Each of these propositions was voted on at the convention, and it seems likely that voting on them should be correlated. In fact, voting on Propositions 14 and 15 is highly correlated with a chi-square test statistic of 98.5 and a p-value of 0.000 indicating rejection of the null hypothesis of no correlation. Interestingly, voting on Propositions 14 and 16 is weakly correlated, with a p-value of 0.078, and voting on Propositions 15 and 16 is uncorrelated, with a p-value of 0.573.

Proposition 48 created an eligibility index—a sliding scale of academic requirements that a student must meet in order to receive a scholarship.[6] The actual indexes adopted in 1986 and in 1992 are shown in Appendix 1. Like the votes on basketball scholarships, the imposition of an eligibility index did not sit well with some NCAA member institutions. Much of the subsequent debate focused on the fate of "partial qualifiers" after they spent a year at an institution improving their academic ability. The "partial qualifier" provision adopted in 1987 is effectively a back door around the eligibility index adopted in 1986. It allows an institution to admit students who do not meet the eligibility index and award them an athletic scholarship following a 1-year probationary period, thus relaxing the effective academic requirements placed on student-athletes.[7]

In addition to the roll-call vote data, we collected data on institutional characteristics and on-field athletic success for all of the institutions with recorded roll-call votes. The institutional characteristics data come from the National Center for Educational Statistics' Integrated Postsecondary Educational Data System (IPEDS) and include financial and fall enrollment data. The on-field athletic success variables, including football and basketball won-loss records, postseason appearances, final poll rankings, national championships, and recruiting violations, were collected from a wide variety of web and print sources, including NCAA publications.

Table 4.4 contains some descriptive data on the institutions in the sample that voted on Proposition 16 in 1986. Although 304 institutions voted on this proposition, we have data on only 266 of these institutions after accounting for data missing from IPEDS and omissions from the roll-call voting tables published by the NCAA. Most of the institutions are public and slightly less than 39% (103) played football at the highest level of the divisional hierarchy in the NCAA in 1986.

---

[5] See, for example, Fleisher et al (1990) and Fleisher et al (1992).

[6] Fleisher et al (1990) and Fleisher et al (1992) studied voting on this proposition for evidence supporting the hypothesis that the NCAA is a cartel. Some of that analysis is very similar to what we do below, though we use a much broader sample of Division I institutions than they do.

[7] The genesis of Proposition 48 is, in itself, an interesting story. Fleisher et al (1992) report that Vince Dooley, the head football coach at the University of Georgia, responded to public criticism and a lawsuit against the university that alleged that student athletes were not treated as rigorously in academics as other students by proposing higher academic standards for the entire Southeastern Conference. Once agreed to by the institutions in the conference, these teams found themselves at a competitive disadvantage and pushed for the higher standards for all NCAA member institutions.

Table 4.4 Institutional characteristics

Institutions		266
	Division IA	103
	Division IAA	38
	Division I	125
	Public	176
	Private	90

Table 4.5 Summary statistics, 1986 votes

Variable	Mean	Std. dev.
FTE Enrollment, 1986	11,794	8,667
FTE Undergraduate Enrollment, 1986	9,550	6,817
FTE Graduate Enrollment, 1986	2,243	2,409
Current Dollar (1986) Expenditure/FTE	$11,371	7,881
Current Dollar Endowment, 1986	$3,875,991	12,000,000
NCAA Basketball Appearances, 1975–85	1.7	2.3
Div IA Bowl Appearances, 1975–85	3.1	3.2

Table 4.5—Summary Statistics—contains sample statistics for the institutions as of 1986. All dollar values on this table are in current 1986 dollars. The average full-time equivalent enrollment of institutions in the sample is just under 12,000. Undergraduates comprise about 80% of the student body, on average. Current dollar expenditure per FTE student was $11,371 in the 1985–1986 academic year, and the average size of the endowment was about $3.8 million dollars. This endowment variable has a sizable left tail and many observations piled up at or near zero. On average, schools that played Division I basketball made slightly fewer than two appearances in the NCAA Basketball Tournament in the decade prior to the 1986 votes. Schools that played Division IA football made three bowl appearances during this period.

4.3.2 Defining "Power Schools"

The behavioral model explicitly includes heterogeneity among the principal member teams in the form of two different groups: "power teams" and "non-power teams." In order to empirically investigate the predictions of this model, we need to divide the group of institutions that voted on the proposals described above into two or more mutually exclusive groups. There is no objective method for grouping institutions. Simply defining "power" teams as those institutions that play Division I basketball and/or football in Division IA—the top divisions in these sports in the NCAA hierarchy—would appear to be one objective method for grouping the sample. However, as Fleisher et al (1992) make clear, the power schools are a limited subset of the Division I institutions.

Intuitively, we think of "power" teams as longstanding national football powers like the University of Notre Dame, the University of Texas, and the University of Southern California or basketball powers like Duke University, the University of North Carolina, and the University of Kentucky. While these teams are members of Division IA football or Division I basketball, these divisions also include small academically prestigious private universities like Vanderbilt University, large public urban universities with little football tradition like Temple University, and small liberal arts colleges and universities like the University of the Pacific. The power team group and the non-power team group have to be relatively homogeneous, and we wonder if the two groups of Division IA football and Division I basketball institutions described above are sufficiently homogeneous.

As an alternative, we define power teams in terms of postseason Division IA bowl appearances over the period 1975–1986 or based on appearances in the NCAA basketball championship tournament. Appearing in postseason bowl games generates significant revenues and prestige for football teams, so frequent appearance in these games may be an important indicator of the scope and importance of the football program at an NCAA member institution. Likewise, appearance in the NCAA basketball tournament carries a great deal of prestige and provides an institution with a high-profile or high-exposure experience on a national scale. Because of the somewhat arbitrary nature of these decision rules, we use different criteria to define power teams and estimate our voting models for each group to assess the robustness of our empirical results to the definition of power teams.

The first power team group consists of teams that played in two or more bowl games over the period 1975–1985. The second power team group consists of teams that played in three or more bowl games over the period 1975–1985. The third power team group consists of teams that played in five or more bowl games over the period 1975–1985. The list of power teams can be found in Appendix 2. Similarly, we identify basketball power schools based on 2, 3, and 5 tournament appearances in the 10-year period. These schools are also listed in the Appendix.

The schools we identify as power schools, especially under the criterion of participation in three bowl games between 1975 and 1985, include those that led in the creation of the College Football Association, whose objective was largely to wrest control of television revenues away from the NCAA. However, whole conferences joined the CFA, the Atlantic Coast Conference, the Southeastern Conference, the Big Eight Conference, the Western Athletic Conference, and the Southwestern Conference to be specific, as did many large independents such as Penn State and Miami. Not all members of these conferences would be considered power schools by any reasonable observer of college football. Consequently, our measure based on bowl appearances seems a more accurate identifier of those schools with the greatest stake in college football.

4.3.3 Empirical Model

In this section we define and estimate voting models that explain an institution's vote on NCAA regulations or policies with respect to the number of basketball scholarships member institutions may offer and the eligibility restrictions for freshmen athletes. As our model makes clear, institutions of different types are likely to have different interests or stakes in the outcomes of these votes. Of course, within an institution there may exist tension between tighter academic standards and greater on field (or court) competitiveness. The models that we estimate attempt to capture the range of interests and influences that determine the voting behavior of the colleges and universities. In doing so, we have had to make several compromises for the lack of data. These compromises will be detailed below. At present, we describe the model in general terms before turning our attention to its implementation.

Each institution is assumed to determine how to vote based on maximizing the return described above. If the net benefits from a favorable vote are larger than the net benefits of an opposing vote, then an affirmative vote is cast. Otherwise, a negative vote is cast. Of course, the net benefits are not observed, but the votes are. Let $NB_{ij} = X_{ij}\beta + \epsilon_{ij}$ be the net benefits to institution i from policy j, X is a vector of explanatory variables, β is a vector of parameters to be estimated, and ϵ is a normally distributed random error term.

The ith institution votes in favor of the proposal if net benefits are positive or if $-\epsilon_{ij} < X_{ij}\beta$. In other words, the probability of a yes vote is equal to the probability that $-\epsilon_{ij} < X_{ij}\beta$. More formally, $\Pr(V_{ij} = 1 \mid X_{ij}) = \Pr(-\epsilon_{ij} < X_{ij}\beta)$. The probability of a no vote is $1 - \Pr(V_{ij} = 1 \mid X_{ij}) = 1 - \Pr(-\epsilon_{ij} < X_{ij}\beta)$. We estimate the model using maximum likelihood methods.[8]

The vector X_{ij} contains variables that proxy for the variables in the cost and benefit functions in the theoretical section. The ability to accurately represent these variables is key to the success of this exercise, so we err on the side of inclusiveness in the analysis. For example, the model suggests that some institutions have great interest in academic quality with relatively little direct interest in erecting barriers to entry into the upper echelons of the collegiate sporting world. Other colleges and universities have relatively stronger interest in capturing and maintaining a degree of athletic superiority. To capture these disparate effects, we use a variety of variables in our analysis, including the "power" variables described above.

Other variables indicate affiliation with either Catholic or protestant religious denominations. Our hypothesis is that religiously affiliated institutions will be more likely to favor greater academic standards than will other colleges and universities. Likewise, we include a variable indicating public sector control of an institution.

---

[8] Because of the high correlation in voting on Propositions 14 and 15, we estimate those voting equations using a bivariate probit approach which allows us to improve the efficiency of the estimates.

Institutions from the south are hypothesized to behave differently than those from other regions for two reasons. First, southern public educational systems generally rank lower than those systems elsewhere in the country. If colleges and universities recruit predominantly local students, then southern colleges and universities would naturally have weaker students from which to draw and would, therefore, have an interest in lower academic requirements for their athletes. The largely southern phenomenon of the historically black colleges and universities may also be related to this interest in somewhat lower academic requirements, and more scholarships, as these would be means of compensating for often poorer primary and secondary educations available for black students. Second, until recently, few southern states had professional sports franchises, making college sports effectively the "major leagues" for fans from those states.

Lower academic requirements would be deemed desirable by fans from those states to assure team competitiveness. The dummy variable for south is an indicator of stronger than average fan intensity as included in the theoretical model. The theoretical model suggests that power schools should be influenced differently than non-power schools when voting on lower academic quality requirements for incoming students. Specifically, southern power schools should be less likely to vote for Proposition 48 than other schools, because they have lower quality students from which to recruit whether because of relatively poor public education systems or because of the desire to provide access to higher education to relatively more weakly prepared black students. Power and non-power schools should be affected similarly in voting on reduced numbers of basketball scholarships, the entry barrier issue. We include a variable to identify those institutions that are located in urban areas. We hypothesize that collegiate sports may be less of a focus in an urban area and, therefore, that pressures to be highly successful may be less intense. For example, in an urban area, relative to a rural area, there will be a wider array of entertainment options. In addition, urban campuses are more likely to be "commuter" schools than more rural institutions. If students spend great amounts of time away from the collegiate environment, as they might if they are commuters, then they may have less interest in the success of their institutions sports teams. All of this translates into a lower probability of supporting entry restrictions. The urban environment may also encourage enhanced academic standards as the wider array of entertainment activities will include some of the intellectually stimulating forms of entertainment that would be favored by better educated who would find high academic standards desirable.

We include a measure of the cost to the student of the education provided by the institution. This variable is the total tuition receipts divided by the number of full-time equivalent undergraduates. Higher tuition is expected to induce greater desired academic quality. We also include the number of full-time equivalent undergraduate and postgraduate students. The former is intended to address a greater demand for athletic success and the latter a greater demand for academic quality.

The Carnegie Foundation classifies colleges and universities based upon the missions and accomplishments of the institutions. We identify institutions' "degrees offered" levels by their Carnegie classification. Institutions that do not offer any

4 Conflicting Objectives of Cartel Members: Analysis of Voting Behavior in... 75

Table 4.6 Variable definitions and descriptive statistics

Variable	Definition	Obs.	Mean	Std. dev.	Min	Max
pi1	Power index 1—D1A, D1AA	266	0.39	0.49	0	1
pi2	Power index 2—2 bowls in 10 years	266	0.16	0.37	0	1
pi3	Power index 3—3 bowls in 10 years	266	0.14	0.34	0	1
pi5	Power index 5—5 bowls in 10 years	266	0.09	0.28	0	1
Tuition	Total tuition per undergraduate FTE	264	5,259	5,444	0	31,746
Hcug	Undergraduate head count enrollment	264	11,045	7,949	804	50,706
Catholic	Affiliation with Catholic order	266	0.11	0.32	0	1
Protest	Affiliation with Protestant denomination	266	0.06	0.24	0	1
Hcpg	Post graduate head count enrollment	264	3,414	3,151	0	14,303
Public	Public institution	266	0.66	0.47	0	1
South	Located in the south	266	0.38	0.49	0	1
Urban	Located in an urban area	266	0.28	0.45	0	1
Prestige1	Level of degrees offered—doctoral	266	1.53	0.59	0	2
Prestige2	Level of degrees offered—doctoral split	266	1.90	0.96	0	3
Pibb2	Basketball Power index 2 in 10 years	266	0.27	0.45	0	1
Pibb3	Basketball Power index 3 in 10 years	266	0.20	0.40	0	1
Pibb5	Basketball Power index 5 in 10 years	266	0.08	0.26	0	1

graduate degrees are coded as prestige of 0. Masters granting institutions are coded as prestige level 1 and doctoral granting institutions as prestige level 2. Because doctoral institutions and research institutions may have different levels of prestige, an alternative coding splits these, with research institutions having prestige of 3. The theory indicates that power and non-power schools may be influenced differently by the level of prestige when voting on academic standards for incoming athletes.

Finally, we include two measures of the size of institution. The first of these is the head count undergraduate enrollment, and the second is the head count postgraduate enrollment. Our hypothesis is that more undergraduates will result in a greater emphasis on athletic success, and hence to favorable votes to raise entry barriers, but that more graduate students will correlate with a greater emphasis on academic quality, all other things equal. Once again, theory indicates that the effects of more students on the optimal level of academic quality differ between power and non-power schools.

Table 4.6 lists the variables and descriptive statistics for 1986, the year of the first vote we study. Means and standard deviations for the variables are consistent from year to year. A correlation matrix with p-values is available upon request.

4.3.4 Empirical Results

We estimate the empirical voting models for each of the five votes using different definitions of "power" schools. Because we focus on the different effects of various institutional characteristics depending on whether the school is or is not a "power" school, interaction terms are needed. When these interactions are created, estimation often becomes problematic because of high degrees of collinearity among the explanatory variables with their interactions or because some cases become perfectly identified by the included variables. These considerations lead us to report only those estimations based on the power level 3 and omit the power level as a separate explanatory variable.

Table 4.7 reports the results of probit estimation of the voting behavior on Proposition 48 (v8616) which created an eligibility index. This vote was the subject of the analysis by Fleisher et al (1990, 1992), though we use more than three times as many institutions in our analysis. The first pair of columns reports the coefficient estimates and p-values using the power index for at least three bowl appearances in the 1976–1985 period.

The results clearly indicate that the interaction of the power index with the south, undergraduate enrollment, and prestige variables and the level of the prestige variable are jointly statistically significant (the chi-square statistic reported in the last line of the table), and the first three of these are individually significant at the 5% level. Indeed, with the exception of the undergraduate enrollment variable, these are the only individually significant coefficients. The prestige and public variables each have a p-value of 0.101, so these are very close to individually significant at the 10% level. The south dummy is next with a p-value of 0.149.

Table 4.7 Proposition 48 (v8616) creating eligibility index

Variable	Coefficient	P-value	Coefficient	P-value
Tuition	0.000	0.677	0.000	0.856
hcug/1000	0.103	0.000	0.080	0.003
Catholic	0.147	0.700	0.055	0.887
Protest	0.364	0.444	0.292	0.537
Hcpg/1000	−0.072	0.236	0.000	0.393
Public	−0.737	0.101	−0.664	0.138
South	−0.301	0.149	−0.427	0.040
Urban	0.002	0.993	−0.009	0.968
south*pi3	−1.645	0.020		
hcug*pi3	−0.093	0.040		
prestige2*pi3	0.952	0.017		
south*pibb3			−0.355	0.405
hcug*pibb3			−0.019	0.632
prestige2*pibb3			0.198	0.427
prestige2	−0.229	0.101	−0.215	0.119
Constant	0.637	0.198	0.810	0.104
Pseudo R-squared	0.129		0.104	
P-value LR test	0.000		0.001	
Chi-square (4)	10.110	0.039	3.220	0.522
Observations		264		264

Recall that the south variable is intended to capture greater than average fan intensity. These results suggest that greater than average fan intensity lowers the likelihood that an institution will vote to impose higher academic restrictions on student athletes and that this effect is the strongest among the power schools. On the other hand, more prestigious schools are also less likely to vote to raise academic quality of the student athletes, but for the power schools, an increase in prestige raises the support for these restrictions. Finally, greater undergraduate enrollment raises the likelihood an institution will support the eligibility restrictions, though this effect is mitigated for the power schools.

The last two columns in Table 4.7 report the results of the probit on Proposition 48 when the power index is defined based on NCAA basketball tournament appearances in the 10 years prior to 1986. The results are for power index three pibb3, which takes the value of 1 if the institution was in three or more of the tournaments between 1976 and 1985. The interesting points to note from these results are that the interaction terms and prestige variable are not jointly significant using this specification, though the signs are the same as when the football power index is used. This suggests that on this general issue of eligibility, football power is of more relevance than basketball power.

The model developed above predicts that the effects of changes in fan intensity, prestige, and size should have opposite signs for power and non-power schools. Consider the results for the football bowl appearances power variable. In this case, fan intensity, identified by the south variable, is negative and significant for the power schools, but not different from zero for the non-power schools. Prestige is positive and significant for the power schools and has a negative coefficient for non-power schools though it is not statistically significant. Size has the opposite signs for power and non-power schools, and both coefficients are individually statistically significant.

Looking at the results based on the basketball tournament index of power, fan intensity (south) has a negative and significant coefficient for non-power schools and a negative but not different from zero coefficient for power schools, prestige has opposite signs but neither is significant, and size has the opposite sign for power and non-power schools, but only the non-power schools variable is significant. In sum, there is some weak support for the theory in these results.

It is useful to compare our results with those of Fleisher et al (1990, 1992). First, recall that our sample includes three times as many Division I institutions as their sample. Their model includes both the SAT score of the institution and the average SAT score of the institution's conference. We use neither of these variables. To do so eliminates a large number of observations because of missing values. Moreover, the school's own SAT score is not statistically significant in any of their regressions, and that is what we find when we include that variable as well. They find that the average SAT in the conference is statistically significant, leading them to conclude that "higher quality academics lead to support for stricter rules" on eligibility, specifically lower support for using the sliding scale index between SAT scores and high school GPA. Our finding that the prestige and prestige interaction variables are jointly statistically significant may be consistent with their conclusion about higher quality academics to some extent, except our result provides some nuance to that conclusion. Specifically, non-power higher quality academic institutions are more likely to support stricter restrictions on eligibility, that is, are less likely to favor using the sliding scale, than power institutions, but power schools with high-quality academics are more likely to favor use of the sliding scale.

In a similar vein, Fleisher et al (1990, 1992) find that enrollment is statistically significant in explaining voting outcomes, which they interpret as more support for looser restrictions (support for the use of the sliding scale). Our enrollment variable is also statistically significant, but enrollment interacted with the power school dummy is also statistically significant and of the opposite sign and very nearly the same magnitude. If greater enrollment is a good proxy for greater demand, then this means that when demand is greater at non-power schools, those schools are more likely to favor use of the sliding scale. However, greater demand, as proxied by enrollment, at power schools has essentially no effect on support for the eligibility index. This may mean that enrollment is not a good proxy for demand. It may also mean that non-power schools with strong demand for athletic success believe they are more likely to attain elite status if they can recruit and enroll players who are weaker academically.

Power schools, on the other hand, may not need this edge and may be put at a competitive disadvantage, finding it more difficult to maintain their elite status if other schools can recruit weaker students for their teams. Viewed this way, these results are consistent with the conclusion of Fleisher et al (1990, 1992, p. 132) that when voting on Proposition 48 "schools are pursuing their competitive self-interest." Finally, this finding may be an artifact of the way proposition 48 came onto the agenda. If it is the case that Proposition 48 was a response by the University of Georgia, a power school, to criticism of its academic standards for athletes, with the support of the Southeastern Conference, whose membership includes Georgia and four other schools counted as power schools, then it may be that the lack of an effect of enrollment on the support for the sliding scale on the part of power schools is idiosyncratic to this particular vote.

Table 4.8 reports the bivariate probit results of estimating the model on the votes on Propositions 14 and 15. Recall that Proposition 14 would have eliminated all use of SAT and ACT scores in determining eligibility to participate in intercollegiate athletics as a freshmen, while Proposition 15 would allow those scores to be used in determining placement, but not in determining eligibility.

The evidence in Table 4.8 clearly reveals that the regression errors are strongly and statistically significantly correlated (rho $= 0.886$ with a p-value of 0.043). This means that estimating the equations this way improves the efficiency of the estimates over single-equation methods. Public schools, urban institutions, and power schools from the south are all statistically significantly (at the 5% level or better) more likely to vote in favor of eliminating the use of the SAT and ACT in determining eligibility. Non-power southern schools are less likely to vote favorably on Proposition 15 than power schools with large undergraduate enrollments and those offering more prestigious and graduate degrees.

Table 4.8 Proposition 14 and 15 (1986) on SAT and ACT for eligibility—bivariate probit estimation

Variable	Coefficient	P-value	Coefficient	P-value
Tuition/100	0.002	0.592	−0.002	0.711
Hcug/1000	−0.010	0.728	−0.007	0.774
Catholic	0.324	0.425	0.285	0.438
Hcpg/100	−0.008	0.164	−0.002	0.686
Public	1.005	0.032	0.526	0.229
South	−0.268	0.222	−0.460	0.039
Urban	0.523	0.027	0.131	0.560
south*pi3	1.289	0.026	−0.347	0.557
hcug*pi3/100	0.002	0.698	−0.008	0.081
prestige2*pi3	−0.497	0.315	0.458	0.146
prestige2	−0.110	0.508	−0.269	0.077
Constant	−1.353	0.014	−0.376	0.424
P-value LR test		0.000		
Chi-square (8)	25.69	0.001		
Rho	0.886	0.043		
Observations		264		264

The chi-square statistic reported in the table is for the null hypothesis that none of the power interactions or prestige variables is statistically significant in determining voting on either Proposition 14 or Proposition 15. This test rejects the null hypothesis, indicating that power and non-power schools are influenced differently by these variables. Note also that undergraduate enrollment (hcug) interacted with the power indicator is of opposite signs, though not different from zero in the Proposition 14 voting model, while the interacted variable is negative and statistically different from zero at the 10% level in the Proposition 15 equation. The null that these four variables all have zero coefficients is easily rejected at the 5% level, suggesting that enrollment has different effects at power and non-power schools.

Likewise, the four south and south-power interaction variables are jointly significant, at the 5% level, and of opposite signs in the Proposition 14 equation. The prestige variables and their interactions also do not all have zero coefficients, and this is better than the 1% level. In the Proposition 15 equation prestige and prestige interacted with power have opposite signs, prestige is significant at the 10% level, and the interaction variable is significant at the 15% level.

These results on the interaction variables all lend some support to the implication of the model that power schools and non-power schools are influenced differently by the same institutional characteristics. Moreover, there is also support for the hypothesis that the effects are in opposite directions for some variables.

Table 4.9 uses the same specifications as in Table 4.7 to examine voting in 1991 on the proposal to reduce the number of basketball scholarships a school can offer from 15 to 13. We contend that support for fewer scholarships is consistent with

Table 4.9 Reducing basketball scholarships from 15 to 13

Variable	Coefficient	P-value	Coefficient	P-value
Tuition	0.023	0.503	0.043	0.226
Hcug	0.046	0.113	0.042	0.117
Catholic	0.735	0.153	0.577	0.278
Protest	0.545	0.376	0.432	0.486
Hcpg	−0.006	0.934	−0.058	0.368
Public	−0.306	0.575	0.044	0.938
South	0.006	0.980	−0.211	0.359
Urban	−0.399	0.099	−0.223	0.346
south*pi3	−0.796	0.112		
hcug*pi3	−0.019	0.620		
prestige2*pi3 south*pibb3	−0.051	0.863	−0.665	0.150
hcug*pibb3			−0.055	0.156
prestige2*pibb3			0.523	0.086
prestige2	−0.241	0.112	−0.387	0.012
Constant	1.138	0.073	1.165	0.078
Pseudo R-squared	0.129		0.101	
P-value LR test	0.002		0.015	
Chi-square (4)	15.07	0.005	8.62	0.071
Observations		264		264

an attempt to reduce entry barriers to Division 1 by lowering the cost of running a competitive basketball program. Consider now the results from Table 4.9. First, the power index based on football bowl appearances dominates that based on basketball tournament appearances, at least insofar as the interactions and the prestige variable are jointly significant at better than the 1% level using the football power variable, but only at the 10% level using the basketball power variable. This is striking as the issue at hand affects basketball directly and affects football, and other scholarship sports, only indirectly. On the other hand, none of the variables is individually significant, using the football power index, but prestige and prestige interacted with the basketball power index variable both are significant at the 10% level or better.

Most of the variables have very similar coefficients across the two different specifications. The principle difference is in the prestige and prestige power interaction variables. In the basketball power index equation, as prestige rises for the non-power schools, the likelihood of voting to reduce basketball scholarships falls. However, as prestige rises for the basketball power schools, the likelihood of voting to reduce basketball scholarships rises. Interestingly, one cannot reject the null hypothesis that these two effects are of equal magnitude but opposite sign. The implication of this result is that non-power schools are less likely to support reducing basketball scholarships as the prestige of the institution rises, but that the effect of enhanced prestige is completely undone by status as a basketball power. The theory developed above suggests that the effects for power and non-power schools should work in the same direction on the decision to reduce entry barriers. The results here are especially weak. The three pairs of variables are not statistically significant in the football power equation, and only the prestige pair is significant in the basketball equation, but the two prestige variables have opposite signs. The size variables also have opposite signs, though, as reported, they are not statistically significant.

The analysis so far does not control for the quality of the students enrolled in the institution. Fleisher et al (1990) used the average SAT score of the incoming class to capture the academic quality of the student body and, by extension, the institution. Unreported results find that using the average SAT score and that variable interacted with the power index has little explanatory power in either vote, with or without the presence of our prestige variable and its interaction term with the power index. Our results suggest, therefore, that the academic quality of incoming students is a poor proxy for the "prestige" of the institution.

We estimated the empirical voting models above for the other votes listed in Tables 4.2 and 4.3. The results are broadly consistent with those reported here. Specifically, the football power index does a much better job than the basketball power index, whether the vote applies to all sports or applies directly only to basketball. Second, interaction terms between power status and other explanatory variables are often individually and jointly significant. This suggests that power and non-power schools' voting behavior is affected differently by institutional characteristics.

4.4 Conclusion

This chapter models NCAA member institutions to develop and test hypotheses related to the trade-off between an institution's academic quality and athletic success. The model assumes the existence of two types of schools: power schools with prominent, continuously successful athletic departments that generate large revenues and non-power schools with lower profile athletic departments. The model predicts heterogeneity in voting on NCAA regulations based on the level of fan intensity, the type of degrees offered by institutions or the prestige of its academic mission, and the size of the student body. The model generates different predictions about voting on NCAA academic and recruiting regulations by power and non-power schools.

We test the predictions made by this model using data on the voting behavior of NCAA institutions at the annual conference on three motions to change freshman eligibility based on test scores and high school GPA taken at the 1986 annual convention and to two motions to change the number of scholarship athletes on men's basketball teams taken at the 1991 and 1992 annual conventions. We find evidence of empirical support for the model in that votes by power and non-power athletic institutions are affected differently by prestige, fan intensity, and the size of their student body.

Appendix

See Tables 4.10, 4.11, and 4.12 for additional information about eligibility indexes and power schools.

Table 4.10 Eligibility indexes specified by Proposition 16

1986 requirements			1992 requirements		
GPA	SAT	ACT	GPA	SAT	ACT
2.200–Above	660	13	2.500-Above	700	17
2.100–2.199	980	14	2.375–2.499	750	18
2.000–2.099	700	15	2.250–2.374	800	19
1.900–1.999	720	16	2.125–2.249	850	20
1.800–1.899	740	17	2.000–2.124	900	21

Table 4.11 Power teams

Group 1: 2+ bowls	Group 2: 3+ bowls	Group 3: 5+ bowls
Alabama	Alabama	Alabama
Auburn	Auburn	Arkansas
Arizona St.	Arizona St.	UCLA
Arkansas	Arkansas	Southern Cal
UCLA	UCLA	Florida St.
Southern Cal	Southern Cal	Florida
Colorado	Air Force	Georgia
Air Force	Florida St.	Notre Dame
Florida St.	Florida	Louisiana St.
Florida	Miami	Maryland
Miami	Georgia	Michigan
Georgia	Notre Dame	Nebraska
Illinois	Iowa	North Carolina
Notre Dame	Louisiana St.	Ohio St.
Iowa	Maryland	Oklahoma
Kentucky	Michigan	Penn St.
Louisiana St.	Missouri	Pittsburgh
Maryland	Nebraska	Tennessee
Navy	North Carolina	Houston
Boston College	Ohio St.	Texas A&M
Michigan	Oklahoma St.	Texas
Missouri	Oklahoma	Brigham Young
Nebraska	Penn St.	Washington
North Carolina	Pittsburgh	
North Carolina St.	Clemson	
Ohio St.	South Carolina	
Oklahoma St.	Tennessee	

(continued)

4 Conflicting Objectives of Cartel Members: Analysis of Voting Behavior in... 83

Table 4.11 (continued)

Group 1: 2+ bowls	Group 2: 3+ bowls	Group 3: 5+ bowls
Oklahoma	Baylor	
Penn St.	Houston	
Pittsburgh	Southern Methodist	
Clemson	Texas A&M	
South Carolina	Texas	
Tennessee	Brigham Young	
Baylor	Washington	
Houston	West Virginia	
Southern Methodist	Purdue	
Texas A&M		
Texas		
Brigham Young		
Washington		
West Virginia		
Wisconsin		
Purdue		

Table 4.12 Basketball power teams

Group 1: 3+ NCAA tournaments		Group 2: 5+ NCAA tournaments
Alabama-Birmingham	Houston	Alabama
Alabama	Lamar	Arkansas
Arkansas	Brigham Young	UCLA
UCLA	Utah St.	Georgetown
Pepperdine	Utah	Depaul
San Francisco	Weber St.	Indiana
Georgetown	Virginia Tech	Notre Dame
Depaul	Virginia Commonwealth	Iowa
Illinois	Virginia	Kentucky
Indiana	Marquette	Louisville
Notre Dame	Purdue	Maryland
Iowa		Missouri
Kansas		UNLV
Kansas State		St. Johns
Kentucky		Syracuse
Louisville		North Carolina
Western Kentucky		Oregon St.
Louisiana St.		Penn
Maryland		Villanova
Boston College		Tennessee

(continued)

Table 4.12 (continued)

Group 1: 3+ NCAA tournaments	Group 2: 5+ NCAA tournaments
Western Kentucky	Oregon St.
Louisiana St.	Penn
Maryland	Villanova
Boston College	Tennessee
Northeastern	Marquette
Michigan	
Alcorn St.	
Missouri	
UNLV	
Princeton	
Rutgers	
Iona	
St. Johns	
Syracuse	
Duke	
North Carolina A&T	
North Carolina	
North Carolina St.	
Wake Forest	
Ohio St.	
Oklahoma	
Oregon St.	
La Salle	
Penn	
Villanova	
Memphis St.	
Middle Tennessee St.	
Tennessee	

References

Bowen WG, Levin SA (2003) Reclaiming the Game. Princeton University Press, Princeton

Carroll K, Humphreys BR (2016) Opportunistic behavior in a cartel setting: effects of the 1984 supreme court decision on college football television broadcasts. J Sports Econ 17(6):601–628

Coates D, Humphreys BR (2002) The supply of university enrollments: university administrators as utility maximizing bureaucrats. Public Choice 110(3–4):365–392

Coates D, Humphreys BR, Vachris MA (2004) More evidence that university administrators are utility maximizing bureaucrats. Econ Gov 5:77–101

DeBrock L, Hendricks W (1996) Roll call voting in the NCAA. J Law Econ Organiz 12(2):497–516

Fleisher AA, Goff BL, Tollison RD (1990) NCAA voting on academic requirements: public or private interest? In: Goff B, Tollison R (eds) Sportometrics. Texas A&M University Press, College Station

Fleisher AA, Goff BL, Tollison RD (1992) The National Collegiate Athletic Association: A Study in Cartel Behavior. The University of Chicago Press, Chicago

Garvin D (1980) The Economics of University Behavior. Academic, New York

Humphreys B, Ruseski J (2009) Monitoring cartel behavior and stability: evidence from NCAA football. Southern Econ J 75:720–735

James E (1990) Decision processes and priorities in higher education. In: Hoenack SA, Collins EL (eds) The Economics of American Universities: Management, Operations, and Fiscal Environment. State University of New York Press, Albany, pp 77–106

Koch JV (1978) The NCAA: a socio-economic analysis: The development of the college sports cartel from social movement to formal organization. Am J Econ Sociol 37(3):225–239

Koch JV (1986) The intercollegiate athletic industry. In: Adams W (ed) The Structure of American Industry, 7th edn. Macmillan Publishing Company, New York

Lawrence PR (1987) Unsportsmanlike Conduct: The National Collegiate Athletic Association and the Business of College Football. Praeger, New York

Pacey PL (1985) The courts and college football: new playing rules off the field? Am J Econ Sociol 44(2):145–154

Shulman JL, Bowen WG (2001) The Game of Life. Princeton University Press, Princeton

Sperber M (2000) Beer and Circus: How Big-Time College Sports is Crippling Undergraduate Education. Henry Holt and Company, LLC., New York

Chapter 5
Get Psyched! An Empirical Analysis of Colorado's Legalization of Psychedelic Drugs

Adam Witham and Lillian Fitzgerald

Abstract This chapter empirically explores the relationship between demographic and economic characteristics of individuals and the proportion of Colorado's electorate voting to legalize psychedelic drugs in Colorado in 2022. Proposition 122, introduced with the ballot, offered voters the option to support or reject the legal use of psychedelics. Utilizing county-level data on political party registrations, education, gender, median age, median income, and controls for if a county is urban, we find evidence that there is a positive, statistically significant relationship between the share of Democratic registered voters and the proportion of voters approving Proposition 122. This chapter serves as an application of the Median Voter Theorem in evaluating how characteristics of Colorado voters impact the legalization of psychedelic drugs.

5.1 Introduction

When Colorado introduced legislation in 2012 to allow for the legal, recreational use of marijuana, it started a movement across states. By 2015, Colorado, Washington, Alaska, and Oregon all had legalized marijuana for recreational use, and 18 other states had legalized it for medicinal use (Kim and Monte 2016). As of 2024, 24 states have legalized recreational marijuana, and all but three states (Idaho, Kansas, and Nebraska) have legalized marijuana or CBD at least partially for medicinal or recreational purposes (Bink 2023). Colorado pioneered the road for marijuana legalization in the United States, and we can look to its past when considering potential new legislation.

Proposition 122, introduced with the Colorado ballot in 2022, presented voters with the option to legalize the usage of psychedelic fungi and plants as natural medicines for individuals aged 21 years or older (Ballotpedia 2024d). Psychedelic

---

A. Witham (✉) · L. Fitzgerald
Salve Regina University, Newport, RI, USA
e-mail: adam.witham@salve.edu; lillian.fitzgerald@salve.edu

© The Author(s), under exclusive license to Springer Nature Switzerland AG 2025
J. Hall, K. Starr (eds.), *Empirical Applications of the Median Voter Model*, Studies in Public Choice 45, https://doi.org/10.1007/978-3-031-87179-5_5

drugs, or psychedelics, are hallucinogenic substances that are associated with distorted perception for users; however, there are observations that psychedelics can be used clinically or medically for managing depression and addiction (Nichols 2016). With Oregon already having legalized the usage of hallucinogenic mushrooms with Measure 109 (Jacobs 2023), Colorado's Proposition 122 passed with 53.64% of voters in support of allowing for the legal use of psychedelic fungi and plants (Ballotpedia 2024d). Whereas this affirmative vote appears to capture a narrow victory with only slightly more than a majority of Coloradans in favor of psychedelics, we can better analyze the characteristics of voters and Colorado counties to understand the voting outcome.

The purpose of this chapter is to (1) review the history of drug policies and legalization in Colorado and other states, (2) collect county-level data for Colorado in 2022 toward voter registrations and Proposition 122 votes in connection to county characteristics, and (3) empirically model the preference or likelihood of voters in supporting Proposition 122. The consideration of Colorado's vote serves as an application of the Median Voter Theorem as we can evaluate how factors such as education, age, income, political party affiliation, and employment impact one's likelihood of voting for or against a policy. What we observe is that there is strong statistical significance for political party registration (either Republican or Democrat) impacting the likelihood of county voters supporting Proposition 122. We similarly find that there is evidence of median income, gender, and median age affecting the vote for psychedelic drug legalization.

With Colorado and Oregon having now both legalized marijuana and psychedelic plants, extensions of this research could be toward the likelihood of other states in supporting psychedelic drugs or other substances. It can also be analyzed how this policy compares or fits with national policy toward psychedelic drugs (Samenow et al. 2023). For states other than Colorado and Oregon considering legalization of psychedelics, what would be the likelihood of their representative voter supporting a similar ballot measure? This research could also be used in understanding if perceptions over substances, such as marijuana and psychedelics, change following their legalization. Moreno et al. (2016) explore public opinion over marijuana in two states, one of which legalized marijuana (Washington) and one which did not (Wisconsin); this study finds that among college-age students, there is little deviation in opinion changes about marijuana.[1] Colorado similarly could be evaluated over time to see if public opinion remains consistent toward psychedelics or if it shifts as individuals have greater access to them.

---

[1] Moreno et al. (2016) note, however, in their study that there is evidence of perspective changes regarding the safety of marijuana. By legalizing marijuana, individuals anticipate that it should be safe for them to use.

5.2 Background

Colorado's legalization of psychedelics through Proposition 122 can be analyzed through economic viewpoints on drug legalization, Colorado's past history of drug legalization (i.e., marijuana) along with its voting record and politics, and economic theory regarding the median voter. Literature and discussion related to each of these areas is provided in the following subsections.

Specific to the median voter theorem and its application to the legalization of psychedelic drugs, many studies speak to the social costs and benefits toward legalization. The importance in variables and the unknown is first brought to attention on this topic (Warner 1991). Since this piece, most of the conversation finds that some degree of legalization or decriminalization of psychedelic drugs would benefit the economy in ways of reduced price in drugs, reduced penalties for dealers, reduced cost by government in drug prevention, reduced crime, and overall a small effect on health (Niskanen 1992). Even more so, in specific regard to the United States, Cussen and Block (2000) support the legalization of drugs for constitutional freedom along with all covered aspects in the Niskanen (1992) paper. Another study finds similar outcomes if legalization is enacted in America and also adds exemplary models such as harm reduction and medicalization (Miron and Zwiebel 1995). The conclusion states these example models have been most successful when laws and regulations are relaxed and therefore suggests the loosening and legalization of drug laws in America.

5.2.1 Economics of Drug Legalization

There is extensive literature in economics on the issue of drug legalization. As emphasized by Warner (1991), there are both social costs and social benefits from increasing access to drugs. For example, governments can consider the implementation of excise taxes on them, as well as potential changes for prices based on changing demand and its elasticity. Related to cost-benefit analysis, there is also conversation that some degree of legalization or decriminalization of psychedelic drugs would benefit the economy in ways of reduced price in drugs, reduced penalties for dealers, reduced cost by government in drug prevention, reduced crime, and overall a small effect on health (Niskanen 1992). Also in connection to benefits of legalization specifically in the United States, Cussen and Block (2000) emphasize that legalization of drugs aligns with constitutional freedom. Separately, legalization of drugs may lead to harm reduction and potential use as a medical treatment, as noted by Miron and Zwiebel (1995). Related to the cost side of the analysis, there may be increased usage of drugs following their legalization and potential addiction. Both Walkins and Scrimgeour (2000) and Burrus et al. (2007) note that one of the costs or implications of drug legalization is that it may lead to more consumers of them. By applying this reasoning to psychedelic drugs, their legalization in

Colorado may lead to more individuals using them. Hesitation or unfavorable perception surrounding psychedelics is also evidenced with psychologists, who may not unilaterally recommend them as a medicinal treatment (Davis et al. 2022).

Thornton (2007) pools perspectives from a variety of economists toward drug public policies, related to illegal drugs generally and psychedelics. A majority of the summarized viewpoints are in support of drug legalization and find that some leeway can be found toward drug liberalization or decriminalization. A case study comparison is drawn in Smith and Appelbaum (2021) between two states (California and Oregon) on the issue of psychedelics legalization. Similar to how Moreno et al. (2016) utilize a case study comparison in the context of marijuana, this paper examines the effect of psychedelic access through a cost-benefit analysis. In particular, Downey et al. (2021) underscore the risks or consequences that may be faced by legalizing the drugs. What is generally observed across this literature is that there is a trade-off between the benefits and costs of drug legalization. To better understand the decision process of Colorado to legalize psychedelics, we can look to its policy history on marijuana.

5.2.2 Marijuana Legalization in Colorado

In 2012, Colorado's Amendment 64 was introduced through a ballot to decide whether those over the age of 21 years would be legally allowed to consume marijuana. Roughly 55.32% of the electorate supported it, leading to its passage (Ballotpedia 2024b). Stores for the recreational use of marijuana opened at the beginning of 2014, and it is noted by Felix (2018) that taxation of marijuana sales in Colorado had contributed to roughly 2% of the state's revenue. As a consequence of marijuana legalization and consumption, usage of alternative drugs and crime can be considered as well. Plaksa (2021) highlights that the availability of marijuana in Colorado may lead to less usage of alternative drugs, such as opioids. Relatedly, Dills et al. (2016) assert that there does not appear to be changes in monthly crime statistics in Denver or Fort Collins following the passage of Amendment 64 or at time of dispensaries opening in 2014. However, there is evidence that the availability of marijuana for legal recreation use has led to surges in possession for counties bordering Colorado (Hao and Cowan 2020). This point especially may resonate with psychedelic drugs in Colorado now as bordering states have not legalized them.

5.2.3 Voting and Politics in Colorado

Colorado's legalization of marijuana and now psychedelic drugs can additionally be considered with its voting record. Though Colorado's electoral candidates have gone to the Republican candidate in roughly 48% of presidential elections since 1900, its electoral votes have gone to the Democratic candidate in every presidential election since 2008 (Ballotpedia 2024f). This shift toward the Democratic Party in Colorado may shed light on the state's legalization history. Caldwell and Davis (2021) identify that Democrats may be more inclined to legalizing marijuana than Republicans.

Other than Proposition 122, ballot measures introduced in 2022 in Colorado included gaming licenses and alcohol (Ballotpedia 2024a). Amendment was proposed to Colorado's state constitution that would allow for charitable gaming licenses to be granted after a period of 3 years instead of 5 years and enable compensation for charitable gaming management; it was defeated with 59% voting in opposition (Ballotpedia 2024c). The ballot proposals related to alcohol, however, were split in their outcomes. Proposition 124 was decisively defeated (Ballotpedia 2024a), which would have allowed more liquor store licenses to be held by a person; Proposition 125, presenting a new classification of license which enables stores to sell wine in addition to beer, narrowly passed with approximately 51.77% of voters supporting it (Ballotpedia 2024e).

In thinking about the rationale of Colorado voters choosing to legalize psychedelic drugs, Marlan (2019) iterates that this may be due to the fact that Colorado voters seek medical value in the legalization of drugs, promote religious freedom, and place importance on cognitive liberty. Furthering the point of cognitive liberty, Lopez (2016) finds that the more educated a population is, the more likely they are to be in favor of drug legalization. This result will be a major avenue of exploration in our research along with other characteristics of Colorado voters who spearheaded their "yes" vote toward the decriminalization of psychedelic drugs.

5.2.4 Extensions of the Median Voter Theorem

The Median Voter Theorem has applications across a myriad of policy issues, as originally posited by Black (1948). It has been used to explore business viability, such as with Waldfogel (2008), and prohibition of alcohol, such as with Dinan and Heckelman (2019). It has been rigorously tested empirically, such as with Holcombe (1980). Using a dataset of over 200 school districts in Michigan, Holcombe finds strong evidence that the Median Voter Theorem can be applied in attempt to understand the median citizen or voter in the world around us. Similarly, Rice (1985) evaluates how the theorem is applicable in the United States toward understanding median and mean income gap along with trends in redistribution programs. Through regression analysis, Rice (1985) finds that voter turnout is significant in determining the outcome; voter turnout decreases with respect to time, leading to misrepresentation of the median American in wage gaps. The result of this study is insightful in policy analysis as it does not disprove the Median Voter Theorem, but instead it emphasizes that turnout is meaningful when looking to measure the representative or typical voter.

Similar to Holcombe (1980), Mathis and Zech (1986) investigate the empirical viability of the Median Voter Theorem. A main goal of this paper is to disprove some of the criticisms of the theorem. To avoid criticism concerning lack of voter turnout, this paper ties voters to their income and then uses income to explain educational expenditures. Mathis and Zech find that median income is statistically significant and has high explanatory power of education expenditures, further proving the applicability of the Median Voter Theorem.

A subsequent study Mathis and Zech (1989) argues that while their previous paper empirically supports the Median Voter Theorem through a single-dimensional analysis, it becomes rather challenging to capture the complexity without a multi-dimensional framework. This observation connects to the hurdle of researchers in analyzing the *reason* why voters may or may not support a policy; there may be layers of reasoning. Holcombe (1989) rebuts criticisms and literature against the Median Voter Theorem by honing in on previous model approaches. Moreover, Holcombe (1989) states that the ideology on the feasibility of the Median Voter Theorem in multidimensional models does not disprove the theory's validity in all models. A final paper to consider on the topic of the Median Voter Theorem explores the foundational work it provides in explaining the world (Congleton 2003). The paper echoes much of what Holcombe (1980) asserts and expands on it with the idea that the Median Voter Theorem serves as a stem for public policy research for which more complex models can expand.

The usage of the Median Voter Theorem to analyze preferences of voters and outcomes of elections can be applied further to Colorado's legalization of psychedelic drugs in 2022. By exploring the characteristics of residents across Colorado and their turnout in the election, we can better understand the outcome of Proposition 122.

5.3 Data

We collect our data at the county level for Colorado in 2022 to help us better characterize the "median" voter in the state. This is to ultimately measure their likelihood for voting in favor of legalization of psychedelic drugs. Rather than assuming a homogeneous population across the state of Colorado, we consider, for example, how a voter in urban Denver County may differ from voters in rural Cheyenne County. With 64 counties in Colorado, disaggregating state voter data by county can parse out the distinctions for education, employment, income, age, gender, and political party affiliation.

5.3.1 Variables and Sources

Our data is collected through the Federal Reserve Bank of St. Louis (FRED), the New York Times, Colorado Secretary of State, City Population, and the Colorado Child Welfare Scholars Consortium. Additional details on our variables along with their units of measurement and sourcing information can be found in Table 5.1.

5 Get Psyched! An Empirical Analysis of Colorado's Legalization of... 93

Table 5.1 Variables, descriptions, and sources of data collected

Variable	Description	Source
Bachelor's or greater	The fraction of voters that have a Bachelor's Degree or greater level of education	FRED
Democrat share	The fraction of registered voters by county that are registered as Democrat out of all registered voters in that county	Constructed from Colorado Secretary of State
Female	The fraction of individuals in a county who are female	FRED
Median age	The median age in years for individuals in a county	FRED
Median income	The median income in dollars	FRED
Population density	Estimated population in 2022 of a county divided by the square area in kilometers	CityPopulation.de
Proportion vote yes	The fraction of voters by county that voted in favor of Proposition 122	New York Times
Republican share	The fraction of registered voters by county that are registered as Republican out of all registered voters in that county	Constructed from Colorado Secretary of State
Unemployment rate	Annual unemployment rate by county	FRED
Urban	Binomial variable identifying if a county is urban or rural	Colorado Child Welfare Scholars Consortium

Two measurements that we construct include the Democrat and Republican shares out of all registered voters. Since the county data on votes for the legalization of psychedelic drugs is presented as a proportion or share, we similarly construct the political party shares to create consistency in later empirical modeling. The Democrat and Republican shares are listed below, respectively, for a county i:

$$Democrat\ Share_i = \frac{total\ registered\ Democrats_i}{total\ registered\ voters_i}$$

$$Republican\ Share_i = \frac{total\ registered\ Republicans_i}{total\ registered\ voters_i}.$$

We next proceed with the presentation and discussion of descriptive statistics for each of our variables.

5.3.2 Descriptive Statistics

Table 5.2 presents the descriptive statistics of our variables. Though we observe rough normality for most of our variables of interest, we note that there is some evidence of positive skewness for both median income and population densities.

Table 5.2 Descriptive statistics for variables

Variable	Minimum	Median	Maximum	Mean	Standard deviation
Bachelor's or greater	0.13	0.30	0.63	0.35	0.14
Democrat share	0.05	0.22	0.54	0.23	0.11
Female	0.27	0.49	0.51	0.48	0.04
Median age	32.2	41.3	59.2	43.21	6.52
Median income	36,970	68,829.5	140,768	72,992.58	21,812.21
Population density	0.27	4.23	1799	67.71	253.21
Proportion vote yes	0.22	0.47	0.79	0.47	0.14
Republican share	0.10	0.35	0.65	0.35	0.15
Unemployment rate	0.02	0.03	0.06	0.03	0.01
Urban	0	0	1	0.19	0.39

We also consider potential correlation between our independent variables, noting that there is a clear relationship between a county's urban/rural classification and its population density in addition to the Republican and Democrat shares; we therefore choose not to include these pairs of controls together in a model.

In surveying the data, we present the fraction of the county populations that voted in favor of Proposition 122 against the share of voters in that county who are registered Republican (in Fig. 5.1) and the share of voters who are registered Democrat (in Fig. 5.2). We observe that there is a strong negative relationship in the case of Republican registrants and a positive relationship in the case of Democrat registrants. However, it does appear that there is more variation between counties for the relationship between registered Democrat voters and the percent of voters that voted to legalize psychedelic drugs. These observations in Colorado support the findings of Caldwell and Davis (2021) toward political party alignment of voters on drug legalization. In Fig. 5.3, we subsequently consider if there appears to be a relationship in counties surrounding education and likelihood for voting in favor of Proposition 122; again, we observe a positive relationship. This supports the findings of Lopez (2016) in the context of Colorado. We next proceed with our empirical modeling of the vote for legalization.

5.4 Modeling and Empirical Analysis

5.4.1 Models

In our empirical modeling of county voting for Proposition 122, we utilize Ordinary Least Squares (OLS) estimation. Our base model for consideration is

$$Proportion\ Vote\ Yes_i = \beta_0 + \beta_1 Democrat\ Share_i + \epsilon_i, \tag{5.1}$$

where i denotes a county in Colorado. We similarly estimate the proportion of the population voting against the legalization of psychedelics with the Republican share:

$$Proportion\ Vote\ No_i = \beta_0 + \beta_1 Republican\ Share_i + \epsilon_i. \tag{5.2}$$

We choose to consider these models separately because (1) the Democrat share, made up of the number of registered Democrats out of total registered voters, is highly correlated with the Republican share, (2) there are voters in Colorado who are registered with other political parties or not registered, and (3) we expected the likelihood of supporting the legalization of psychedelic drugs to sharply differ by political party based on the findings of Caldwell and Davis (2021). Since political party affiliation is not represented purely as a binomial variable, we opt to run these models separately. For the purposes of extended analysis, however, we choose to focus on the Democrat share as a control variable to explore a Colorado voter's likelihood for supporting Proposition 122.

We additionally consider extended models that incorporate controls for if a county is urban, as well as its degree of urbanization through its population density. Again noting that both of these variables are, in general, measuring the same characteristic (urban status), we run the following alternative models:

$$Proportion\ Vote\ Yes_i = \beta_0 + \beta_1 Democrat\ Share_i + \tag{5.3}$$
$$\beta_2 Population\ Density_i + \epsilon_i$$

$$Proportion\ Vote\ Yes_i = \beta_0 + \beta_1 Democrat\ Share_i + \beta_2 Urban_i + \epsilon_i. \tag{5.4}$$

Instead of measuring characteristics of a county though through its urban status, we alternatively account for demographic characteristics of a county's residents as controls. This includes the fraction of residents with a bachelor's degree or greater, the fraction who are female, and the median age of a county's residents. This model can be written as

$$Proportion\ Vote\ Yes_i = \beta_0 + \beta_1 Democrat\ Share_i + \tag{5.5}$$
$$\beta_2 Bachelor's\ or\ Greater_i + \beta_3 Female_i + \beta_4 Median\ Age_i + \epsilon_i.$$

Finally, we consider adding in controls for economic characteristics of a county's residents as an expansion of the previous model. This integrates measures for the annual (average) unemployment rate and median income.

$$Proportion\ Vote\ Yes_i = \beta_0 + \beta_1 Democrat\ Share_i +$$
$$\beta_2 Bachelor's\ or\ Greater_i + \beta_3 Female_i + \beta_4 Median\ Age_i +$$
$$\beta_5 Median\ Income_i + \beta_6 Unemployment\ Rate_i + \epsilon_i.$$

Table 5.3 Expected coefficient algebraic signs

Variable	Expected sign
Bachelor's or greater	+
Democrat share	+
Female	−
Median age	−
Median income	−
Population density	+
Republican share	−
Unemployment rate	+
Urban	+

As to the expected algebraic signs of the coefficients in each of these models, we next discuss our hypotheses along with supporting literature.

5.4.2 Hypotheses

We can look to past economics literature and studies on legalization of marijuana as a guide in forming expectations about ballots on psychedelic drugs. Table 5.3 records the expected algebraic signs of the coefficients in our earlier presented empirical models.

It is first important to note that, in general, attitudes toward drug legalization are becoming more favorable in the United States (Galston and Dionne Jr. 2013). This can be seen in the short time that it has taken marijuana to become legal for recreational use in some states and the current strides being taken in psychedelic legalization and decriminalization. In thinking about the relationship between education and drug policy stances, we anticipate a positive coefficient for *Bachelor's or Greater*. Frendreis and Tatalovich (2020) identify, using a county-level analysis, a positive relationship between support for marijuana and college education of voters; we would expect a similar finding for psychedelics.

Another important finding of Galston and Dionne Jr. (2013) is the gender impact on drug legalization, which finds that women are more likely to vote no than men on drug freedom policies. The difference between the male and female acceptance of drug legalization is around 10%. Matheson and Le Foll (2023) similarly note that females are less likely to consume or try marijuana than males. This leads us to project that the coefficient for *Female* will be negative in our regressions.

The median age coefficient is a very unique one in our case. As age increases, there is a significant drop in support for drug legalization (Galston and Dionne Jr. 2013). This is commonly found in other studies such as Campbell et al. (2017) and Spetz et al. (2019). In fact, Campbell et al. (2017) find that in data surveying multiple cohorts of Americans throughout several years, as each cohort ages, support for drug legalization decreases. This is especially interesting because it suggests that age of an individual does play a role in attitudes toward legalization rather than there just being a difference in overall attitudes throughout generations accounting for the current older generation's beliefs on strict drug regulations. This study shows that decrease in support for drug legalization as age increases is a trend that follows and tracks over the course of time. This leads us to expect a negative coefficient for *Median Age*.

Our hypothesis about the coefficient for *Median Income* is guided by Galston and Dionne Jr. (2013) in its conclusion that as income increases, generally agreeableness for drug legalization decreases by a few percent. Further, this factor follows median age in that people typically earn more as they age. However, both Galston and Dionne Jr. (2013) and our summary statistics in Table 5.2 reflect little variance between age groups. So we will note this before proceeding with our regression analysis. In connection to economic characteristics of voters, we anticipate that the *Unemployment Rate* coefficient will be positive. This is furthered by Spetz et al. (2019), which finds unemployed populations more favorable toward marijuana legalization. There is, however, statistical evidence that there may be limited connections between labor markets and marijuana (Popovici and French 2014).

The projected coefficients for the *Democrat Share* (+) and *Republican Share* (−) are opposite to represent the difference in beliefs and values between the political parties. Looking at the support in legalization of marijuana, it is widely referenced that Democrats are more likely to approve of drug legalization than Republican voters (Caldwell and Davis 2021; Galston and Dionne Jr. 2013; McGinty et al. 2017; Spetz et al. 2019). For example, Galston and Dionne Jr. (2013) indicate that Republicans may perceive the use of marijuana (as well as other drugs) as morally wrong, leading to little support for legalization. In McGinty et al. (2017), the authors found 13 reasons why people would be for legalization of marijuana and 13 reasons that people would be against its legalization. In those results, they found that Democrats are likely to agree with more than ten of the pro-legalization rationales; in contrast, Republicans are likely to agree with 11 or more of the anti-legalization rationales.

The two remaining coefficient signs, *Urban* and *Population Density*, can be evaluated through the breakdown of Republican and Democratic populations that live in urban areas compared to rural. Jokela (2022) explores the relationship between party affiliation in urban and rural areas, noting that Republicans are more likely to live in rural areas. By extension, Democrats are more likely to live in urban areas. This study also finds that those who are Republican are more likely to move out of urban areas and into rural areas. Before proceeding with our regression analysis, we inspect for possible correlation between the Democrat share in a county and a county's classification as urban. We find the correlation in our dataset between the Democrat share and Colorado county being urban is 0.275; we similarly find that the correlation in our dataset between the Republican share and Colorado county being urban is −0.333. We again find similar correlations when considering the correlations between population density and the political party shares. This leads us to conclude that these sets of variables are not strongly correlated with

Table 5.4 Regressions (1) and (2)

Variables	(1)	(2)
Democrat share	0.944 ***	
	(0.152)	
Republican share		0.833 ***
		(0.051)
Constant	0.256 ***	0.234 ***
	(0.031)	(0.019)
Robust std. errors?	Yes	No
R^2	0.553	0.814
F-stat	38.7	271.23
Observations	64	64

Note: * $p < 0.10$, ** $p < 0.05$, *** $p < 0.01$ in two-tailed t-test for difference in means

each other and can be used simultaneously in regression analysis. Moreover, even within an urban area, a higher population density would suggest a higher share of Democrats, giving the population density a positive coefficient in line with the Democrat coefficient as well (Jokela 2022).

5.4.3 Regressions and Empirical Analysis

Table 5.4 includes the regression results for our base models (1) and (2). The coefficients for variables in the models are reported alongside their respective standard errors. We additionally test for heteroscedasticity in each of our regressions, including robust standard errors when appropriate.

We identify that there is statistical significance at the 1% level for both the Democrat and Republican shares of voters impacting the proportion of votes for Proposition 122 in Colorado. From (1), for a 1% increase in Democratic registered voters relative to the total number of registered voters, there is a 0.944% increase in the proportion of votes in favor of psychedelic drug legalization. Similarly in (2), we find that with a 1% increase in Republican registered voters relative to the total number of registered voters, there is a 0.833% increase in the proportion of votes *against* psychedelic drug legalization. This supports our hypotheses that political party affiliation of the median voter in Colorado counties may closely affect voting outcomes. We next proceed with Table 5.5, which presents the regression results integrating controls for if a county is urban or rural.

Again, we observe in both (3) and (4) statistical significance at the 1% level of significance for the Democrat share and the proportion of votes in favor of legalization. However, there appears to be little change on the explanatory power of the model by including a control for if a county is urban or its population density. We fail to find any statistical evidence (despite a positive algebraic coefficient) of a relationship between *Urban* and *Population Density* on the proportion of vote in

5 Get Psyched! An Empirical Analysis of Colorado's Legalization of...

Table 5.5 Regressions (3) and (4)

Variables	(3)	(4)
Democrat share	0.932 ***	0.937 ***
	(0.172)	(0.170)
Population density	0.000	
	(0.000)	
Urban		0.007
		(0.026)
Constant	0.258 ***	0.257 ***
	(0.033)	(0.032)
Robust std. errors?	Yes	Yes
R^2	0.554	0.553
F-stat	99.58	35.58
Observations	64	64

Note: * $p < 0.10$, ** $p < 0.05$, *** $p < 0.01$ in two-tailed t-test for difference in means

Table 5.6 Regressions (5) and (6)

Variables	(5)	(6)
Democrat share	0.641 ***	0.615 ***
	(0.076)	(0.103)
Bachelor's or greater	0.006 ***	0.005 ***
	(0.001)	(0.001)
Female	−0.004 *	−0.004 **
	(0.002)	(0.002)
Median age	0.002 *	0.002 *
	(0.001)	(0.001)
log(median income)		0.076
		(0.049)
Unemployment rate		0.021 *
		(0.012)
Constant	0.243 **	−0.651
	(0.111)	(0.553)
Robust std. errors?	No	No
R^2	0.831	0.848
F-stat	72.6	53.16
Observations	64	64

Note: * $p < 0.10$, ** $p < 0.05$, *** $p < 0.01$ in two-tailed t-test for difference in means

favor of psychedelic drugs. We then proceed with Table 5.6, including regression results with controls for demographic and economic factors.

We observe increases to explanatory power for regressions (5) and (6) relative to earlier models through the inclusion of additional controls. In (5), we again observe strong statistical significance between the Democrat share of a county and the proportion of voters in support of legalization. We also find statistical significance at the 1% level for the fraction of voters with a bachelor's degree or higher level of education and the fraction of voters supporting Proposition 122. The algebraic signs of the coefficients for *Bachelor's or Greater* and *Female* also align with the previous findings of Frendreis and Tatalovich (2020) in addition to Galston and Dionne Jr. (2013). In particular, the analysis of these coefficients is insightful for understanding the median voter in Colorado and perspectives on psychedelic drugs. What is surprising though is the positive and statistically significant (at the 10% level) coefficient for *Median Age*. As the median age of residents in Colorado county increases, the proportion of voters supporting legalization increases. Part of the rationale behind this result may be acclimation of the Colorado electorate following the past legalization of marijuana in 2012. In (6), we not only observe similar findings with previous variables but also find statistical significance at the 10% level of a relationship between the average unemployment rate of a county and support for Proposition 122; there is no evidence of a statistical relationship between the log of median income and the proportion of support for legalization. In general, we observe algebraic signs of our coefficients (excluding the unemployment rate) consistent with past literature and hypotheses in estimating Colorado's voting outcome.

5.5 Conclusion and Discussion

The legalization of psychedelic drugs in Colorado with Proposition 122 in 2022 can be analyzed through the characteristics of voters and economic conditions of counties. What we observe is that there is a strong, positive, statistically significant relationship between the proportion of voters who support the legalization of psychedelic drugs in Colorado and the fraction of registered voters who are Democratic. Additionally, we find that as both median age and the percentage of residents who are college-educated increase, the likelihood of supporting Proposition 122 increases. However, there is negative association between the percentage of individuals who are female in a county and the fraction voting in favor of legalization. Evaluating county controls and voter attributes helps us to connect a typical voter's background with the roughly 53.64% of Coloradans deciding to legalize psychedelic drugs (Ballotpedia 2024d).

This empirical analysis on Colorado may help us in considering similar policy proposals in the future, such as successive legalization policies in states. Further, future areas of research could be through synthetic control approaches in estimating a state's likelihood for moving toward legalization. Additionally, a more granular, individualized level could be considered as opposed to the county in understanding the Median Voter. As in the case with Moreno et al. (2016), survey data could be collected regarding perspectives on the legalization of psychedelics. Where the economic effects and consequences of accessible psychedelic drugs may be uncertain to predict at this point, Colorado's progressive steps may lead to a more widespread movement across the United States.

Appendix

See Figs. 5.1, 5.2, and 5.3.

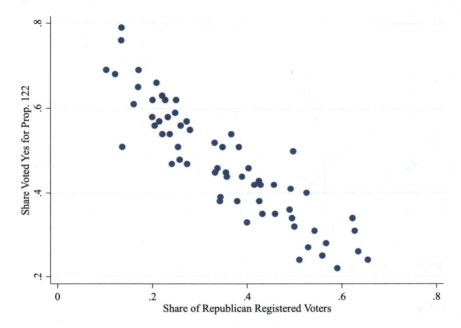

Fig. 5.1 Scatterplot of republican share and vote yes share

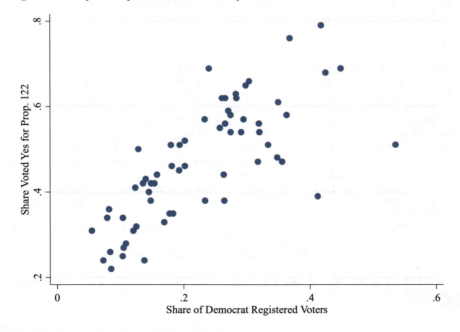

Fig. 5.2 Scatterplot of democrat share and vote yes share

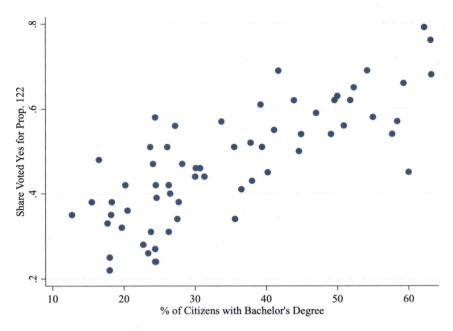

Fig. 5.3 Scatterplot of % with bachelor's degree or greater and vote yes share

References

Ballotpedia (2024a) Colorado 2022 ballot measures. Ballotpedia 26 March 2024
Ballotpedia (2024b) Colorado amendment 64, regulation of marijuana initiative (2012). Ballotpedia 1 April 2024
Ballotpedia (2024c) Colorado amendment f, charitable gaming measure (2022). Ballotpedia 26 March 2024
Ballotpedia (2024d) Colorado proposition 122, decriminalization and regulated access program for certain psychedelic plants and fungi initiative (2022). Ballotpedia 26 March 2024
Ballotpedia (2024e) Colorado proposition 125, wine sales in grocery and convenience stores initiative (2022). Ballotpedia 26 March 2024
Ballotpedia (2024f) Presidential voting trends in Colorado. Ballotpedia 26 March 2024
Bink A (2023) Map: where marijuana will be legal in 2024. The Hill 29 December 2023
Black D (1948) On the rationale of group decision-making. J Polit Econ 56(1):23–34
Burrus R Jr, Sackley W, Sollars D (2007) Illicit drugs and economics: examples for the principles classroom. J Econ Finance Edu 6(2):75–86
Caldwell J, Davis W (2021) Is there a difference between democrat and republican states in the percentage of male high school students who have ever used marijuana? Lincoln Memorial Univ J Human Soc Sci 1(2):1
Campbell W, Twenge J, Carter N (2017) Support for marijuana(cannabis) legalization: untangling age, period, and cohort effects. Collabra Psychol 3(1):1–9
Congleton RD (2003) The median voter model. The Encyclopedia of Public Choice. Springer, Boston, pp 707–712
Cussen M, Block W (2000) Legalize drugs now!: an analysis of the benefits of legalized drugs. Am J Econ Sociol 59(3):525–536

Davis A, Agin-Liebes G, España M, Pilecki B, Luoma J (2022) Attitudes and beliefs about the therapeutic use of psychedelic drugs among psychologists in the united states. J Psychoact Drugs 54(4):309–318

Dills A, Goffard S, Miron J (2016) Dose of reality: the effect of state marijuana legalizations. CATO Institute Policy Analysis No. 799

Dinan J, Heckelman J (2019) Voting on prohibition: disentangling preferences on alcohol and decentralization. Soc Sci History 43(1):113–130

Downey L, Sarris J, Perkins D (2021) Legalization of psychedelic substances. JAMA 326(23):2434–2435

Felix A (2018) The economic effects of the marijuana industry in Colorado. Federal Reserve Bank of Kansas City 15 April 2018

Frendreis J, Tatalovich R (2020) Postmaterialism and referenda voting to legalize marijuana. Int J Drug Policy 75:102595

Galston WA, Dionne Jr E (2013) The New Politics of Marijuana Legalization: Why Opinion Is Changing. The Brookings Institution, Washington, DC, pp 1–16

Hao Z, Cowan B (2020) The cross-border spillover effects of recreational marijuana legalization. Econ Inq 58(2):642–666

Holcombe RG (1980) An empirical test of the median voter model. Econ Inq 18(2):260–274

Holcombe RG (1989) The median voter model in public choice theory. Public Choice 61(2):115–125

Jacobs A (2023) Legal use of hallucinogenic mushrooms begins in Oregon. The New York Times 3 January 2023

Jokela M (2022) Urban-rural residential mobility associated with political party affiliation: the U.S. national longitudinal surveys of youth and young adults. Soc Psychol Personal Sci 13(1):83–90

Kim H, Monte A (2016) Colorado cannabis legalization and its effect on emergency care. Ann Emergency Med 68(1):71–75

Lopez M (2016) Does education affects attitudes towards marijuana legalization. Universidad San Francisco De Quito USFQ

Marlan D (2019) Beyond cannabis: psychedelic decriminalization and social justice. Lewis Clark Law Rev 23(3):851–892

Matheson J, Le Foll B (2023) Impacts of recreational cannabis legalization on use and harms: a narrative review of sex/gender differences. Front Psychiatry 14:1127660

Mathis EJ, Zech CE (1986) An examination into the relevance of the median voter model: empirical evidence offers support for the model and certain uses. Am J Econ Sociol 45(4):403–412

Mathis EJ, Zech CE (1989) The median voter model fails an empirical test: the procedure, useful in the absence of a better one, is not valid for multidimensional issues. Am J Econ Sociol 48(1):79–87

McGinty EE, Niederdeppe J, Heley K, Barry CL (2017) Public perceptions of arguments supporting and opposing recreational marijuana legalization. Prevent Med 99:80–86

Miron JA, Zwiebel J (1995) The economic case against drug prohibition. J Econ Perspect 9(4):175–192

Moreno M, Whitehill J, Quach V, Midamba N, Manskopf I (2016) Marijuana experiences, voting behaviors and early perspectives regarding marijuana legalization among college students from two states. J Am College Health 64(1):9–18

Nichols D (2016) Psychedelics. Pharmacol Rev 68(2):264–355

Niskanen WA (1992) Economists and drug policy. Carnegie-Rochester Confer Ser Public Policy 36:223–248

Plaksa J (2021) The effects of marijuana legalization in Colorado: more neutral than expected. Drug Enforcement and Policy Center, No 37 Ohio State's Legal Studies Research Paper No. 671

Popovici I, French M (2014) Cannabis use, employment, and income: fixed-effects analysis of panel data. J Behavioral Health Serv Res 41(2):185–202

Rice TW (1985) An examination of the median voter hypothesis. Western Polit Q 38(2):211–223

Samenow D, Kung K, Ludwig R (2023) State psychedelic regulation: Oregon and Colorado taking the lead. DLA Piper

Smith W, Appelbaum P (2021) Two models of legalization of psychedelic substances: reasons for concern. JAMA 326(8):697–698

Spetz J, Chapman SA, Bates T, Jura M, Schmidt LA (2019) Social and political factors associated with state-level legalization of cannabis in the united states. Contemp Drug Probl 46(2):165–179

Thornton M (2007) Prohibition versus legalization: do economists reach a conclusion on drug policy? Indep Rev 11(3):417–433

Waldfogel J (2008) The median voter and the median consumer: local private goods and population composition. J Urban Econ 63(2):567–582

Walkins C, Scrimgeour F (2000) Economics and the legalisation of drugs. Agenda 7(4):333–344

Warner KE (1991) Legalizing drugs: lessons from (and about) economics. Milbank Q 69(4, Confronting Drug Policy: Part 2):641–661

Chapter 6
The Racial Political Economy of Bank Entry Restrictions

James Dean

Abstract While previous research has shown that branching restrictions reduced overall credit supply, more recent research suggests that some borrowers benefitted from these restrictions as credit was kept within a community. However, the impact of unit banking on racial outcomes is still theoretically ambiguous. On the one hand, unit banks tended to favor the wealthy. Thus, branching restrictions could lead to banks not expanding into primarily Black areas, leading to many being underbanked. On the other hand, branching restrictions led to the creation of many Black-owned banks devoted to serving primarily Black areas. Using data from the 1920s, I empirically test these competing arguments using an empirical median voter model.

6.1 Introduction

Banking in the United States has always been a regulatory labyrinth, as a bank must meet national regulations, individual state regulations, and regulations specific to a bank's charter. A bank's required reserve ratios, capital requirements, and loan regulations depended on whether it was state or nationally chartered and in what state it was headquartered. Further, while today banks in the United States are largely free to open branches and expand business into new markets, this is a fairly new development in the history of banking. State-by-state branching restrictions have meant it has been more common for regulations to require a bank to serve only its local community than for a bank to be a national fixture.

After the Civil War, national banks were allowed to be chartered but could only operate in individual states. The Comptroller of the Currency, one of the national banks' regulators, restricted national banks from establishing branches throughout a state until the McFadden Act of 1927. For a state-chartered bank, the landscape

---

J. Dean (✉)
Western Carolina University, Cullowhee, NC, USA
e-mail: jdean@wcu.edu

© The Author(s), under exclusive license to Springer Nature Switzerland AG 2025
J. Hall, K. Starr (eds.), *Empirical Applications of the Median Voter Model*, Studies in Public Choice 45, https://doi.org/10.1007/978-3-031-87179-5_6

was somewhat similar. States often outlawed branching for all banks, and even more states restricted branching to within a city's limits. In fact, it was not until the Riegle-Neal Act in 1994 that cross-state mergers and acquisitions were allowed (Calomiris 2000).

This "one-town, one-bank" structure had a large effect on credit access and banking quality. Specifically, unit banking made banks less regionally diversified and more susceptible to region-specific shocks (White 1983; Calomiris 2000). This, in turn, led to a higher bank failure rate and worse economic performance during the Great Depression in states with branching restrictions (Mitchener 2005). Indeed, as banks shifted toward more liberalized branching laws, their statewide banking system became more stable, and banks better diversified their assets (Gart 1994; Hubbard 1994). However, more recent research using individual bank data casts some doubt on these results. Calomiris and Mason (2000) and Carlson (2004) find that unit banks were less likely to fail than branched banks because they opted to reduce their reserves rather than diversify their portfolio. This conundrum was further examined in Carlson and Mitchener (2006), finding that allowing branching increased competition in a state, forcing weaker banks to exit. This strengthened the regional banking system without specifically strengthening branched banks. In short, the competition from branching improved bank stability more than banks geographically diversifying.

While branching restrictions repressed the number of banks to which a consumer had access, it also lowered the quality of banking the consumer received. Calomiris and Ramirez (2004) find that branching restrictions led to slightly lower interest rates received on deposits and higher interest rates paid on loans. Rajan and Ramcharan (2011) similarly find that credit was costlier and more limited in states with branching restrictions. As states shifted toward allowing statewide branching after the Great Depression, the improved credit conditions led to mechanization in the state's agriculture industry and growth in manufacturing (Dehejia and Lleras-Muney 2007).

Despite the largely consistent evidence that branching restrictions led to worse outcomes, states were slow to reform. In fact, a motion to permit branching was defeated in a referendum in Illinois in 1924 (White 1985). Economides et al. (1996) theoretically examine the political economy of these branch restrictions. Their model suggests branching restrictions were introduced for political reasons. Specifically, unit banks did not want to compete with large, branching banks. In turn, these unit bankers lobbied their state to enact and retain these branching restrictions to protect their business. Calomiris and Ramírez (2018) expand on this, developing a model that shows unit banking can be beneficial to certain borrowers, namely land owners in high-wealth states. Put simply, these borrowers benefited from the bank having fewer loan options, increasing their own credit availability.

While unit banking often led to worse outcomes and underbaking community-wide, black communities were often particularly underbanked. Black-owned banks rose to try to fill this void and supply credit and banking services. During the height of bank branching restrictions from 1900 to 1934, 130 black-owned banks, along with 50 additional savings and loans and credit unions, were created in the

United States. These black-owned banks peaked in size in 1926, holding roughly $13 million in assets (Baradaran 2017). These banks created during this time only put a small portion of their assets into industrial businesses, stocks, and bonds, opting instead to lend to churches, mutual aid societies, and service businesses in their local community (Ammons 1996). In turn, these black-owned banks played an important role in black entrepreneurs gaining access to credit, as these entrepreneurs were often discriminated against at non-black-owned community banks (Black et al. 1978, 2001). Because these banks lent to more liquidity-constrained borrowers than other community banks, they ran on tighter margins, leading to higher interest rates charged on loans and lower deposit rates (Brimmer 1971; Kwast and Black 1983). As a result, black-owned banks were hit harder during the Great Depression, and only nine remained in business by the late 1930s.

This chapter examines the racial political economy of these bank branching restrictions. There are two competing arguments for how branching restrictions affected black communities. First, as discussed earlier, unit banks tended to benefit wealthy landowners, leading to inefficient community-wide outcomes at the benefit of the wealthy. These branching restrictions could have prevented banks from opening branches in primarily black communities. In this line of reasoning, black communities would likely favor lighter branching restrictions, as more branches could lead to a greater supply of credit and better banking. Alternatively, black-owned banks played an important role in credit supply in black communities. Lighter branching restrictions could favor financially stronger banks, potentially putting these black-owned banks out of business and reducing community-wide banking. In this scenario, black communities would favor branching restrictions, better protecting the regions black-owned banks and proving better banking services overall.

To test these competing arguments, I utilize an empirical median voter model. Overall, I find that a greater share of black residents significantly decreased the likelihood a state had branching restrictions. Even more, a greater share of black residents pushed a state toward lighter branching laws through each of our four branching classifications. I then examine how these restrictions impacted the quality of banking at the county level. I find that black residents in states with harsher branching restrictions had fewer bank options and paid higher interest rates on their loans. Overall, results are consistent with the theory that a greater share of black residents pushed the median voter toward a preference for bank branching.

6.2 Data and Estimation

I use data on banks from the 1920s, taking advantage of a cross-sectional variation across states' banking laws. I use a state's legal status of bank branching restrictions in 1924, taken from White (1985). This divides states into four categories: (1) states that allow branching in the entire state, (2) states that allow only limited branching, which typically restricts branching to a city, (3) states that did not specifically

Table 6.1 Legal status of branching in various states

Legal status 1	Legal status 2	Legal status 3	Legal status 4
Statewide branching permitted	Limited branching permitted	Judicial/administrative prohibition	Branching prohibited by state law
Arizona	Louisiana	Iowa	Alabama
California	Maine	Kansas	Arkansas
Delaware	Massachusetts	Montana	Colorado
Georgia	New York	Nebraska	Connecticut
Maryland	Ohio	New Hampshire	Florida
North Carolina	Mississippi	New Jersey	Idaho
Rhode Island	Pennsylvania	North Dakota	Illinois
South Carolina	Kentucky	Oklahoma	Indiana
Tennessee	Michigan	Vermont	Minnesota
Virginia		West Virginia	Missouri
		Wyoming	Nevada
			New Mexico
			Oregon
			Texas
			Utah
			Washington
			Wisconsin

Source: White (1985)

prohibit branching, but instead had a judicial or administrative prohibition, and (4) states that permit branching by law. Table 6.1 lists the states by their branching restrictions, and Fig. 6.1 shows a map of branching restrictions. As seen in the figure, branching restrictions were common in the Great Plains through the Pacific Northwest, while branching was more commonly permitted in near the East Coast and through the Northeast.

I obtain state characteristics from the 1920 Census, the *Statistical Abstract of the United States*, and Lleras-Muney (2002). To control for the influence of manufacturing on the state banking landscape, I use the percentage of the workforce employed in manufacturing, and to control for the influence of farm owners, I include a state's number of farms per capita. I control for other factors that might influence the regulator regime, such as income per capita, percentage of the population living in urban areas, and the percentage of population born outside of the USA.

Next, I use bank data from the *FDIC Data on Banks in the United States, 1920-1936*. This data gives, at the county level, the total number of banks, the amount held in deposits, the number of state or nationally chartered banks, the number of banks suspended, and the average interest rate charged on loans at each bank. In turn, this data allows us to examine whether branching restrictions (or deregulation) led to better banking, giving a clearer picture of the state's banking landscape.

6 The Racial Political Economy of Bank Entry Restrictions

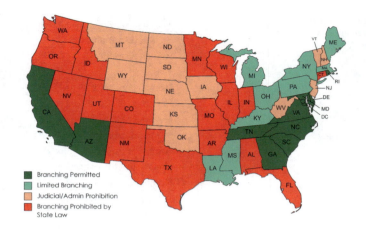

Fig. 6.1 State branching restrictions in 1924

I use a cross section of states in the 1924 for several reasons. First, the mid-1920s allows us to take advantage of heterogeneity among states prior to the Great Depression. The widespread bank closures, and especially black-owned bank closures, during the Great Depression made the political economy of a state's branching restrictions less relevant as banks failed at a high rate. In turn, the Great Depression would complicate any result derived from post-1920s data. Second, as discussed previously, rural bank failures led to significant changes in bank branching regulation across states. As such, the mid-1920s gives substantial cross-sectional variation as this change happened prior to the Great Depression. Third, a wider variety of bank data was available in the 1920s compared to previous years, and the FDIC data is only available as early as 1920. Finally, as noted in Calomiris and Ramírez (2018), cars had become more available to middle-class households by the 1920s. This should have increased competition among nearby unit banks, as consumers could simply drive to the next bank. In turn, the 1920s limited the rents a unit bank can extract. Summary statistics for each variable are in Table 6.2.

I first examine a state's bank branching regime in using the median voter model. This model states that a government is responsive to the electorate, so its policies can be reflective of the median voter (Hotelling 1929). In this context, the state's selected bank branching regime is representative of the median voter. Further, this median voter is representative of the state's racial makeup, so a greater share of black residents leads to greater black representation in the median voter.

I first examine the racial political economy of a state's branching regime by estimating a probit regression on whether or not the state restricts bank branching. Here, a state that restricts branching is coded as a "1" and consists of categories (3) and (4) in the 1924 data detailed above: It is equal to one if a state explicitly prohibits branching or had administrative or judicial prohibitions and is zero otherwise. Next, I decompose the probit results by examining a state's specific branching regulations through an ordered probit model. In this model, the dependent variable is coded

Table 6.2 Comparison of state-level and county-level variables

Variable	Mean	Std. dev.
State-level variables		
Branch restriction	0.604	0.494
% Black	0.099	0.146
Income per capita	15,278.74	1632.09
% Urban	0.423	0.214
% Foreign	0.123	0.08
% Manufacturing	0.065	0.048
Farms per capita	68.83	36.16
County-level variables		
Number of banks	10.42	10.45
Average interest rate	6.414	0.877
% Black	0.127	0.194
Branch restriction	0.591	0.492
% Urban	0.195	0.242
Illiteracy rate	0.042	0.041
Log(population)	9.878	0.909
% Farms w/mortgage	0.245	0.144
Land area	0.941	1.310
Log(wage)	2.734	1.578

according to the four categories detailed in Table 6.1. As such, this variable is coded as the lowest branching restrictions (branching allowed statewide, equal to one) to the greatest branching restrictions (branching prohibited statewide, equal to four). These regressions take the form:

$$\Pr(Restrictions = 1 \mid Black, X) = \Phi(\beta_0 + \beta_1 \text{Black}' + \beta_2 X' + \epsilon) \quad (6.1)$$

$$\Pr(Restrictions = i \mid Black, X) = \Phi(\beta_1 \text{Black}' + \beta_2 X' + \epsilon) \quad (6.2)$$

where $i = 1, 2, 3, 4$. R represents the percentage of the state's population who is black, and X are state controls. Specifically, I use the state's income per capita, percentage of population residing in urban areas, percentage of population born outside the USA, percentage of employment in manufacturing, and the number of farms per capita.

Next, I want to examine whether these branching restrictions (or lack of restrictions) leads to better banking throughout the state and how a state's racial makeup influences this. For this estimation, I use county-level data on the number of banks and the average interest rate charged on loans. While branching restrictions were a state-level policy, examining the data at the county level, given the state's branching regime, allows us to more deeply examine the role of race in the local banking market. I construct these regressions of the form:

$$B_i = \beta_0 + \beta_1 \text{Black}'_i + \beta_2 \text{Restriction} + \quad (6.3)$$
$$\beta_3 \text{Black}_i \times \text{Restriction} + \beta_4 X'_i + \theta V_i + \epsilon_i$$

where B_i is the number of banks in the county and average interest rate charged, *Race* is the county's black population share, Restriction is whether the state restricts branching (coded as above), X_i are county controls for the illiteracy rate, log population, percentage of farms with a mortgage, land area, income per capita, and percentage of population in urban areas. Finally, V_i are county-level fixed effects, and standard errors are clustered at the state level.

6.3 Empirical Results

Results for the probit and ordered probit are given in Table 6.3, and results for the county-level regressions are given in Table 6.4. Column (1) gives results for the probit regression. Notably, the coefficient on black population share is negative and statistically significant, even when controlling for farm and manufacturing industries. Thus, a greater share of black population decreases the likelihood that a state enacts any kind bank branching restrictions. Column (2) gives results for

Table 6.3 Probit regression results

Variable	Branch	Legal status
% Black	−0.056**	−0.030*
	(−2.48)	(−1.86)
Income per capita	−0.147	−0.210*
	(−1.09)	(−1.92)
% Urban	−0.024	0.009
	(−0.87)	(0.47)
% Foreign	−0.009	−0.02
	(−0.20)	(−0.62)
% Manufacturing	−0.801	−0.022
	(−0.09)	(−0.62)
Farms per capita	0.001	0.002
	(0.15)	(0.28)
Constant	4.235	–
	(1.78)	
N	48	48
Chi^2 statistic	17.56	13.41
Prob > Chi^2	0.0074	0.0370
Pseudo R^2	0.2803	0.0883
Log likelihood	−23.191	−59.292

Note: t-statistics in parentheses. **$p < 0.05$, *$p < 0.1$

Table 6.4 Regression results from county-level banking regressions

	(1)	(2)	(3)	(4)
%Black	5.641*	1.513	0.666	1.133**
	(2.44)	(0.70)	(1.60)	(3.07)
Restriction	4.725***	2.925*	0.174	0.378*
	(3.87)	(2.45)	(1.08)	(2.20)
%Black*Restriction	−14.06***	–	1.593*	–
	(−4.33)		(2.48)	
Illiteracy rate	−58.75***	−59.61***	4.285*	4.383*
	(−4.42)	(−3.72)	(2.45)	(2.43)
Log(population)	9.236***	9.085***	−0.177**	−0.160*
	(8.77)	(8.54)	(−2.75)	(−2.46)
% Farms w/mortgage	6.185	7.638*	−0.171	−0.336
	(1.73)	(2.20)	(−0.25)	(−0.47)
Land area	0.231	0.188	0.156***	0.161***
	(1.46)	(1.28)	(4.89)	(4.89)
Log(wage)	−0.684**	−0.777***	−0.0655*	−0.0549
	(−3.34)	(−3.77)	(−2.54)	(−1.95)
%Urban	−3.239*	−2.945	0.104	0.0710
	(−2.19)	(−1.87)	(0.47)	(0.31)
Constant	−82.48***	−80.17***	7.753***	7.492***
	(−8.28)	(−7.98)	(12.51)	(11.82)
N	2837	2837	2837	2837
R^2	0.547	0.535	0.414	0.393
State FE?	Y	Y	Y	Y

Note: t-statistics in parentheses. ***$p < 0.01$, **$p < 0.05$, *$p < 0.1$. The number of Banks is the dependent variable in Columns 1 and 2. The Average Interest Rate is the dependent variable in Columns 3 and 4

the ordered probit regression. Here, the coefficient on black population share is still negative and statistically significant, controlling for the same factors. Thus, not only does a higher share of black population decrease the likelihood of any branching restriction, but it also decreases the likelihood of each level of branching restriction, leading to freer branching. Per the median voter theorem, this is consistent with the conclusion that, as there was greater black representation in the median voter, there tended to be lower likelihood of any branching restriction and a greater tendency toward freer bank branching.

Table 6.4 builds on these results by examining how the share of black population impacts banking access and quality, given these branching restrictions. Columns (1) and (2) use the total number of banks as the dependent variable, while columns (3) and (4) use the average interest rate. Standard errors are clustered at the state level. The coefficient on black population share is positive and statistically significant in Column (1), but the interaction between black population share and a state's branching regime is negative and significant. In turn, this means a greater share of black population increases the number of banks on the aggregate, but a greater black population share in restricted branching states leads to fewer banks. This is consistent with the hypothesis that black residents in states with branching restrictions were underbanked. The regression in Column (2) omits this interaction, and the coefficient on black population share is not statistically significant. Notably, the coefficient on branching restrictions is positive and significant in both regressions, so greater branching restrictions increase the number of banks. Column (3) shows similar results to Column (1): a greater black population share leads to statistically significant increase in the average interest rate paid on loans, and greater black populations in states with branching restrictions paid higher rates on loans. Indeed, this result reinforces the theory that black communities in branching restricted states had lower quality banking opportunities. Column (4) omits the interaction term, and the coefficient on black population share and branching regime is positive and significant, as intuition would largely dictate.

6.4 Conclusion

This chapter empirically examines the racial political economy of branching restrictions in the 1920s United States. Some borrowers benefited from the more localized credit markets of restricted branching. Indeed, black-owned banks often stepped in to provide banking services to underbanked black communities. However, unit banks often favored the wealthy and could have prevented banks from opening branches in black communities. This begs the question: what is the role of race in a state's branching regime?

Overall, results show that a higher black population share was associated with a lower likelihood of branching restrictions and decreased levels of branching restrictions. According to the empirical median voter model, as black residents were better represented in the median voter, the median voter preferred freer bank branching. What is more, black residents in states with branching restrictions were subject to worse banking quality and access, seen through a decline in the number of banks and an increase in the interest rate paid on loans.

References

Ammons L (1996) The evolution of black-owned banks in the United States between the 1880s and 1990s. J Black Stud 26(4):467–489

Baradaran M (2017) The Color of Money: Black Banks and the Racial Wealth Gap. Harvard University Press, Cambridge

Black H, Schweitzer RL, Mandell L (1978) Discrimination in mortgage lending. Am Econ Rev 68(2):186–191

Black HA, Robinson BL, Schweitzer RL (2001) Comparing lending decisions of minority-owned and white-owned banks: is there discrimination in mortgage lending? Rev Financ Econ 10(1):23–39

Brimmer AF (1971) The black banks: an assessment of performance and prospects. J Finance 26(2):379–405

Calomiris C, Ramirez C (2004) The Political Economy of Bank Entry Restrictions: Theory and Evidence from the US in the 1920s. Columbia University, Working Paper

Calomiris CW (2000) US Bank Deregulation in Historical Perspective. Cambridge University Press, Cambridge

Calomiris CW, Mason J (2000) Causes of US Bank Distress During the Depression. National Bureau of Economic Research, Working Paper 7919

Calomiris CW, Ramírez CD (2018) The political economy of bank entry restrictions: a theory of unit banking. In: Hall J, Witcher M (eds) Public Choice Analyses of American Economic History: Volume 2. Springer, New York, pp 99–119

Carlson M (2004) Are branch banks better survivors? evidence from the depression era. Econ Inq 42(1):111–126

Carlson M, Mitchener KJ (2006) Branch banking, bank competition, and financial stability. J Money Credit Banking 38(5):1293–1328

Dehejia R, Lleras-Muney A (2007) Financial development and pathways of growth: state branching and deposit insurance laws in the United States, 1900–1940. J Law Econ 50(2):239–272

Economides N, Hubbard RG, Palia D (1996) The political economy of branching restrictions and deposit insurance: a model of monopolistic competition among small and large banks. J Law Econ 39(2):667–704

Gart A (1994) Regulation, Deregulation, Reregulation: The Future of the Banking, Insurance, and Securities Industries. Wiley, New York

Hotelling H (1929) Stability in competition. Econ J 39(153):41–57

Hubbard RG (1994) Money, the Financial System, and the Economy. Addison-Wesley Publishing Company, Boston

Kwast ML, Black H (1983) An analysis of the behavior of mature black-owned commercial banks. J Econ Business 35(1):41–54

Lleras-Muney A (2002) Were compulsory attendance and child labor laws effective? an analysis from 1915 to 1939. J Law Econ 45(2):401–435

Mitchener KJ (2005) Bank supervision, regulation, and instability during the great depression. J Econ History 65(1):152–185

Rajan RG, Ramcharan R (2011) Land and credit: a study of the political economy of banking in the United States in the early 20th century. J Finance 66(6):1895–1931

White EN (1983) The Regulation and Reform of the American Banking System: 1900–1929. Princeton University Press, Princeton

White EN (1985) Voting for costly regulation: evidence from banking referenda in Illinois, 1924. Southern Econ J 51(4):1084–1098

Chapter 7
The Political Economy of Public Pension Reform

Dashle G. Kelley

Abstract Public pension plans in the United States face unprecedented insolvency risk form unfunded liabilities. Reforming state-level public retirement systems requires legislative action in most states, exposing the process of pension reform to various political influences. This chapter examines financial as well as political factors of public pension plans, comparing possible political motivations for pension reform. The empirical results suggest that pension reform decisions are largely independent from political biases and are primarily a response to pension underfunding. In addition, the chapter examines a hypothesis that news media have an important role in the political process of pension reform by providing low cost information to pension stakeholders. Empirical evidence confirms that dissemination of popular information on public pensions is a significant positive predictor of legislative reforms.

7.1 Public Pension Reforms

Unfunded public pension liabilities increase the probability and severity of potential fiscal crises for sponsoring governments as well as their current and future beneficiaries. In several states the current imbalance is large enough to pose major funding and budgetary problems. Munnell (2012) deduces that major unfunded liability problems are largely the consequence of inadequate contributions to the states' pension funds. Moreover, Novy-Marx and Rauh (2009) suggest that public pension accounting methods considerably understate the "true" levels of unfunded liabilities,

---

D. G. Kelley (✉)
Grand View University, Des Moines, IA, USA
e-mail: dkelley@grandview.edu

given the overly optimistic assumptions on the pension portfolios' expected rates of return (somewhat synonymous with discount rates in public pension accounting).[1]

Novy-Marx and Rauh (2011) estimate unfunded liabilities at $2.49 trillion when discounting future benefit promises at the Treasury bill rate and using the actuarial asset values of the plans for June 2009. Nonetheless, estimates of state-level unfunded pension liabilities tend to be in the range of $700 billion to $1 trillion when using plan discount rates and plan accounting numbers (Congressional Budget Office 2011; Wilshire Consulting 2012). Most pension researchers agree that the risks of a pension crisis are state specific (Mitchell 2012; Munnell 2012), although analysts disagree in their assessments of the risks confronted. Given that the total annual budgetary expenditure for all states is around $1,650 billion, current unfunded liabilities present a considerable risk for taxpayers and state budgets.

Responding to these fiscal troubles, state legislatures have enacted a variety of public pension reforms, which either reduce promised payments or increase contributions from employees, employers, or other areas of the budget. These legislative decisions regarding pension reform, therefore, reflect both state fiscal conditions as well as state politics, in addition to the standard influences of pension management. This chapter analyzes the relative importance of these factors as determinants of state-level public pension reforms.

This chapter examines four possible political explanations for state-level pension reforms—the median voter theorem, special interest group theory, a benevolent government (or technocrat) model, and a combined model of the three. If the pure median voter model holds true for legislative pension reforms, taxpayer preferences as well as fiscal variables—such as income, age, mobility, life expectancy, etc.— determine the timing and magnitude of the reforms. In the case of the pure special interest group model, public sector unions seek to maximize compensation—a strategy that might include supporting pension reforms in certain funding scenarios. Moreover, public worker special interest groups have an incentive to become informed for the purpose of altering political outcomes in their favor. Alternatively, public pension reform legislation could be solely determined by pension financials. In a pure technocrat (or benevolent government) model, legislative pension reform decisions are independent from the influences of the median voter or the political manipulations of special interest groups, and the determinants of reform include pension contributions, expected retirement rates, and the demographics of the pension system. Of course, the origins of legislative pension reform are in reality quite dynamic. In instances of pension crises, factors from all three models might synthesize to encourage reform and discourage pension insolvency.

The three alternative explanations are subjected to statistical analysis using data that includes 47 states from 2001 to 2010. Tennessee and Connecticut are excluded because of biannual reporting, and the retirement systems of the State

---

[1] The calculation of the present value of a future lump sum requires a discount rate that is positively correlated with the riskiness of the future payment. Riskier investments, such as junk bonds, necessitate larger discount rates and consequently command larger required returns.

of Washington are excluded because of their complexity and numerous tiers. A bivariate probit estimation strategy is used given that the two initial dependent variables are binary dummies that indicate employee contribution increases and pension benefit reductions as was shown on the Pew Research Center website. To capture the magnitude of pension reforms, a new pension reform variable is created using the annual legislative reports of Snell (multiple years). The new measure is used as the dependent variables in count data analysis. The empirical analysis provides credence to the technocrat model, since the funding ratio is the strongest predictor.

Although neglected in most studies, it bears noting that information has an integral function in the political process for legislative pension reforms. Politicians, voters, and the public workforce use information to form preferences on pension issues as well as to maneuver and strategize within the political process. In addition, information is essential for detecting potential crises and shaping pension reform legislation. Low-cost information should have a greater influence on special interest groups, the median voter, and politicians, since pension practitioners are likely aware of problems before the media. The substantial and recent public pension reforms are largely a response to the widespread perception of considerable pension underfunding and consequent insolvency risks. The somewhat steady increase in media focus on public pension issues during the sample period perhaps stems from greater risks, more awareness of present risks, or simply hysteria. Glaeser and Ponzetto (2014) create a political economy model of public worker pension compensation in which the "true" value of pension promises is "shrouded"—meaning that voters are unaware of the true costs.

The next section of the paper provides background information on pension plans for state and local public workers in the United States, focusing on funding concepts and the standard characteristics of the public defined benefit plans. Section 7.3 explores in greater detail the different political scenarios that offer explanations for public pension reforms (the median voter, special interest group influence, and a fiscally responsible government) in addition to examining the integral role of information distribution by the news media. A detailed discussion of the data is presented in Sect. 7.4 along with a presentation of the bivariate probit and negative binomial models. The empirical results are shown in Sect. 7.5, and Sect. 7.6 concludes.

7.2 Background on State-Level Public Pensions in the United States

7.2.1 Characteristics of Public Plans

State and local public sector workers in the United States are primarily covered by traditional defined benefit pension plans. Defined benefit plans guarantee the employee a specified amount upon retirement typically either in the form of a lump-sum payment or a life annuity. The benefit level usually derives from the standard benefit formula, which is the product of the number of years of service, the final salary, and the benefit multiplier.[2] Defined contribution plans, the main alternative, have individual accounts for each employee, and individual plan members usually control the investment decisions of their own personal accounts. Given that future defined benefit pension payments to public sector workers and retirees have strong legal protections in most states, state governments and taxpayers retain most of the risk in a defined benefit system. The sponsoring government, if need be, is responsible for any shortfalls—either through taxation or budget reallocation.

Pension challenges such as unfavorable demographics and unexpectedly low market returns are universal to both public and private sector plans. Beginning in the 1980s, private companies began to transition from defined benefit retirement schemes to defined contribution plans, effectively transferring retirement risk from the employer to the employee. Employees with defined contribution plans incur the full consequences of inadequate savings and poor portfolio management. After the dot-com bust, private sector plans were criticized for inadequate pension funding and overly optimistic investment expectations (Wiedman and Goldberg 2002). In turn, companies, aided by government regulators, reformed some private pension methods. It bears noting that public sector employees have much stronger legal claims to their pension benefits than private sector employees. As a consequence, private sector pension plan sponsors command greater leeway when addressing pension underfunding. For example, many private sector sponsors implemented pension freezes during the recent financial crisis. Pension freezes, which guarantee pension benefits that are already accrued but stop further accumulation, are infeasible for most public sector pension systems because prospective benefits are legally protected in many states.

The Employee Retirement Income Security Act of 1974 (ERISA), the guiding force for private sector retirement plans, is practically inapplicable to government sponsored pension plans.[3] Henceforth, state legislatures have considerable liberty with the structuring of their pension systems. Some states have one universal pension system that covers all state and local government employees; other states have separate pension systems for each type of worker—one for state employees, one for teachers, one for firefighters, etc.—or for combinations of these. Pension programs for state legislators and judges are smaller with different benefit formulas, since employees tend to enter these positions later in their careers. Some state and local public workers do not participate in Social Security because the original law did not apply to nonfederal government workers; however, compensation for

---

[2] For example, with a final salary of $60,000, a work tenure of 30 years before retiring, and a benefit multiplier of 2%, a public employee would receive an annual retirement benefit of $36,000.

[3] The government plans were excluded from ERISA because there was little available information on public plans at the time of the law.

nonparticipatory workers tends to be comparable to participatory workers, if not slightly more generous.[4]

Although there is no ERISA equivalent for public sector plans, the Governmental Accounting and Standards Board (GASB) issues nonbinding statements to guide management and reporting of public pension plans. Most large plans follow the GASB guidelines, and some state legislatures require compliancy. The GASB does not advocate a single actuarial method but instead provides multiple acceptable options. The large degree of accounting flexibility reduces the comparability of pension reporting across states. Novy-Marx (2013) criticizes the current GASB methodology for encouraging riskier pension portfolio investment strategies—in particular for favoring equities over cash. The GASB issued new statements in 2012 to address the lack of comparability across plans and the discount rate issue; however, Munnell et al. (2012) argue that these changes will be ineffectual.

7.2.2 Public Pension Plan Funding

The estimates of unfunded public pension liabilities largely depend on the chosen discount rates (Brown et al. 2011). Pension practitioners discount future pension liabilities at the expected long-run rate of return on the plans' portfolio (around 8%)—a rate that most economists argue is too high because it reflects neither the low-risk nature of public pension promises, nor the recent declines in expectations of long-term market returns (Brown and Wilcox 2009). Brainard (2010) and most practitioners, however, contend that discounting at the historical rate of return is appropriate, since state and local governments are ongoing entities with low risks of default.

The standard measure of pension funding is the funding ratio—the actuarial value of the pension portfolio's assets to the present value of projected pension obligations. It bears noting that the actuarial value differs from the market value. The actuarial value, which typically uses a 5-year smoothing method to reduce the volatility, is a determinant of the actuarial required contribution (ARC)—the GASB's suggested contribution amount.

Public defined benefit pension funds are rarely ever fully funded in practice, despite the fact that public plans tend to be compared to the 100% funded ideal. Pension underfunding creates additional risks, increasing the probability of a pension crisis as well as increasing the urgency and severity of public pension reforms. States with substantially underfunded pension systems can theoretically transition to pay-as-you-go (PAYG) systems with current contributions financing

---

[4] Due to concerns about the constitutionality of Social Security for state and local public employees, state and local government employees were excluded from the original law. When the constitutional uncertainty was clarified later, public workers at the state and local levels of government were allowed to participate; some public retirement systems, however, have remained independent from the U.S. Social Security System. See (Munnell 2012, 24-27) for further reading.

current benefits. However, PAYG systems are costly; Schieber (2012) suggests that budgetary costs would increase 33% for Illinois or Louisiana (two states with largely underfunded pension plans) if they were to switch to a PAYG system. Bohn (2011) shows that unfunded pension (PAYG) systems are optimal, for taxpayers (the majority of whom are debtors) generally receive a greater benefit from reducing their debt levels rather than contributing to pension funds that earn the market rate of return.

Upside risks are present in public pension funding, although the downside risks (funding crises) receive considerably more attention from media sources and policymakers. An overfunded governmental fund might tempt state legislators to transfer resources toward other areas of the budget. In scenarios of pension overfunding, public sector special interest groups might shortsightedly lobby for benefit increases. If previous fund surpluses were diverted to other areas or were used as a basis for larger benefit promises, a public pension may have insufficient funds when the time comes to pay beneficiaries. Most state-level pension funds were overfunded in the dot-com boom of the late 1990s, and many state legislatures increased benefits on the premise that fund portfolios would continue to generate 8% annual returns.[5] Snell (2001) finds that many states were continuing to increase pension benefits in their 2001 legislative sessions. To capture the reality that full funding is probably neither optimal nor necessary, the Government Accountability Office (2005) considers plans with funding ratios of 80% adequately funded.

7.3 Politics of Pension Reform

The legislative decision-making process for public pension reforms can be understood as a dynamic process of political interaction between self-interested parties—politicians, taxpayers, current and future beneficiaries, and the other affected parties. Hence, an examination of public pension reforms ought to focus on political factors as well as standard pension variables. This chapter compares four public choice scenarios—the median voter theorem, special interest group theory, a technocrat model (the unbiased political outcome), and a combined model. The methodology and model comparisons of this chapter are similar to previous studies that compare median voter and special interest groups explanations of outcomes of the political process (Congleton and Shughart 1990). My paper adds a technocrat model to account for scenarios where reforms are primarily determined by pension factors not politics. Insofar as there are several plausible models of the politics of pension reform, the empirical results and the comparison of the models drive the conclusions of the paper, rather than a priori suppositions.

---

[5] California Senate Bill 400 in 1999 exemplifies these benefit increases; on the premise of the 128% funding ratio of CALPERS, the legislature enacted retroactive pension benefit increases for members and retirees, leading to considerable underfunding after the dot-com bust.

"Reform," for the purposes of this chapter, occurs when a state legislature alters the characteristics of a pension plan for the purpose of sustainability by either reducing outflows or increasing inflows. Types of reform that reduce outflows include increasing the retirement age, reducing the cost-of-living adjustments (COLAs), lowering benefit levels, and cost-effectively transitioning to a defined contribution system. The figure below shows the total employee contribution increases and/or benefit decreases for each year of the sample period as determined by the Pew Research Center's website. There is a noticeable rise in reforms after the financial crisis of 2008–2009.

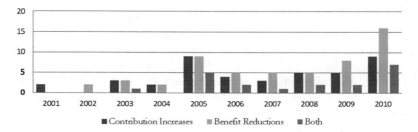

Three models are discussed below, each of which reflects the interests of different subsets of the stakeholders in state pension reform. The median voter model represents the political outcome that is determined by taxpayers; the median voter prefers public pension reforms that maximize utility from the public sector while reducing present and future tax costs. Special interest group theory characterizes the preferences of the public workers and retirees, but the success of public sector unions and their lobbying efforts at altering political outcomes is somewhat ambiguous, due to differing time horizons and preferences of union members. The unbiased political model represents a scenario where politicians are making decisions independent of outside political influences. In addition, all stakeholders rely on information to form preferences on pension issues and to utilize the political process for their own self-interested objectives.

7.3.1 The Median Voter Theorem

Taxpaying voters clearly have a financial interest in the political outcome of public pension reforms, being the ultimate backstop of severely underfunded public pension plans. For the purpose of winning elections, politicians may adopt the preferences of the median voter—a middle-aged taxpayer in most states. If voter preferences are single peaked with perfect information, this strategy is successful for politicians, and the median voter's preferences manifest themselves as political outcomes (Downs 1957). Failure of a legislature to address pension insolvency concerns can be costly for taxpayers, since larger funding shortfalls correspond to more devastating pension crises. Nonetheless, the median voter, who is concerned about utility, stands to incur tax increases and reductions in government services from budget reshuffling to alleviate pension shortfalls.

Unfunded liabilities function similar to deficit spending, delaying costs (labor costs in the case of public pensions) of public sector spending. Given that employment compensation consists of wages as well as other benefits, lower wages in the present and larger pension benefits in the future can be substitutes. If a link exists between compensation and productivity in the public sector, citizens' utility from the public sector goods and services likely increases along with the wages and retirement benefits of public sector employees.

Increases in public utility from unfunded pension liabilities may saddle future taxpayers with larger tax costs. Nevertheless, the actions of private individuals might nullify the intertemporal transfer of wealth from unfunded liabilities, if citizens change their present behavior in anticipation of future tax increases and Ricardian equivalence holds (Barro 1974). Ricardian equivalence assumes that there are intertemporal linkages between generations (such as bequests) and that individuals save in anticipation of future tax increases. Ricardian equivalence is unlikely to materialize at the state level, given that individuals and their children can relocate to states with less indebtedness to avoid future tax burdens. Instead, public debt may affect the values of goods, such as property, that are immobile and commonly taxed. Debt capitalization, an alternative equivalence mechanism, occurs when current property values decline in response to public borrowing and expectations of larger tax costs in the future (Daly 1969). Thus, individuals bear the burden of public borrowing in the present through lower property values.

Independent from the success of these equivalence mechanisms, the median voter is likely unaware of the "true" intertemporal distribution of the costs and benefits of public borrowing. Buchanan (1960) applies the term "fiscal illusion" to the scenario where individuals inaccurately perceive to benefit from public borrowing at the expense of future taxpayers. In summary, a self-interested median voter likely supports public pension reforms that appear to maximize public and private utility while minimizing tax costs, regardless of the actual incidence of public borrowing and unfunded liabilities.

7.3.2 Special Interest Group Theory

Public sector special interest groups have a clear stake in the outcome of the political processes that determine pension reforms. Members of state-level public retirement systems are active in the political process and have a greater incentive than the median voter to become informed of pension policymaking.[6] In addition

---

[6] The recent Wisconsin recall elections provide evidence of the magnitude of public sector employee involvement in the politics. $43.9 million was spent on the recall elections for nine state senators in August of 2011, and over $60 million was spent in the recall election of Governor Walker in June of 2012; previously, the most expensive race in Wisconsin was the 2010 gubernatorial election at $37.4 million (Davey 2012; Mayers 2011).

to collective bargain powers, public worker special interest groups utilize various channels of the political process to influence compensation levels.

Special interest groups may be successful at altering political outcomes in their favor by contributing to reelection campaigns of politicians and extracting rents from the political process (Stigler 1971). Public sector workers are in a natural position to lobby state legislatures and influence political outcomes, since retirees are already organized for collective bargaining purposes. Becker (1983) depicts the political arena as a process of numerous competing special interest or pressure groups.[7] Successful rent seeking is not always in the form of explicit increases in retirement benefits but includes lower retirement ages and changes in actuarial assumptions.

To address severe pension underfunding, state legislatures have two options: reduce pension benefits to current and future pensioners or increase contributions to the plan. Public sector workers prefer the latter remedy to the extent that contribution increases come from taxpayers and other areas of the budget not employee wages. Rattso and Sorensen (2004) suggest that the constituency of public employees functions as a swing voter with blocking power, overcoming its non-majority status to promote the status quo and prevent unfavorable reforms. In addition to collective bargaining and political involvement, public sector unions use the legal system to discourage unfavorable reforms. Strong legal protections of public pension promises by governments to employees significantly limit the ability of state legislatures to reduce the pension benefits of current workers. Hence, public sector unions virtually always challenge legislative benefit reductions in court, creating legal costs for governments.

The time horizons of unions' leaderships likely influence special interest group objectives and lobbying (Mitchell and Smith 1994). Focusing primarily on the short term, union leaders may encourage high-profile agenda items and resist prudent reforms to the point of jeopardizing the long-term sustainability of the pension system. On the other hand, public sector union leaders with long-term time horizons can guide policymakers with management and reforms of the pension system, being incentivized to acquire high-cost information on their plans. Thus, the impact of effective public sector special interest groups is unclear.

7.3.3 Benevolent Government Model

Most states have adopted institutions, such as independent boards, that attempt to insulate pension fund management from politics. Insofar as the legislature defers to their fund managers and pension actuaries, decision-making for public pension

---

[7] When groups compete for resources within the political processes for state budgeting, no natural opposition group to public pensioners clearly exists. Nevertheless, municipal bondholders oppose pensioners in the instance of bankruptcy. Gerson (2012) discusses possible conflicts between public sector workers and other constituencies within the Democratic Party.

systems may be largely independent from the preferences of the median voter and the political influences of special interest groups. In such cases, reforms may be based entirely on future pension fund characteristics, such as the anticipated outflows, expected employee contributions, reserves, and the funding level. In a scenario with a fiscally responsible government, a low funding ratio is the primary factor that signals to policymakers a need for pension reform.

An assumption of the other two models is that politicians are self-interested and that they make decisions to promote their own political careers whether it is aligning with the median voter in order to win elections or aligning with special interest groups in order to receive larger campaign contributions. The benevolent model suggests that that politicians may be less self-interested (or more sophisticated in determining their long-term interests) than the median voter and special interest group models assume.

7.3.4 The Role of Information

The stakeholders of the pension reform process rely on information to form opinions on the timing and magnitude of pension reforms. Since only a few voters and/or interest group members carefully study the annual pension fund reports of state fund administrators, it seems clear that the extent of information available from mass media sources is integral to the political process for most stakeholders.

For example, perfect information is a necessary assumption for the median voter model to operate perfectly. Politicians can only represent the interests of the median voter if the median voter and elected officials are aware of one another's preferences. If public pension information is costly for the median voter to obtain, given the complex actuarial methods and the nonstandard accounting principles, voters may not know their true interests or, indeed, may largely ignore the issue entirely (Congleton 2007). The median voter is incentivized to become rationally ignorant of public pension funding and other issues. It bears noting that Ricardian equivalence and debt capitalization require an informed populace. Similar informational problems also affect the typical member of large interest groups, such as public officials.

This creates a void the news media can fill by lowering the cost of obtaining the information through collection, analysis, and mass distribution. By looking at the front page of a newspaper or at the headlines of Yahoo News, taxpayers can more easily get a general idea about the funding of the public pension plans, for which they are fiscally responsible, than by searching through government reports. Consequently, their preferences for reform are at least partly induced by mass media sources.

Public workers have a greater incentive to become informed of the true risks affecting their public pension plans, but also have information costs and associated biases. Nevertheless, the leadership of special interest groups can use information to their advantage by releasing information at advantageous times and manipulating facts in the ways suggested by Mueller and Stratmann (1994). Likewise, politicians have little incentive to delve deeper than the Certified Annual Financial Report of their public pension systems—such as examining actuarial assumptions—unless voters and/or the mass media do.

Given that the outcomes of pension reforms are dependent on the quality of information available to policymakers, the media play an integral role when outcomes are unaffected by the biases of the median voter and special interest group influence.

Due to the fact that pension issues are not on the radar of most pension stakeholders, pension reform is somewhat dependent on the ability of the media to inform the public of possible pension risks. Boeri and Tabellini (2012) suggest that citizens are more likely to acquiesce to benefit reductions from their countries' social insurance and pension systems if mass media coverage significantly improves available information on these systems. The quality and quantity of information available on state and local public pension plans in the United States have both increased over the past decade. Highlighting both the importance of low-cost information and the opaqueness of pension reporting, MacKay (2014) finds evidence of debt capitalization in Los Angeles property values after the release of a report that showed unfunded liabilities of the city were considerably understated.

7.4 Data and Methodology

7.4.1 Exogenous Variables

The statistical analysis of legislative public pension reforms examines data from 2001 to 2010 for 47 states with 95 large state-level plans.[8] Table 7.1 reports the descriptive statistics for the exogenous variables of the empirical analysis. The state-level public pension data is from the Public Pension Database (PPD) (2010)—a dataset sponsored by the Center for Retirement Research at Boston College and Center for State and Local Government Excellence (2010). Public pension actuarial and accounting methods in the United States are somewhat heterogeneous, partly reducing the comparability of pension statistics across plans. Minor adjustments were made to the PPD numbers in a few instances when differences with the states' CAFR reports were detectable.

The funding ratios in this paper's dataset are cumulative for each state, being compiled from the large state-level public retirement plans in the PPD. Thus, the funding ratio is the quotient of the sum of the actuarial values (not the market values) for a state's large plans and the sum of the corresponding accrued actuarial liabilities. Public pension membership data for each state and year is compiled

---

[8] Connecticut and Tennessee are excluded because of the biannual reporting methods of their large plans, and Washington is not included due to its numerous tiers.

Table 7.1 Descriptive statistics

Variables	Mean	Min	Max	Std. Dev
Median income	51,287	35,582	73,598	7651.8
Median voter age	50.58	45.74	56.02	1.82
Life expectancy MV	29.95	21.7	62.79	4.35
Public union	0.327	0.0311	0.744	0.191
Members to population	0.076	0.027	0.15	0.024
Democratic legislature	0.4	0	1	0.49
Republican legislature	0.35	0	1	0.48
Democratic governor	0.47	0	1	5
Republican governor	0.52	0	1	0.5
Funding ratio	83	39.2	117.9	15.6
Actives to retirees	2.31	1	4.27	0.6
Non-defined benefit	0.19	0	1	0.4
State debt to income	2.94	0	12.1	2.17
Google New Citations	1312.3	203	3010	953.3
NYT1	307.5	127	718	219.8
No social security	0.256	0	0	0.44

similarly for the classifications of active members, inactive members, and retirees. The cumulative totals of these categories, along with state population data from the U.S. Census Bureau, create descriptive ratios, such as the actives to retirees ratio (a measure of transferability to a unfunded pension system) and the ratio of plan membership to population (a gauge of special interest strength). The mean ratio of active members to retired members for the dataset is 2.3, suggesting that on average a state has 23 current public workers for every ten retirees.

Hirsch and Macpherson (2010) calculate detailed estimates of public sector union membership but do not distinguish between federal workers and government employees at the state and local levels. To separate state and local public employee union membership from the federal bias, I adjust the Hirsch and Macpherson (2010) numbers by removing a Bureau of Labor Statistics estimate of the federal workforce, assuming a 60% (the BLS national estimate) federal worker union membership rate in all states.

The median household income data comes from the U. S. Census Bureau and approximates the income of the median voter. The age of the median voter in each state is an estimate by the author using U.S. Census voting numbers for various age ranges, assuming uniform distributions within the given ranges. These estimates of median voter age and state-specific life tables of the Center for Disease Control produce life expectancy estimates for median voters in each state. Table 7.1 illustrates the average characteristics of median voters across states; the median voter has an average income around $51,287 and a mean age of around 50 years old with an estimated average life expectancy of about 30 years.

To identify risk sharing between public employers and employees, the dataset includes a binary variable that indicates if a state has a non-supplemental defined contribution pension plan or hybrid plan that is an optional or mandatory alternative to the state's traditional defined benefit plan (Munnell 2012).[9] About 19% of the state years in sample represent an optional or mandatory defined contribution or hybrid plan for new or current public employees.

The analysis uses binary indicator variables to denote the party of the governor and legislature of each state, which are obtained from National Council of State Governments. During the sample period, more state legislatures were controlled by the Democratic Party, but Republican Party candidates held more of the governorships. The ratio of state debt to state income is from Moody's Investor Services (2010)—a report that primarily focuses on public borrowing at the state level and excludes unfunded liabilities.

Testing the secondary informational hypothesis of the paper requires explanatory variables that approximate the availability of low-cost information in the media. The initial variable Goog is the total number of Google News Citations for each year for the search terms "state," "pension," and "crisis" on March 1, 2012 (Munnell 2012). I calculated an additional informational factor from the website specific search engine at the New York Times website on May 29, 2013. The variable is the number of article search hits with the terms "public" and "pensions" as NYT1.

7.4.2 Estimation Specification and Dependent Variables

The initial empirics utilize two dichotomous variables from the Pew Research Center website that indicate whether a state increases employee contributions and/or reduces benefits during the sample period of 2001–2010. The paper uses probit analysis to confine regression estimates to the probabilistic range between zero and one. Moreover, likelihood of interdependence between legislative decisions for reducing benefits and increasing employee contributions suggests a bivariate probit model as shown in Eq. 7.1.

The bivariate probit model assumes a joint distribution—the bivariate normal distribution, ϕ_2, to obtain the joint probabilities for the dependent variables. *Reform*1 and *Reform*2 are binomial variables that indicate whether a state legislature enacts a pension reform with payout reductions or employee pension contribution increases, respectively, in a given year. The index variables i and t represent state and year, respectively. The exogenous variables form the matrices X_{1it} and X_{2it}, with the beta vectors containing parameter estimates. Rho is a correlation parameter, signifying the degree of covariance between the two sublevel probability models of the bivariate probit model. No covariance of the residuals exists if rho equals zero, and the two dependent variables are perfectly positively (negatively) correlated with one another when rho equals one (negative one).

---

[9] A hybrid plan has both defined benefit and defined contribution components.

Table 7.2 Index of pension reform

Values	
Zero	363
One	61
Two	24
Three	14
Four	5
Five	3
Six	0
Seven	0
Index factors	
1. Employer contribution increases	
2. Employee contribution increases	
3. Reduce COLA	
4. Increase retirement age	
5. Reduce benefit multiplier	
6. Modify salary calculations to reduce benefits	
7. Implement a defined contribution or hybrid plan	

$$\text{Prob}(Reform1_{it} = 1, Reform2_{it} = 1)$$
$$= \int_{-\infty}^{\mu_{1it}} \int_{-\infty}^{\mu_{2it}} \phi_2(X_{1it}\beta_1, X_{2it}\beta_2, \rho) du_{1i} du_{2i} \tag{7.1}$$

$$u_{1it} = \eta_{it} + \varepsilon_{1it} \tag{7.2}$$

$$u_{2it} = \eta_{it} + \varepsilon_{2it} \tag{7.3}$$

Equations 7.2 and 7.3 present the compositions of the residuals for the individual ancillary probit models of dependent variables that comprise the bivariate probit model analysis. Each error term consists of a portion, η, which is common in both models and another part, ϵ, which is unique to each ancillary probit model. The interaction between the residuals of the two ancillary probit models captures the interdependence of the two legislative decisions to reduce benefits and increase contributions.

The binary probit analysis fails to distinguish between insignificant and substantial legislative pension reforms. Thus, I compile an index to capture the magnitude of pension reforms, using the annual legislative reports of Ronald Snell at the National Conference of State Legislatures.[10] Table 7.2 shows the distribution of the new variable of pension reform, which represents the extent of pension reforms for each state and year during the sample period. The values of the pension reform

---

[10] The new pension reform measure derives from Snell (2001, 2002, 2003, 2004, 2005, 2006, 2007, 2008, 2009, 2010).

variable derive from numerations of seven different types of possible legislative pension reforms for each state and year of the sample period. The seven reforms include the following: increases in the employee contribution rate, increases in the employer contribution rate, reductions in the COLA, increases in the retirement age, reductions in the benefit multiplier, modifications of the definition of pensionable compensation (the salary used to calculate benefits), and implementations of a nonsupplementary defined contribution or hybrid pension plan.

The non-continuousness and discreteness of the pension reform variable cause standard OLS regressions to yield inefficient estimates. Attributes of the new reform variable favor a count data interpretation. Nevertheless, the Poisson model's assumption that counts be random and independent events is not met, since a legislature that implements one type of pension reform in a legislative session is more likely to implement others. In preliminary Poisson regressions, overdispersion—inequality of the mean and variance—is detected with Cameron and Trivedi's regression-based tests, violating another Poisson assumption. Negative binomial models relax these assumptions by introducing an unobserved effect in the error term with a gamma distribution but have the same expected coefficient values as the Poisson model. This paper estimates negative binomial models, using quasi-maximum likelihood estimation with robust standard errors from a "sandwich" of the inverse of the Hessian and the outer product of the gradient.

$$P(X=k) = \frac{\Gamma(\alpha+k)}{\Gamma(\alpha)\Gamma(k+1)} \left(\frac{\alpha}{\alpha+\lambda}\right)^\alpha \left(\frac{\lambda}{\alpha+\lambda}\right)^k \qquad (7.4)$$

$$E(y \mid x) = \exp\left(x'\beta\right) \qquad (7.5)$$

The paper uses the more common Negbin II specification with $\theta = \lambda/\alpha$, $\alpha = \sigma^{-2}$, and $\lambda = \exp(x'\beta)$. Alpha and theta are parameters that are greater than or equal to zero. Equation 7.4 shows the probability function. Equation 7.5 shows the conditional probability of the dependent variable y, in this chapter the new reform variable, on a matrix of the independent variables x.

7.5 Empirical Results

This chapter compares a median voter model, a special interest group model, a technocrat model, and a combined model of the three to gain perspective on the determinants of legislative public pension reforms. Bivariate probit regression analysis captures the interdependence between the two reform variables from the Pew Research Center—increases to employee contributions and reductions in the benefits of pensioners and future pensioners. The new public pension reform variable captures reform magnitude. Characteristics of the new variable suggest a count data interpretation and quasi-maximum likelihood negative binomial models estimations.

Table 7.3 presents the empirical results of the bivariate probit model analysis for the two binary dependent variables from the Pew Research Center. Statistical tests on the rho correlation coefficients for all five models suggest that significant interdependence between the two dependent variables exists, indicating the suitability of the bivariate probit model. Indeed, state legislatures that reduce benefits are more likely to increase employee contributions and vice versa. In addition, an indicator variable of Social Security participation controls for structural differences between these two types of plans.

The median voter coefficient effects in column 1 are statistically insignificant, suggesting that median voter preferences do not influence the political process of public pension reforms. In the special interest group model, state and local public sector union membership negatively corresponds to the probability that a legislature enacts employee contribution increases, and a Democratic Party majority in a state legislature is a significant positive predictor of legislative reductions in retirement benefits.

The technocrat model in column 3 outperforms the median voter and special interest group models as the log likelihood ratios and subsequent Wald tests show. A lower funding ratio—a measure of insolvency risk—leads to an increase in the likelihood of both types of pension reform, as statistically significant coefficient effects indicate. Moreover, the presence of a non-supplemental defined contribution or hybrid plan in a state is a significant negative predictor of employee contribution increases. Public pension systems that promote risk sharing between employers and employees may better manage insolvency risks. The ratio of public debt to state income corresponds to legislative employee contribution rate hikes with a significant as well as negative coefficient effect.

The combined model in column 4 explains more of the variation in the dependent variables, given that it includes all the explanatory variables of other three political models. The coefficient effect of the union membership variable loses significance as shown in column 4. Nevertheless, the exogenous factors of the technocrat model remain consistent in sign and in statistical significance in the combined model. The addition of the informational factor in column 5 captures the influence of information distribution by media sources, improving the explanatory power of the combined model. The informational factor dominates the funding ratio variable for both types of reforms. Interestingly, the age of the median voter becomes a significant negative predictor of reductions in public pension benefits in column 5, supporting the hypothesis that older voters tend to defer pension problems.

Table 7.4 presents the empirical results for the new reform variable with quasilikelihood maximization negative binomial regression estimation. The coefficient estimate of median voter life expectancy is the only significant coefficient in the median voter model in column 1. The result suggests that a greater life expectancy for a median voter corresponds to a reduction in the probability and severity of a legislative pension reform—at the ratio of one year to about negative one-tenth of the new reform measure. For the special interest group models (shown in column 2), only the political party indicator variable for a Republican legislature has a

7 The Political Economy of Public Pension Reform

Table 7.3 Regression results for pew data

Increase employee contributions	Median voter (1)	Special interest groups (2)	Benevolent government (3)	Combined (4)	Information (5)
Constant	2.1 (0.58)	−1.37*** (−4.34)	0.78 (1.25)	4.49 (0.86)	8.31 (1.45)
Median income	−0.0000034 (−0.29)			0.00001 (0.000005)	0.00000051 (0.36)
Median voter age	−0.045 (−0.81)			−0.059 (−0.14)	−0.14* (−1.7)
Life expectancy MV	−0.033 (−0.75)			−0.047 (−0.64)	−0.062 (−0.84)
Pubic union		−0.96** (−2.1)		−0.66 (−0.93)	−0.33 (−0.46)
Members to population		4.19 (1.22)		4.47 (1.14)	3.83 (0.97)
Leg_Dem_DUMMY		0.12 (0.71)			
Fund ratio			−0.014** (−2.14)	−0.013* (−1.95)	−0.0081 (−1.1)
Actives to retirees			−0.16 (−0.88)	−0.23 (−1.05)	−0.12 (−0.52)
Non-defined benefit			−0.7** (−2.53)	−0.73** (−2.56)	−0.79** (−2.72)
State debt to income			−0.18*** (−3.4)	−0.16*** (−2.81)	−0.17*** (−2.85)
No social security	−0.23 (−1.08)	−0.26 (−1.24)	−0.26 (−1.2)	−0.29 (−1.3)	−0.35 (−1.51)
Google news cites					0.00029*** (2.59)
Reduce pension benefits					
Constant	−1.27 (−0.45)	−1.63*** (−5.47)	0.47 (0.86)	−0.23 (−0.007)	3.85 (1.07)
Median income	−0.0000003 (−0.0003)			0.000008 (0.66)	−0.0000022 (0.17)
Median voter age	0.014 (0.29)			0.009 (0.18)	−0.085 (−1.47)
Life expectancy MV	−0.024 (−0.94)			−0.021 (−0.73)	−0.025 (−0.78)
Public union		−0.32 (−0.77)		−0.45 (−0.72)	−0.12 (−0.18)
Members to population		4.29 (1.37)		3.35 (0.94)	2.64 (0.72)
Leg_Dem_DUMMY		0.33** (2.07)			
Fund ratio			−0.012** (−2.07)	−0.011* (−1.87)	−0.0044 (−0.66)

(continued)

Table 7.3 (continued)

Increase employee contributions	Median voter (1)	Special interest groups (2)	Benevolent government (3)	Combined (4)	Information (5)
Actives to retirees			−0.26 (−1.59)	−0.27 (−1.39)	−0.12 (−0.59)
Non-defined benefit			−0.19 (−0.92)	−0.17 (−0.78)	−0.26 (−1.14)
State debt to income			−0.037 (−0.99)	−0.024 (−0.58)	−0.022 (−0.51)
No social security	0.32* (1.84)	0.2 (1.2)	0.2 (1.12)	0.24 (1.25)	0.19 (0.96)
Google new cites					0.0004*** (3.89)
Observations	470	470	470	470	470
Log likelihood	−287.53	−283.65	−273.69	−270.98	−262.01
RHO	0.657	0.653	0.662	0.67	0.65
Chi-squared stat	40.67	39.25	38.38	37.69	33.75

Note: Z-stats shown in parenthesis. The results above are for a bivariate probit model with the reform data from The Pew Research Center. Z-statistic tests are two tailed; asterisks denote significance at the 1% (***), 5% (**), and 10% (*) levels

significant coefficient estimate; Republican legislatures are less likely to enact pension reforms.[11]

The technocrat model for the reform variable in column 3 improves upon the other two political models with three factors that are economically and statistically significant. Lower pension funding ratios in states increase the probability of legislative pension reforms. The ratio of active members to retirees, another factor of the technocrat model, gauges the costliness of switching from a traditional defined benefit pension plan to a pay-as-you-go (or unfunded) system; retirement systems with more workers and fewer retirees can pay current benefits with the contributions of current employees. The coefficient estimate of the actives to retirees ratio is significant and negative. Thus, it appears that the ability to economically switch to an unfunded pension system discourages legislatures from implementing pension reforms. The indicator variable for non-defined benefit plans is a significant negative predictor of pension reform. Hence, greater risk sharing between public employers and employees corresponds to fewer and lesser public pension reforms; perhaps these plans are better managed.

The combined model in column 4 slightly outperforms the technocrat model. The factors of funding ratio, state debt, and median voter life expectancy remain significant with consistent signs and effects in the combined model; however, the

---

[11] Regressions with other political party indicator variables—Republican governors, Democratic governors, and Democratic legislatures—are not significant and consequently not shown in Table 7.4.

7 The Political Economy of Public Pension Reform

Table 7.4 Regression results for new measure of pension reform

	Median voter (1)	Special interest (2)	Benevolent government (3)	Combined model (4)	Information (5)	Information (6)
Constant	1.88 (0.55)	−0.091*** (−2.68)	2.68*** (4.19)	5.61 (1.51)	10.31** (2.5)	10.21** (2.45)
Median income	0.000002 (0.18)			0.000012 (0.68)	0.0000049 (0.28)	0.000006 (0.34)
Median voter age	−0.00028 (−0.004)			−0.023 (−0.37)	−0.13** (−2.00)	−0.12* (−1.83)
Life expectancy MV	−0.103*** (−3.39)			−0.1*** (−2.63)	−0.11** (−2.43)	−0.11** (−2.45)
Public union		−0.51 (−0.92)		0.007 (0.008)	0.32 (0.40)	0.23 (0.30)
Members to population		3.15 (0.76)		4.09 (0.89)	3.08 (0.70)	3.15 (0.72)
Leg_GOP		−0.501*** (−2.28)				
Fund ratio			−0.03*** (−4.24)	0.029*** (−4.06)	−0.022*** (−2.98)	−0.024*** (−3.20)
Actives to retirees			−0.38* (−1.84)	−0.33 (−1.43)	−0.17 (−0.77)	−0.22 (−0.98)
Non-defined benefit			−0.45 (−1.54)	−0.4 (−1.34)	−0.43 (1.46)	−0.41 (−1.42)
State debt to income			−0.11** (−2.31)	−0.11** (−2.13)	−0.102* (−1.83)	−0.101* (−1.84)
No social security	0.42* (1.67)	0.22 (0.96)	0.13 (0.52)	0.21 (0.77)	0.063 (0.26)	0.071 (0.29)
Google News Cites					0.00039*** (3.55)	
NYT1						0.0014*** (2.79)
Alpha	2.8*** (5.36)	2.82*** (5.76)	2.31*** (5.21)	2.25*** (4.9)	2.01*** (4.55)	2.07*** (4.59)
Observations	470	470	470	470	470	470
Log likelihood	−375.95	−377.19	−367	−364.82	−360.2	−361.64

Note: Regression results are for negative binomial models with the new measure of pension reform as the dependent variable. Z-statistics are in parentheses; asterisks denote significance at the 1% (***), 5% (**), and 10% (*) levels on a two-tailed test

active to retiree ratio loses statistical significance when the political variables are added.

Information has a strong positive effect on public pension reforms as shown by the statistical significance of two different information variables in columns 5 and 6. One could conclude that an electorate with greater levels of information is more likely to encourage (or at least acquiesce to) public pension reforms. The coefficient effects of these informational explanatory variables are difficult to interpret, since it is unlikely that one New York Times article directly causes state legislatures to reform a certain number of public pension reforms. Thus, these informational variables only approximate the total distribution of public pension information by news media sources across the country.

To summarize, pension funding and the distribution of pension information by the media have the largest influence on the legislative decision to enact public pension reform. The funding ratio is statistically significant and consistently negative throughout all of the negative binomial regression models as well as in both the technocrat model and combined model in Table 7.3. In addition, the informational factors are significant when included in regressions.

7.6 Concluding Remarks

State and local government retirement plans in the United States face unprecedented insolvency risks in the aftermath of the 2008–2009 Financial Crisis. State legislatures enact pension reforms that either reduce benefit payments or increase contributions, or both, to increase the sustainability of their public pension systems. Since 2009, 43 states have reformed their pension systems with some of these states doing so in multiple years (Snell 2012). This chapter examines public pension reforms from 2001 to 2010 for 47 states and compares three conjectural political explanations—a median voter model, a special interest group model, and a technocrat model—along with a combination of these models. In addition, I create a new measure of pension reform magnitude and test the hypothesis that information has a significant role in the process of public pension reforms.

The empirical results suggest that pension underfunding is the most significant determinant of public pension reform. Nevertheless, the effectiveness of the median voter and special interest groups in the political process should not be hastily dismissed. Although state legislatures appear to primarily focus on pension financials, the preferences of all stakeholders may align to avoid a pension default when a public pension plan is hazardously underfunded. The median voter and other taxpayers potentially face a decline in government services, greater public borrowing costs in the future, and larger tax burdens. Public sector unions are incentivized to become informed of their pension plans and be active on public pension issues, for public pensioners of severely underfunded plans could lose their pension benefits for period time in a worst-case scenario, as took place during the bankruptcy of Prichard, Alabama.

The statistical significance of the informational factors supports the hypothesis that the distribution of low-cost information on public pensions by the mass media encourages public pension reforms. Voters, politicians, and members of public sector special interest groups likely rely on news stories and online articles to form opinions and operate within the political process, foregoing the reading of annual financial reports and the studying of actuarial assumptions and accounting methods.

In practice, benefit reductions for current public sector workers and retirees rarely occur without significant pension underfunding, and benefit payment cuts to the pensions of current public employees are almost always challenged in court by public sector unions. Consequently, most pension reform legislation only applies to the benefit structures of future hires. It bears noting that high-profile and large-scale pension reforms have been attempted since the end of the paper's sample period: Most notably the public pension reforms led by State Treasurer Chaffee in Rhode Island and the bankruptcy filing of Detroit. The judicial conclusions of these and other legal cases will likely clarify the latitude that policymakers have when reforming public pensions. Nonetheless, this paper sheds a somewhat favorable light on the recent wave of pension reforms: for, it appears that pensioners' benefits are not being reduced aimlessly or arbitrarily, but in contrast, for the purpose of addressing insolvency risks.

References

Barro RJ (1974) Are government bonds net wealth? J Polit Econ 82(6):1095–1117
Becker GS (1983) A theory of competition among pressure groups for political influence. Q J Econ 98(3):371–400
Boeri T, Tabellini G (2012) Does information increase political support for pension reform? Pub Choice 150(1):327–362
Bohn H (2011) Should public retirement plans be fully funded? J Pension Econ Finance 10(2):195–219
Brainard K (2010) Public Pension Plan Investment Return Assumptions. National Association of State Retirement Administrators, Lexington
Brown JR, Wilcox DW (2009) Discounting state and local pension liabilities. Am Econ Rev 99(2):538–42
Brown JR, Clark R, Rauh JD (2011) The economies of state and local pensions. J Pension Econ Finance 10(2):161–172
Buchanan JM (1960) Fiscal Theory and Political Economy. University of North Carolina Press, Chapel Hill
Center for Retirement Research at Boston College and Center for State and Local Government Excellence (2010) Public Pension Database. Center for Retirement Research, Boston
Congleton RD (2007) Informational limits to democratic public policy: the jury theorem, yardstick competition, and ignorance. Pub Choice 132(3):333–352
Congleton RD, Shughart I W F (1990) The growth of social security: electoral push or political pull? Econ Inquiry 28(1):109–132
Congressional Budget Office (2011) The UnderFunding of State and Local Pension Plans. Congressional Budget Office, Washington DC
Daly GG (1969) The burden of the debt and future generations in local finance. Southern Econ J 36(1):44–51
Davey M (2012) Frenzied campaigning on eve of Wisconsin vote. New York Times 4 June
Downs A (1957) An Economic Theory of Democracy. Harper and Row, New York
Gerson M (2012) Unions are driving a wedge between democrats. Washington Post 6 June
Glaeser EL, Ponzetto GA (2014) Shrouded costs of government: the political economy of state and local public pensions. J Pub Econ 116(1):89–105

Government Accountability Office (2005) Social Security: Coverage of Public Employees and Implications for Reform. Government Accountability Office, Washington DC

Hirsch B, Macpherson D (2010) The union membership and coverage database from the CPS. Union Stats, Atlanta

MacKay RC (2014) Implicit debt capitalization in local housing prices: an example of unfunded pension liabilities. Natl Tax J 67(1):77–112

Mayers J (2011) Nearly $44 million spent on Wisconsin recall elections. Reuters 21 September

Mitchell OS (2012) Public pension pressures in the United States. In: Conti-Brown P (ed) When States Go Broke: The Origins, Context, and Solutions for the American States in Fiscal Crisis, Cambridge University Press, Cambridge, pp 57–76

Mitchell OS, Smith RS (1994) Pension funding in the public sector. Rev Econ Stat 76(2):278–290

Moody's Investor Services (2010) 2010 State Debt Medians Report. Moody's Investor Services, New York

Mueller D, Stratmann T (1994) Information and persuasive campaigning. Pub Choice 81(1):55–77

Munnell AH (2012) State and Local Pension: What Now? Brookings Institution Press, Washington DC

Munnell AH, Jean-Pierre A, Hurwitz J, Quinby L (2012) How would GASB proposals affect state and local pension reporting? J Gov Finan Manag 61(2):18–24

Novy-Marx R (2013) Logical implications of the GASB's methodology for valuing pension liabilities. Financ Analy J 69(1):26–32

Novy-Marx R, Rauh JD (2009) The liabilities and risks of state-sponsored pension plans. J Econ Perspect 23(4):191–120

Novy-Marx R, Rauh JD (2011) Public pension promises: how big are they and what are they worth? J Finance 66(4):1211–1249

Rattso J, Sorensen RJ (2004) Public employees as swing voters: empirical evidence on opposition to public sector reform. Pub Choice 119(3):281–310

Schieber SJ (2012) The Predictable Surprise: Unraveling the U.S. Retirement System. Oxford University Press, New York

Snell RK (2001) Pensions and Retirement Plan Enactments in 2001 State Legislatures: Final report. National Conference of State Legislatures, Washington DC

Snell RK (2002) Pensions and Retirement Plan Enactments in 2002 State Legislatures. National Conference of State Legislatures, Washington DC

Snell RK (2003) Pensions and Retirement Plan Enactments in 2003 State Legislatures. National Conference of State Legislatures, Washington DC

Snell RK (2004) Pensions and Retirement Plan Enactments in 2004 State Legislatures. National Conference of State Legislatures, Washington DC

Snell RK (2005) Pensions and Retirement Plan Enactments in 2005 State Legislatures. National Conference of State Legislatures, Washington DC

Snell RK (2006) Pensions and Retirement Plan Enactments in 2006 State Legislatures. National Conference of State Legislatures, Washington DC

Snell RK (2007) Pensions and Retirement Plan Enactments in 2007 State Legislatures. National Conference of State Legislatures, Washington DC

Snell RK (2008) Pensions and Retirement Plan Enactments in 2008 State Legislatures. National Conference of State Legislatures, Washington DC

Snell RK (2009) Pensions and Retirement Plan Enactments in 2009 State Legislatures. National Conference of State Legislatures, Washington DC

Snell RK (2010) Pensions and Retirement Plan Enactments in 2010 State Legislatures. National Conference of State Legislatures, Washington DC

Snell RK (2012) Highlights of Pension Reform in 2012. National Conference of State Legislatures, Washington DC

Stigler GJ (1971) The theory of economic regulation. Bell J Econ Manag Sci 2(1):3–21

Wiedman CI, Goldberg DG (2002) Pension accounting: coming to light in a bear market. Ivey Business J 66:38–41

Wilshire Consulting (2012) 2012 Report on state retirement systems: Funding levels and asset allocation. Wilshire Associates Incorporated, Santa Monica

Chapter 8
Determining If a State Will Adopt a Renewable Portfolio Standard

Laura Lamontagne

Abstract Increasing concerns over climate change and volatile energy prices have led several state governments to consider legislation to mitigate these matters. At the state level, Renewable Portfolio Standards (RPS) have emerged as a popular tool to motivate the transition away from fossil fuels, reduce carbon emissions, and diversify electricity supply. This study examines the economic, social, and political factors that prompt a state to adopt a Renewable Portfolio Standard. A fifty-state panel data set over the years 1990–2010 was assembled from the United States Energy Information Administration, Bureau of Economic Analysis, the Database of State Incentives for Renewables and Efficiency (DSIRE), and state legislative data from Indiana State University. Using the data set complied for this study, I estimate a probit model to determine the probability a state will adopt an RPS in a year given its present political and economic climate. Results show that a deregulated electricity market, a high per-capita GDP, a strong democratic presence in the state legislature, high renewable capacity, and a strong incidence of natural gas are indicators a state will pass an RPS. Whether or not a state is a net importer or exporter of electricity is not a significant indicator of adoption of an RPS within a state.

8.1 Introduction

As worldwide concern over climate change and environmental degradation grows, the use of clean and renewable energy has become increasingly common. In the United States, public concern regarding the environment has helped persuade policymakers to implement various policies and regulations that promote the development of renewable technologies. These include cap and trade programs, where government limits the amount of pollution a firm may emit and any unused allowances may be traded on the market, a renewable energy production tax credit,

---

L. Lamontagne (✉)
Framingham State University, Framingham, MA, USA
e-mail: llamontagne@framingham.edu

© The Author(s), under exclusive license to Springer Nature Switzerland AG 2025
J. Hall, K. Starr (eds.), *Empirical Applications of the Median Voter Model*, Studies in Public Choice 45, https://doi.org/10.1007/978-3-031-87179-5_8

where renewable energy producers are given the motivation to produce renewables by means of a tax incentive, a simple Pigouvian taxes, where polluters are held responsible for the damages they impose on society and Renewable Portfolio Standards. A Renewable Portfolio Standard (RPS) is a form of legislation that requires an increased production of electricity generation to come from renewable energy sources. Currently 30 states and the District of Columbia have adopted RPS mandates.

The ultimate goal of an RPS is to motivate production of renewable energy as a means of promoting energy sustainability. At the state level, RPSs have grown increasing popular as a means of influencing the transition away from conventional fossil fuels to the growth of renewable energy. An RPS is initially proposed by a state legislature. It is designed to meet a state's goals based on current renewable capacities, resource endowments, political considerations, and growth potentials. Each state designs its mandate by specifying an absolute number of megawatt hours or by a percentage of overall electricity generation produce that must be produced from renewables by a targeted future date. To prove compliance a utility may generate its own renewable energy or purchase Renewable Energy Credits (RECs). An REC represents one megawatt hour of renewable energy. At the end of each year RECs are submitted to the state regulator in order to prove compliance with the RPS. In order to ensure compliance with the standard, an RPS will establish penalties for utilities that fail to meet its specified targets. These penalties are set above REC prices, thus creating the incentive to invest in renewables and comply with the standard rather than pay the penalty.

Renewable Portfolio Standards have been grown increasing popular throughout the global. National RPS policies have been passed throughout the majority of Europe, parts of South America, Japan and Australia and New Zealand. Upon entering office, President Barak Obama initially proposed a standard that would require 25% of the United States' electricity to be generated from renewables by the year 2025. As of June 2013, there has been no national RPS has been passed. Although there has been no adoption of a federal standard, RPSs have become increasing popular at the state level.

The emergence of RPS regulations at the state level is a relatively recent phenomenon. Of the 30 states with binding RPS mandates, 22 have implemented them after the year 2000. Additionally, eight other states have established renewable portfolio goals. States with renewable goals are Vermont, North Dakota, South Dakota, Virginia, Utah, Oklahoma, and Indiana. These goals are nonbinding, and thus utilities within the state do not face penalties for noncompliance. For purposes of this study, these states will be viewed as having no RPS because there is no incentive to comply with the RPS mandate.

This study examines the economic, social, and political factors that prompt a state to adopt a Renewable Portfolio Standard. A 50-state panel data set over the years 1990–2010 was assembled from the United States Energy Information Administration, Bureau of Economic Analysis, the Database of State Incentives for Renewables and Efficiency (DSIRE), and state legislative data from Indiana State University. Using the data set complied for this study, I estimate a logit and probit model to determine the probability a state will adopt an RPS in a year given the various covariates employed.

This chapter proceeds as follows. Section 2 provides a detailed background regarding RPS policies and provides a literature review while discussing the political economy of adoption of an RPS. Section 3 summarizes that panel data set that was constructed provides descriptive evidence regarding policy adoption and discusses the empirical model. Section 4 examines the empirical results. Lastly, section 5 concludes the study with a summary of principal findings.

8.2 RPS Background and Mechanics

8.2.1 Background on RPS Policies

In 1983, the state of Iowa approved the Alternative Energy Law, creating the very first Renewable Portfolio Standard in the United States. This law required Iowa's two investor-owned utilities to own or contract a total of 105 megawatts of renewable generating capacity and associated energy production (O'Hallearn 2009). However, it was not until the late 1990s that other states followed Iowa's lead. Massachusetts and Nevada enacted their own RPS policies in 1997, followed by Connecticut in 1998. From the turn of the millennium to 2009, 22 states passed RPS legislation. In total through 2010, 30 states and the District of Columbia have some form of RPS. Many of these policies were introduced in states as part of a general restructuring of electricity markets. However, an RPS was passed through voter-approved initiatives in both Colorado and Washington (Wiser and Barbose 2008; Wiser et al. 2007).

Table 8.1 summarizes those states that have adopted an RPS describing the initial year of adoption, size of the goal, and the targeted completion year. In addition states with a binding standard, seven states have nonbinding renewable portfolio goals. It is interesting to note the geographic distribution of states with an RPS. Every state in the Northeast currently has some sort of RPS save for Vermont (though Vermont does have voluntary renewable portfolio goals). In fact, of all states that have no renewable portfolio standards or goals, only four are located outside the southern United States.

The motives for adopting a Renewable Portfolio Standard vastly differ by state. One may simplify the motives into two schools of thought: the existence of a market failure and political motivations. First, an RPS may be used as a tool to mitigate climate change. If climate change is viewed as an externality, the market will not be able to correct for it without the creation of this legislation. An RPS is a means of stimulating the development of renewable energy. By investing in the development of hydro, wind and solar energy production of electricity shifts away from conventional fossil fuels and into clean, green energy that will in turn reduce the amount of greenhouse gasses in the atmosphere and help to mitigate climate

Table 8.1 States with renewable portfolio standards

State	Year initially passed	Compliance year	Standard
Arizona	2006	2025	15.00%
California	2002	2030	33.00%
Colorado	2004	2020	20.00%
Connecticut	1998	2020	23.00%
Delaware	2005	2025	25.00%
District of Columbia	2005	2020	20.00%
Hawaii	2004	2030	40.00%
Iowa	1983		105 MW per year
Illinois	2007	2025	25.00%
Kansas	2009	2020	20.00%
Massachusetts	1997	2020	15.00%
Maryland	2004	2022	20.00%
Maine	1999	2017	40.00%
Michigan	2008	2015	10.00%
Minnesota	2007	2025	25.00%
Missouri	2008	2021	15.00%
Montana	2005	2015	15.00%
North Carolina	2008	2021	12.50%
New Hampshire	2007	2025	23.80%
New Jersey	1999	2021	22.50%
New Mexico	2002	2020	20.00%
Nevada	1997	2025	25.00%
New York	2004	2015	29.00%
Ohio	2009	2025	25.00%
Oregon	2007	2025	25.00%
Pennsylvania	2004	2020	18.00%
Rhode Island	2004	2019	16.00%
Texas	1999	2015	5,880 MW
Washington	2006	2020	15.00%
Wisconsin	1999	2015	10.00%

change. Second is the political motivation involved in the adoption of a Renewable Portfolio Standard. Various political groups may lobby to pass an RPS for their own personal interests. For example, farmers may be in favor of an RPS if the legislation has specific provision for biomass as a source of renewable energy. If a utility could potentially capture federal subsidy money to build a wind farm, it would be in favor of an RPS or it may be as simple as an environmental group lobbying its state legislature. Whichever the reason may be, this study aims to measure which state characteristics are determining factors when an RPS is passed.

While all RPSs aim to increase the amount of electricity generated from renewable sources, the specifics of each standard differ from state to state. This is due to varying objectives, resource endowments, and political landscapes of states across the United States (Chen et al. 2008). Given the political landscape and existing infrastructure, each state defines an assorted list of eligible technologies. All 30 policies count biofuels, biomass, hydropower, solar power, and wind as renewable energy sources, while Ohio is the only state to consider nuclear power a renewable. Additionally, an RPS may require particular goals regarding a specific energy source. For example, Illinois has a target of 25 percent, 18.75% of which must come from wind power, while Nevada, New Mexico, Massachusetts, and New Jersey have specific solar carve outs that utilities must meet. In New Jersey, 4.1% of electricity must be generated by solar energy. North Carolina specifies that 0.2% should come from swine waste, while 900,000 MWH must be generated by poultry waste.

8.2.2 Mechanics of an RPS

An RPS functions by requiring retail electricity suppliers to procure a specific amount (minimum absolute number of megawatts or a percentage) of electricity sales from eligible renewable technologies by a specified date. For examples, under California's RPS utilities must provide a minimum of 33% from eligible renewable technologies by the year 2030, whereas Iowa must produce 105 MW per year from eligible renewable technologies. Additionally, many states have intermediate goals which must be met while attempting to comply with the standard.

In most states, an electric utility can demonstrate compliance with a state RPS in three ways. If the utility is still vertically integrated, it will simply generate its electricity from eligible renewable technologies. If the state has restructured electricity market, generation and distribution are independent. In this scenario, a generator will be issued one Renewable Energy Credit (REC) for each megawatt hour of electricity generated (Wiser and Barbose 2008). An REC is unbundled from the actual electricity generated and is sold as an independent commodity. While the electricity generated from renewables is sold on the grid, the REC is sold as strictly a financial product and exists as a way to supplement the revenue of renewable energy generators. The motivation of this structure is to provide an extra financial incentive to prompt investment in renewable energy. As a financial product, RECs trade on a spot market and can be bought and traded, borrowed, or stored for later years to give utilities flexibility in complying with current or future requirements. Most states allow utilities to purchase RECs to meet standards. Only New York, Hawaii, and Iowa disallow the use of RECs for meeting RPS standards.

RECs are purchased by the utilities by means of either long-term contract or on the spot market. At the end of each year utilities submit their RECS to the state regulator in order to prove compliance with the RPS. To ensure compliance with the standard, an RPS will establish penalties for utilities that fail to meet its specified targets. These penalties may be preestablished or may be left up to the discretion of the state depending on how far short the utility was in meeting its specified requirements. Penalties may also increase for repeat offenders. Typically, these penalties are set above REC prices, thus creating the incentive to invest in renewables and comply with the standard rather than pay the penalty.

8.2.3 Previous Literature

The rapid emergence of Renewable Portfolio Standards over the past decade has brought with it a wealth of new analyses focusing on political economy, cost benefit analyses, price impacts, etc. In a study similar to this one, Huang et al. (2007) explore the factors that influence a state's decision to adopt an RPS. Using a logistic model, they find that states with high Gross State Product (GSP), high growth rates and education levels, and Democratic Party dominance typically will have a higher probability of passing an RPS.

Similarly, Lyon and Yin (2010) conducted an empirical study to try and explain why a state might adopt an RPS. They find that concern surrounding the environment was generally not a motivating factor for states when deciding whether to implement an RPS. Instead, they find that the adoption of an RPS was more dependent on political ideology and renewable energy potential. Essentially, states that adopted regulations already had high levels of renewable potential, were not as reliant on natural gas, and were largely Democratic. Furthermore, they find that states with high unemployment rates are less likely to pass an RPS. This result is unexpected, as many legislators claim the expansion of the renewable energy sector will result in significant job creation.

Chen et al. (2008) conducted a survey of 31 state-level studies on the impact projections from RPS laws finding that, in general, adopting an RPS serves to diversify the state's energy supply and produces substantial environmental benefits. Additionally, the diversified energy supply helps control for potential supply shocks from unpredictable fuel prices. Jaccard (2004) summarizes the importance of RPS regulations for motivating the transition away from fossil fuels sooner rather than later emphasizing the reduction in greenhouse gases that would result from the increased use of renewable technologies.

However other studies point out that these benefits may come at a sizeable cost. The Energy Information Administration conducted studies in 2002 to analyze the impact of a national 10% RPS. Using a computer-based, energy-economic simulation model, they find that this RPS would raise consumer electricity prices by around 1.5%. If the national standard was set at 20%, prices could rise by up to 4% (U.S. Energy Information Administration (EIA) 2002). Palmer and Burtraw (2005) perform a similar simulation to the one done by the EIA. They find that a national RPS of 15% would increase prices by approximately 4%. However, in accordance with the EIA's findings, they find that electricity prices would rise significantly as the standard is raised above 15%. For an RPS of 20%, average electricity prices could increase by as much as 8% by 2020.

Michaels (2008) claims that the estimates made by the EIA are far too low. He reviews state RPS data and claims that, contrary to popular belief, these programs are disorganized and most are already out of compliance with their own goals. He points out how no cost analysis was done to try and find the optimal penalty payments for utilities failing to comply. Owing to this and other factors, he predicts that a national RPS "will at best be an inefficient policy, and at worst it will be outright pernicious." He enforces these claims by analyzing the computer simulation model used by the EIA. He maintains that the simulation was carried out with a fundamentally incorrect understanding of gas markets. While a national RPS may serve to diversify energy supply, Michaels is confident that it will also lead to significantly increased costs and inefficiencies for utilities.

Cooper (2008) contests Michaels' paper. He contends that Michaels' state analysis was intentionally misleading, using outdated and flawed data. Additionally, he suggests that the inefficiencies that do exist in the differing state RPS policies do not mean a national RPS would suffer the same fate. In fact, Cooper argues that a national RPS mandate would bring uniformity and predictability in the electricity market. This would help alleviate the regulatory uncertainty utilities currently face under inconsistent state RPS policies.

Fischer (2010) creates a theoretical model to examine whether it is possible that an RPS could actually lower electricity prices. She finds that the impact of an RPS on electricity prices is ambiguous, as it depends on the elasticities of supply for both conventional fossil fuels and renewable energy sources. According to her model, if the elasticity of supply for renewables is greater than that of conventional fossil fuels, an RPS will actually lower electricity prices. Conversely, if the supply of fossil fuels is more elastic than that of renewables, an RPS will result in rising electricity prices. She also finds that elasticity of demand will only serve to influence the magnitude of these price changes.

Tra (2016) conducted the first empirical estimation in analyzing the impact an RPS has on state electricity prices. Using panel data from 2,602 electric utilities in the United States from 1990 to 2006, he finds that an RPS will, on average, increase the price of electricity by approximately 3.8%. Furthermore, he finds that this price increase is higher for utilities that are subjected to higher renewable standards, but lower in states with high wind and solar energy potential.

8.3 Methodology

8.3.1 Data

The data set complied for this analysis is a cross-sectional panel that includes 50 states over the years 1990–2010. All data concerning electricity prices, generation, sales, the number of customers, and input prices were obtained from the United States Energy Information Administration. Data on retail sales, revenues, prices, and the number of customers in each sector were taken from the EIA's "Annual Electric Power Industry Report, EIA-861. Generation and composition of electricity supply data were taken from the EIA's Annual Electric Generator Report," EIA-860, and the EIA's "Power Plant Operations Report," EIA-923. All data regarding Renewable Portfolio Standards including the presence of the regulation, year an RPS were passed, stringency of the standard and target completion dates were gathered from the Database of State Incentives for Renewables and Efficiency (DSIRE). Finally, all data pertaining to population and income were obtained from the Bureau of Economic Analysis.

Iowa was the first state to adopt an RPS in 1983. For purposes of this study, Iowa has been dropped from the sample as it adopted its RPS prior to the sample period, and thus we are unable to measure the political and economic conditions under which its state legislature passed the standard.

Fifteen years after Iowa passed the first RPS, Nevada and Massachusetts followed suit passing their standards in 1997. By the end of the 1990s a total of seven states had adopted the legislation. In 2002 both California and New Mexico passed an RPS, while all remaining standards were adopted in 2005 and later. Figures 8.1 and 8.2 respectively illustrate the total number of states with an RPS and the number of states adopting an RPS in each year.

Summary statistics for the complete data set used in this study are described in Table 8.2. Table 8.3 further breaks down the data by states that have adopted an RPS during the sample period and those that have not. Across all observations a restructured electricity market is observed only 26% of the time. However, 70% of states that have passed an RPS also have a restructured market versus only 16% of non-RPS states. On average, RPS states have an $8,000 higher per-capita GDP than non-RPS states. Surprisingly, non-RPS states have a higher mean percentage of electricity generation coming from renewable resources than RPS states. Lastly, RPS states have a higher mean percentage of democrats in the state legislature at 59% than non-RPS states with a mean of 52%.

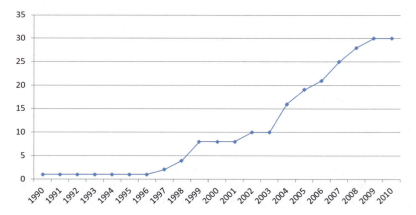

Fig. 8.1 Total numbers of states with an RPS

8 Determining If a State Will Adopt a Renewable Portfolio Standard

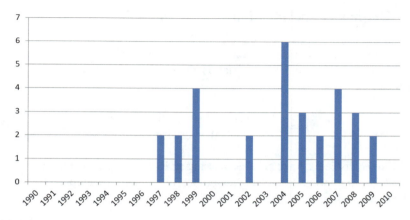

Fig. 8.2 Number of states adopting an RPS in each year

Table 8.2 Summary statistics

Variable	Obs	Mean	Std. dev.	Min	Max
Restructured market	1029	0.266	0.442	0	1
Per-capita GDP	1029	35,227	6185	21,224.92	58,737.12
Coal price	925	205.999	128.411	70.20	2030.49
Natural gas price	923	533.145	292.598	140.90	6123.31
% Generation from coal	1029	0.478	0.302	0	0.985602
% Generation from natural gas	1028	0.155	0.206	0	0.989443
% Generation from renewable	1029	0.140	0.214	0	0.982843
Democrats in state legislature	1008	0.533	0.167	0.086	0.971
Number of customers in the market	1029	2,582,587	2,622,260	236,622	1.48E+07
Net trade ratio	1029	1.144	0.536	0.16	3.75

Table 8.3 Summary statistics, RPS states, vs. non-RPS states

	RPS states			Non-RPS states		
	Obs	Mean	St. dev.	Obs	Mean	St. dev.
Restructured market	199	0.698	0.460	830	0.163	0.369
Per-capita GDP	199	41,903	5967	830	33,626	5067
Coal price	191	266.270	240.297	734	190.316	68.014
Natural gas price	177	672.543	199.253	746	500.070	301.434
% Generation from coal	199	0.346	0.256	830	0.509	0.304
% Generation from natural gas	199	0.259	0.232	829	0.130	0.191
% Generation from renewable	199	0.123	0.170	830	0.144	0.224
Democrats in state legislature	199	0.585	0.145	809	0.520	0.169
Number of customers in the market	199	3,636,163	3,493,723	830	2,329,982	2,298,087
Net trade ratio	199	0.995	0.286	830	1.180	0.575

8.4 Empirical Specification

In this estimation the decision to adopt a Renewable Portfolio Standard is modeled as a binary choice, adopt the legislation or not. It is denoted by the following specification:

$$y_{st} = \begin{cases} 1 \text{ if state s adopts an RPS in year } t \\ 0 \text{ otherwise} \end{cases} \quad (8.1)$$

Given the discrete choice between passing an RPS or not, a conditional probability model is appropriate to estimate the probability a state will adopt an RPS in year t. The model will take the form:

$$\Pr(y_{st} = 1 \mid X_{st}) = F(\alpha + \beta X_{st}) \quad (8.2)$$

where X_{st} is a vector of state-specific covariates and $F(.)$ is a specified cumulative distribution function. We estimate both the probit and logit models where the probit model follows a standard normal cumulative distribution function and assumes the form:

$$\text{Probit}\{P(t, X_{st})\} = \Phi^{-1}(X_{st}\beta) = \Phi\left(X'_{st}\beta\right) \quad (8.3)$$

while the logit follows a logistic CDF taking the form:

$$\text{Logit}\{P(t, X_{st})\} = \log\left(\frac{P(t, X_{st})}{1 - P(t, X_{st})}\right) \quad (8.4)$$

The decision to adopt an RPS will depend on a vector of covariates that are state specific, X_{st}. These include a dummy variable indicating whether or not a state has a restructured electricity market, per-capita GDP, percentage of electricity generation coming from coal, natural gas and renewable energy, the price of coal and natural gas, the total number of customers in each state market, and if the state is a net importer or exporter of electricity. The empirical specification to be estimated is denoted as follows:

$$RPS_{st} = \alpha + \beta_1 Restructure_{st} + \beta_2 GDP_{st} + \beta_3 Coal_{st} \quad (8.5)$$
$$+ \beta_4 NatGas_{st} + \beta_5 \%Renew_{st}$$
$$+ \beta_6 P\_Coal_{st} + \beta_7 P_{Nat}Gas_{st} + \beta_8 NumCustomers_{st}$$
$$+ \beta_9 NetTradeRatio_{st} + \varepsilon_{st}$$

The variable restructured electricity market is a dummy variable that is equal to one if a state has a restructured market in year t and zero otherwise. A restructured market should increase the probability of adopting an RPS as it allows for more flexibility to meet the requirement. A distributor can purchase electricity from a supplier it chooses as long as it also purchases the required number of RECs needed to comply with its RPS. Assuming clean renewable energy is a normal good, a higher per capita should increase the probability of adoption. A higher per-capita GDP should correlate to a higher willingness to pay for renewable technologies and thus increase the likelihood of adoption.

The price of coal and natural gas should have a positive impact on RPS adoption as should a high percentage of existing renewable capacity. As the prices of fossil fuels increase, it becomes more likely that states will want to motivate the transition away from fossil fuels to renewable technologies.

8.5 Results

The results from the probit model are presented in Table 8.4. Column 1 reports the results from a standard probit, while Column 2 presents the marginal effects, and standard errors are reported in the parentheses. These results are consistent with the hypothesized results. Recall that a restructured electricity market separates generation from distribution in the production and sale of electricity. Ultimately, it is the distributor that must prove compliance with the RPS by submitting Renewable Energy Credits (RECs) to the state regulator. The distributor may purchase electricity from any generator it desires so long as it also purchases the

Table 8.4 Probit results

	(1)	(2)
Restructured market	5.4483*** (1.0683)	0.2061*** (0.0371)
Per-capita GDP	0.0007*** (0.0001)	0.00002*** (3.05E–06)
Coal price	0.0384*** (0.0078)	0.0004** (0.0002)
Natural gas price	0.0004 (0.0004)	0.00007** (3.02E-5)
% Generation from coal	7.8457 (3.5318)	0.4672 (0.0962)
% Generation from natural gas	10.6883*** (3.4234)	0.5038*** (0.0970)
% Generation from renewable	9.8327** (4.1242)	0.4719*** (0.0996)
Democrats in state legislature	6.5831** (2.8124)	0.5104*** (0.1059)
Number of customers in the market	6.83E–07*** (2.36E–07)	2.37E–08*** (5.27E–09)
Net trade ratio	0.2227 (1.2182)	0.0222 (0.0273)
_cons	−51.8073*** (5.9522)	
obs	848	848
Log likelihood		−228.236
Pseudo R2		0.473

Dependent variable: Year in which a state adopts an RPS. Column 1 reports the results from a standard probit, while Column 2 presents the marginal effects, and standard errors are reported in the parentheses. *** significant at the 1% level, ** significant at the 5% level, * significant at the 10% level required number of RECs that are needed to conform to the RPS. This unbundling of electricity and RECs allows greater flexibility to meet the RPS at the lowest possible cost to the utility. Thus, having a restructured market increases the probability of adopting an RPS by an estimated 20.6%.

Increases in the price of coal and natural gas also increase the likelihood of RPS adoption, though by a minimal amount. As fossil fuel prices increase, renewable energy becomes more appealing. State legislatures may pass an RPS to motivate the transition away from fossil fuels to renewables. However, a one percent increase in the price of coal or natural gas results in a less than one percent increase in the probability of RPS adoption. Also having a minimal impact on RPS adoption is per-capita GDP. A one percent increase in GDP results in only a 0.002% increase in the probability of adopting an RPS. This is an unexpected result as forcing the transition to renewable energy distorts a utility's investment choice and thus increases electricity prices. Higher incomes are more likely to be willing to pay for renewable energy and thus more likely to adopt an RPS. However, results from this analysis show an increase in household incomes has a minimal impact in determining to adopt a Renewable Portfolio Standard.

The percentage of democrats in the state legislature was found to have the greatest impact on passing an RPS. A strong democratic presence in the state legislature will increase the chances of adopting an RPS by 51%. Also motivating adoption is a large existing percentage of electricity coming from renewable energy. A strong existing renewable infrastructure increases probability of adoption by 47%.

Proving to be insignificant in the adoption of an RPS is whether or not the state is a net importer or exporter of electricity. Although some RPSs impose in state generation requirements, not all states have this obligation. It is very simple to trade electricity across state lines. A utility may purchase RECs from generators in surrounding states to prove compliance with its state RPS mandate. Thus it does not matter is the state is a net import or exporter of electricity. One suspect result is the significance of the high percentage generation coming from natural gas impacting RPS adoption rates. These results may be impacted by the natural gas boom in the late 1990s to early 2000s and the development of fracking. During this time period the market moved away from coal to natural gas. Natural gas provides a "bigger bang for its buck" than coal fired generation, producing a third the carbon dioxide as coal. As the electricity generation from coal to natural gas was occurring during the same time frame as RPS adoption, the results estimated in this study may be influenced by the onset of natural gas.

Table 8.5 presents the results from the logistic estimation. Column 1 presents the estimated coefficients, while Column 2 lists the odds ratios. The results obtained from the logit model are consistent with those from the probit. Positively impact RPS adoption rates are a restructured electricity market, high per-capita GDP, high renewable potential, and a democratic state legislature. A state with a restructured electricity market is 5.6 times more likely to pass an RPS, comparable to the 20.6% produced by the probit. Playing a minimal role in likelihood of adoption are per-capita GDP, coal price, and total number of customers in the market. Each of these estimated ratios is slightly over 1, making them only slightly more prone to adopting

Table 8.5 Logit results

	Coeff.	Odds ratio
Restructured market	11.5304*** (2.9245)	5.5707
Per-capita GDP	0.0014*** (0.0002)	1.0003
Coal price	0.0817*** (0.0202)	1.0052
Natural gas price	0.0008 (0.0008)	1.0001
% Generation from coal	10.6969 (8.1982)	125.6782
% Generation from natural gas	20.4260** (8.0927)	176.2467
% Generation from renewable	19.0957** (9.1419)	141.9737
% Democrats in state legislature	11.2684* (6.0024)	322.8442
Number of customers in the market	1.57E–06*** (5.82E–07)	1.000
Net trade ratio	1.7435 (3.0361)	1.4487
_cons	104.1727*** (13.8762)	
Obs	848	848
Log likelihood		−229.7138
Pseudo R2		0.4696

Dependent variable: Year in which a state adopts an RPS. *** significant at the 1% level, ** significant at the 5% level, * significant at the 10% level

an RPS. Playing a major role in passing an RPS quickly are a democratic state legislator and a large existing renewable generation capacity.

8.6 Conclusion

As Renewable Portfolio Standards have grown increasingly popular over the past decade, it is interesting to observe which states are faster to adopt. To date, 29 states and Washington DC have passed an RPS, and there is discussion in Congress over a national Renewable Portfolio Standard. This study examines the economic, social, and political factors that prompt a state to adopt a Renewable Portfolio Standard. A 50-state panel data set over the years 1990–2010 was assembled from the United States Energy Information Administration, Bureau of Economic Analysis, the Database of State Incentives for Renewables and Efficiency (DSIRE), and state legislative data from Indiana State University.

Using the data set complied for this study, I estimate a probit model to determine critical factors to determine when a state will pass a Renewable Portfolio Standard. Results show that adoption of a mandate is more likely when a state has a restructured electricity market, a strong Democratic presence in the state legislature, high percentage of electricity generation already being produced by renewables, and a high per-capita GDP. The results obtained in this analysis are consistent with previous studies done by Lyon and Yin (2010) and Huang et al. (2007). This study builds on previous research by extending the time span for analysis and incorporating interstate electricity trade. This proves to be insignificant in adoption of an RPS. There are only a limited number of states that have an in-state generation requirement, while most states are able to purchase renewable energy credits from any generator they choose.

References

Chen C, Wiser R, Mills A, Bolinger M (2008) Weighing the costs and benefits of state renewables portfolio standards in the United States: a comparative analysis of state-level policy impact projections. Renew Sustain Energy Rev 13(3):552–566

Cooper C (2008) A national renewable portfolio standard: politically correct or just plain correct? Electr J 21(5):9–17

Fischer C (2010) Renewable portfolio standards: when do they lower energy prices? Energy J 31(1):101–120

Huang MY, Alavalapati JRR, Carter D, Langholtz MH (2007) Is the choice of renewable portfolio standards random? Energy Policy 35(11):5571–5575

Jaccard M (2004) Renewable portfolio standard. In: Cleveland C (ed) Encyclopedia of Energy. Elsevier, New York

Lyon TP, Yin H (2010) Why do states adopt renewable portfolio standards? Energy J 31(3):131–155

Michaels R (2008) A national renewable portfolio standard: politically correct, economically suspect. Electr J 21(3):9–28

O'Hallearn M (2009) The Iowa power fund: making Iowa the energy capital of the world. Drake J Agricult Law 14(1):221–244

Palmer K, Burtraw D (2005) Cost-effectiveness of renewable electricity policies. Energy Econ 27(6):873–894

Tra CI (2016) Have renewable portfolio standards raised electricity rates? evidence from us electric utilities. Contemp Econ Policy 34(1):184–189

US Energy Information Administration (EIA) (2002) Impacts of a 10-Percent Renewable Portfolio Standard. SR/OIAF/2002-03, Department of Energy, Washington, DC

Wiser R, Barbose G (2008) Renewable Portfolio Standards in the United States – A Status Report with Data Through 2007. Lawrence Berkeley National Laboratory, Berkeley

Wiser R, Namovicz C, Gielecki M, Smith R (2007) The experience with renewable portfolio standards in the United States. Electr J 20(4):8–20

Chapter 9
California Voters Reject the "Fair Pricing" for the Dialysis Act

Tuyen Pham, Shishir Shakya, and Alexandre Scarcioffolo

Abstract We examine the intricate interplay of incentives, political dynamics, and public policy outcomes that can lead to counterintuitive or inefficient results. Specifically, we examine the case of Proposition 8, a 2018 California ballot initiative that sought to require dialysis clinics to issue refunds if their revenue exceeded treatment costs by more than 115%. Through our analysis, we demonstrate how the concentrated benefits and diffuse costs inherent in this proposal resulted in policies that may not have been optimal for society as a whole.

9.1 Introduction

The public choice literature divides the electorate into two categories of voters: informed and uninformed. Voters who know the policy position of a candidate or a proposition are considered informed, while voters who do not know those positions and are influenced by campaign expenditures are considered uninformed (Baron 1994). In this chapter, we contribute to the discussion about uninformed voters by examining whether largely heterogeneous funded campaigns impact voting outcomes considering the 2018 California Preposition 8 in limiting dialysis clinics' revenue.

Pro-profit dialysis clinics in the USA have a reputation for elevated treatment costs and low-quality treatment (Thompson 2021). In November of 2018, the Service Employees International Union–United Healthcare Workers SEIU-UHW

T. Pham (✉)
Ohio University, Athens, OH, USA
e-mail: tuyen.pham@ohio.edu

S. Shakya
Appalachian State University, Boone, NC, USA
e-mail: shakyas@appstate.edu

A. Scarcioffolo
Denison University, Granville, OH, USA
e-mail: scarcioffoloa@denison.edu

sponsored the ballot campaign for Proposition 8, which aimed to limit dialysis clinics' revenue and protect patients from poor-quality care. The proposition required that private and for-profit dialysis clinics refund to patients or patients' payers revenue above 115% of the costs of direct patient care and healthcare improvements. Supporters of this proposition argued that the law would force clinics to improve the quality of their healthcare by encouraging additional spending on direct patient care and investments in new equipment and technology.

In the face of having a cap on profits, dialysis companies spent heavily on advertising relative to support groups. They argued that the proposed law would put clinics at risk of closing and, thus, reduce access to healthcare for all patients with severe kidney diseases. Dialysis companies contributed nearly six times more than supporters of the proposition. Ultimately, the voting outcome favored dialysis companies, with an overturn of 59.93% of votes to reject the proposition. In this case, we assume informed voters are people who understand the real benefits of having the new law passed and uninformed voters are people who are easily persuaded by the dialysis giants' heavily funded campaigns and advertisement, who already made high profit margins. The event of a largely heterogeneous funding campaign for California Proposition 8 in 2018 presents a unique opportunity to test the hypothesis that counties with DaVita and FMC clinics, the two dialysis giants, were less likely to support Proposition 8 because uninformed voters in these counties may have been exposed to more advertising against the proposition.

According to Strömberg (2001), advertising (via mass media) can influence voting through at least three channels. First, politicians can convey their promises and beliefs to a forward-looking electorate. Second, advertising can inform voters about politicians' actions that are not directly observable. Third, the media may influence policy by influencing the weight voters put on different issues. In the case of Proposition 8, the third channel may have been most significant since supporters and opponents were able to communicate possible outcomes of approving or rejecting the proposition; hence, it largely impacted uninformed voters. As suggested by Roberts (1992), the media might not only tell voters what to think about but also influence what actions they take based on those thoughts.

Since the media can influence how voters vote, it is crucial to understand the impact of funded campaigns in shaping voting outcomes. Yet, the empirical literature on the impact of advertising on voting finds conflicting results. The classic study by Lazarsfeld et al. (1944) suggests that advertising via mass media has only a small effect on voter behavior. Similarly, Berelson et al. (1986) conclude that radio and printed newspapers have a relative weak direct impact on voting outcomes. More recently, Coppock et al. (2020) find that political advertising in the 2016 US presidential election campaign had a small effect on voting. Additionally, Motta and Fowler (2016) find that advertising's impact on voting outcomes is conditional on the characteristics of the messages being aired and the voters who view them. In contrast, Ferraz and Finan (2008) suggest that mass media such as radio impact voting outcome. The authors analyze the impact of random audits of federally transferred funds in Brazil, finding that municipalities that the local radio presented the information had larger effect on the reelection rates of corrupt legislators.

Additionally, Chiang and Knight (2011) suggest that voters' decisions are shaped by information disseminated by campaigns, but that the degree of influence depends on the direction of bias. Therefore, mass media might have a larger impact on voting behavior when campaigns reveal important and unexpected information (Strömberg 2015).

In this study, we contribute to the literature on voting behavior in response to advertising. We use the case study of the rejected proposition on putting a cap on dialysis clinics' profit in California to show that the media and advertising can influence voters' weighting of an issue and persuade them to vote against their own economic interests. Our findings highlight the importance of advertising on voting outcomes, as counties with the presence of DaVita clinics were 5% less likely to support Proposition 8, while the presence of FMC clinics in a county does not significantly explain voting behavior.

We proceed as follows. The second section explores rationale behind the California Preposition 8. The third section sheds light on the conceptual framework. The data is described in Sect. 9.4. The fifth section presents the empirical results. Finally, the sixth section concludes.

9.2 California Proposition 8: Limits on Dialysis Clinics' Revenue and Required Refund Initiative

Chronic kidney disease (CKD) is an under-recognized public health problem. It affects more than 37 million people in the United States and is the ninth leading cause of death in the country (National Kidney Foundation 2018). If left untreated, CKD can evolve into end-stage renal disease (ESRD). At this stage, patients' kidneys are not capable of removing the body's liquid such as salt and wastes, so they need either a kidney transplant or dialysis. While transplants might enable a better and longer life, in 2017 less than 20% of ESRD patients received a kidney transplant, making dialysis[1] a crucial treatment for those in need (National Kidney Foundation 2018).

ESRD patients need to have dialysis their whole lives, and the treatment is expensive. According to United States Renal Data System's (USRDS) annual report in 2018, the yearly average cost of dialysis ranges from $76,177 to $90,971 per person (USRDS 2018). As of 2018, over 700,000 Americans were being treated for kidney failure, including those who received kidney transplants (Sullivan and Stern 2018). Medicare covers most of the cost of dialysis. In 2018, it spent $35.4 billion

---

[1] There are two types of dialysis: hemodialysis and peritoneal dialysis. The length of each treatment depends on circumstances such as how much waste is in patients' bodies and how big they are. On average, treatments last 4 hours and occur three times per week (National Kidney Foundation 2018). According to the National Kidney Foundation (2018), the average life expectancy on dialysis is 5–30 years depending on patients' condition and how well they follow the treatment.

on fee-for-service expenditures on patients with ESRD, which accounts for over 7% of all Medicare expenditures (USRDS 2018). In California, the estimated average cost of a dialysis treatment is $250 per person with Medicare and $1,000 or more per person with commercial insurance providers (Firozi 2018).

Even though the cost of the life-saving treatment is high and for-profit dialysis companies make billions of dollars in profit, its quality is usually poor. According to data released by the Centers for Medicare and Medicaid Services in 2019, the national average rating of dialysis centers' care quality is 3.9 out of 5, while the California rating (3.67) is below national average. Additionally, for-profit clinics appear to perform worse than nonprofit clinics. Zhang et al. (2010) find that dialysis clinics with a large chain status independently associated with higher mortality rate after controlling for sociodemographic risk factors, patient disease severity, comorbid conditions, and facility characteristics. According to Zhang et al. (2010)'s results, patients at for-profit facilities also had 13% higher mortality compared to patients at nonprofit facilities.

In the face of the high-cost and low-quality treatment, in November 2018 California put Proposition 8 on the ballot. The Limits on Dialysis Clinics' Revenue and Required Refunds Initiative. The measure had three key provisions: (1) limiting dialysis clinics' profits to 15% and refunding profits above the limit to patients or patients' payers, (2) requiring clinics to submit an annual report to the state government, and (3) prohibiting clinics from refusing to treat patients based on the source of payment. In general, the bill was intended to protect patients from poor-quality care and being overcharged by private dialysis clinics.

Supporters argued that Proposition 8 would improve the quality of dialysis by forcing private dialysis clinics to dedicate a higher percentage of their revenues to patient care and healthcare improvement including training, specialists' wages, medical supplies, maintenance, equipment, new technology, and patient education and consulting. Since nine out of ten Americans with kidney failure have Medicare, which pays 80% of the treatment's cost, the proposed law would lower the cost burden on Medicare. According to American Kidney Fund (2022), patients with kidney failure in the USA without Medicare or Medicaid are covered by private insurance through employers or Affordable Care Act health insurance marketplace. Supporters also argue that by putting a cap on clinics' revenue, it would reduce excessive charges to private insurance companies, thus lowering premiums for all Californians. Opponents, including dialysis providers and their employees, argued that Proposition 8 would put dialysis clinics at risk of closing and thus reduce patient access to the treatment and put the lives of ESRD patients at risk.

Though the purpose of the proposition was to protect dialysis patients from poor-quality service and to protect their payers from being overcharged by private dialysis clinics, the measure was defeated. According to California's secretary of state, 59.93% of votes reject the proposition. The committees in support of and opposition to Proposition 8 together raised more than $130 million, making the ballot measure the most expensive of the year. More than $111 million was raised by the opposition, with more than 88% of that figure coming from two dialysis companies: DaVita (59%) and Fresenius Medical Care North America (FMC) (29%). Together the companies operate more than 67% of all clinics in the state, with 316 operated by DaVita and 132 by FMC. Every year, these private clinics make billions of dollars in pretax profit, with a profit margin between 18 and 19% (Hiltzik 2018).

9.3 Conceptual Framework

If Proposition 8 had been enacted, there would be two main potential benefits to consumers. The first potential benefit is improvement in quality of care. If clinics had wanted to keep a bigger portion of their revenue, they would have had to invest more money in direct patient care, which leads to better sanitation, better hygiene, and a lower infection rate. The second potential benefit is that service payers could avoid excessive charges from private clinics. We argue that since the cost of dialysis treatments is mainly paid by Medicare, Medi-Cal, and private insurance companies, the first benefit would have directly affected individual voters, while the lower costs would have benefited payers more than patients in most cases.

While $19 million was contributed to the supporting committees during the campaign, more than $111 million was contributed to the opposition committees, mainly from large dialysis providers.[2] The two dialysis giants, DaVita and FMC, who together run nearly 67% of all dialysis clinics in California, contributed more than $101 million. Of that $101 million, more than $67 million came from DaVita, and the other $34 million came from FMC. During the campaign, the pair put out ads arguing that if the proposition was passed by voters, clinics would be at risk of closing. Therefore, when making their voting decision, voters were confronted with the resulting cost of reduced access to lifesaving treatments.

When voters choose between two alternatives, they weigh the costs and benefits to themselves. If the benefit of passing Proposition 8 is bigger than the cost, voters will be more likely to vote yes; otherwise, they will vote no. Voters weigh improved health care against the cost of losing access to the treatment.

$$B_i = prob_{having\_ESRD} \times b$$
$$C_i = (prob_{reducing\_access} \times c \times prob_{having\_ESRD})$$
$$U_i = B_i - C_i = U_i(prob_{having\_ESRD}, prob_{reducing\_access})$$

Let b be each ESRD patient's direct benefit (the improvement in patient care) if Proposition 8 is passed. Voter i's benefit is B_i. The benefit is determined by an individual's susceptibility to ESRD. When the probability of getting ESRD is higher, the benefit of Proposition 8 is higher.

Let c be each ESRD patient's direct cost (the reduction in access to care) if Proposition 8 is passed. Voter i's cost from the passage of Proposition 8 is C_i. The cost to the voter increases with the odds of getting ESRD and the probability of clinic closures.

---

[2] According to Ballotpedia.org, "California Proposition 8."

Assume the costs and benefits for all ESRD patients are the same, which means b and c are constant.

Let U_i be voter i's utility, which is the benefit minus the cost. Since b and c are constant, U_i is a function of the probability of having ESRD and the probability of clinic closures. The factors that impact these probabilities also impact voters' utility and hence the voting outcome.

During the campaign for Proposition 8, FMC and DaVita spent over $100 million on advertising the message that the proposition would put their clinics at risk of closing. We argue that the existence of FMC and DaVita clinics in a county increases people's access to campaign advertising by these companies and hence increases voters' expected cost of losing access to treatment. Therefore, the existence of FMC or DaVita clinics in a county is expected to reduce the number of yes votes.

Since the probability of getting ESRD increases voters' cost and benefits alike, we do not know whether the net effect of that variable is negative or positive. However, since dialysis is a lifesaving treatment, losing access to care seriously harms patients' health. We argue that the cost c is much bigger than the benefit b. Therefore, the net effect is expected to be negative. This hypothesis can be tested in our empirical approach.

9.4 Data

We use three different data sets. The first is voting outcome data from California's Secretary of State (California Secretary of State 2018). The data set reports the numbers of voters, the number of yes votes, and the number of no votes by county.

The second data set is Dialysis Facilities in the United States (The Centers for Medicare & Medicaid Services 2018). It provides a list of all dialysis clinics in California that registered with Medicare and includes the facilities' names, addresses, chain organization, and services provided. From these data, we calculate the number of clinics in each county, whether FMC clinics or DaVita clinics are in operation in that county, and the number of FMC clinics and DaVita clinics.

The third data set is California's 2018 County Health Rankings report (Givens et al. 2018). The data provides counties' demographic and economic characteristics. The data also reports different health outcomes by county.

After merging the three data sets by county, we get the final data for analysis. The final data shows that there is at least one DaVita clinic in 60% of all counties in California. FMC clinics are present in 30% of all Californian counties. On average, there are five DaVita clinics and two FMC clinics in each county. Table 9.1 shows the descriptive statistics from the final data. On average, there are 11.4 dialysis clinics located in each county in California, and the majority of them are for profit clinics (Table 9.1). DaVita and FMC are the state's largest for profit dialysis chains. DaVita clinics appear in 60% of all Californian counties with the average of 5.4 clinics per county. FMC clinics appear in 30% of all Californian counties with the average of 2.3 clinics per county (Table 9.1).

9 California Voters Reject the "Fair Pricing" for the Dialysis Act

Table 9.1 Descriptive statistics

Statistic	Mean	St. Dev.	Min	Max
Yes	0.4	0.1	0.3	0.6
No	0.6	0.1	0.4	0.7
DaVita	0.6	0.5	0	1
FMC	0.3	0.5	0	1
Household_Income ($)	60,930.10	18,000.90	38,727	110,843
% under 18	22.2	4.2	14	31
% over 65	17	5.1	9.7	28.8
% Black	3	3	0.1	13.8
% Native	3.1	3.3	0.8	22
% Asian	7.7	8.6	0.6	36.5
% Hispanic	30.4	18	7.3	83.8
% White	54.5	19.8	11.1	85.4
% Non-English	6.9	4.9	1	21
% female	49.5	2.1	37.7	51.7
% rural	28.7	28.9	0	100
% diabetes	8.7	1.1	7	11
% obesity	24.2	3.6	18	33
# of facilities	11.4	25.9	0	184
# of stations	228.5	572.8	0	4,129
# of DaVita clinics	5.4	11.3	0	77
# of FMC clinics	2.3	5.6	0	33
# of for profit clinics	10	24.3	0	175
# of not for profit clinics	1.5	2.6	0	14

Numbers of observations $N = 58$

9.5 Empirical Approaches and Findings

In our first empirical approach, we use simple OLS to test the theoretical model. Our dependent variable is the percentage of yes votes in each county. Our independent variables are the factors that affect a county's kidney disease incidence and the probability of a CKD clinic closure.

Since DaVita and FMC spent millions of dollars on advertising the message that they would close their clinics if they were no longer profitable, the presence and number of clinics run by these two big chains in each county might cause voters in these counties (relative to those in counties with no FMC or DaVita clinics) to think that the probability of clinic closure is much higher. Hence, our independent variables include dummy variables that indicate whether there are any DaVita or FMC clinics in a county and the number of clinics run by these two chains. We include the numbers of dialysis clinics and dialysis stations in each county in our models because they might also affect voting behavior.

We do not have county data on the incidence of CKD. However, since people with obesity and diabetes are more likely to develop kidney diseases than others are, we use counties' incidence of obesity and diabetes as indicators for prevalence of kidney diseases. On average, the prevalence to obesity and diabetes in California in 2018 was 24.2% and 8.7%, respectively. We also control for other economic and demographic characteristics such as household income and the racial composition of each county.

The primary results for this OLS approach are reported in Table 9.2. Column 1 reports results from model 1, which includes dummy variables for the existence of DaVita and FMC clinics and also includes the total number of clinics and dialysis stations in each county. Model 2, reported in column 2, includes the numbers of DaVita and FMC clinics in each county. Column 3 shows results for model 3, which includes counties' incidence of obesity and diabetes. Lastly, in column 4, we include controls for the percentage of the population with a high school or college degree (or both) and for the number of clinics per 1,00,000 people. All four models control for demographic characteristics and economic characteristics such as county-level education attainment, mean household income, and racial composition. We find that the presence of DaVita clinics in a county predicts 5% fewer yes votes. The presence of FMC clinics in a county does not affect the voting outcome. The findings are consistent with our conceptual framework. If DaVita clinics are present in a county, voters in that county fear that they will lose access to their care if DaVita closes their clinics when Proposition 8 is passed. In model 3, we also find that a 1% increase in the incidence of obesity in a county decreases the number of yes votes by 0.6%. This supports our hypothesis that ESRD incidence has a net negative effect. However, when controlling for education in model 4, this small negative effect from incidence of obesity becomes insignificant. This suggests a correlation between a county's level of education attainment and its incidence to obesity.

Next as a robustness check, we implement the double-selection post-Lasso method selecting the optimal set of controls from data while avoiding "over-fitting" the models.[3]

---

[3] The LASSO estimator introduced by Tibshirani (1996) simultaneously performs variable selection and coefficient estimation. In its simplest form, LASSO is a basic ordinary least squares (OLS) regression where coefficients are chosen to minimize the sum of the squared residuals and include a penalty term. The penalty term restricts the model's size, in terms of the number of included covariates, through the sum of absolute values of the coefficients (Belloni et al. 2014). Intuitively, the LASSO estimator drops variables whose coefficients are closer to zero and selects the remaining variables as covariates in the model. Belloni et al. (2014) caution against interpreting the model parameters obtained from the LASSO estimator as causal evidence of treatment effects. Instead, Belloni et al. (2014) propose a three-step method for using the LASSO estimator for causal inference. The first step is to apply LASSO to select a set of control variables by regressing the dependent variable on the treatment variable and the set of possible control variables. The second step is to apply LASSO by regressing the treatment variable (in our case, MA-PDMP) on the same set of potential control variables. If the treatment variable is truly exogenous, then no variables would be selected to be included in the model; however, this is not likely the case. This is the double selection approach. The third step is to reestimate the model by regressing the dependent

9 California Voters Reject the "Fair Pricing" for the Dialysis Act

Table 9.2 OLS estimation

	Percentage of voting in favor			
	(1)	(2)	(3)	(4)
DaVita	−5.45**	−5.08**	−4.82**	−5.43**
	(2.15)	(2.31)	(2.28)	(2.68)
FMC	1.88	3.31	3.24	2.25
	(1.94)	(2.23)	(2.23)	(2.21)
# of all facilities	0.39	0.51	0.56	0.71
	(0.67)	(0.73)	(0.71)	(0.75)
# of all stations	−0.02	−0.02	−0.02	−0.02
	(0.03)	(0.03)	(0.03)	(0.03)
# of DaVita clinics		−0.21	−0.12	−0.16
		(0.41)	(0.41)	(0.41)
# of FMC clinics		−0.16	−0.41	−0.45
		(0.35)	(0.36)	(0.36)
% High school degree				−0.03
				(0.06)
% College degree				0.17
				(0.18)
# of facilities per 100,000 population				−0.58
				(1.04)
% Obese			−0.60*	−0.46
			(0.36)	(0.37)
% Diabetes			−0.98	−0.67
			(0.95)	(1.01)
% Not proficiency in English	1.41***	1.40***	1.2**	1.20**
	(0.48)	(0.49)	(0.49)	(0.51)
% Rural	−0.11**	−1.0*	−0.07	−0.13*
	(0.05)	(0.05)	(0.06)	(0.07)
Observations	58	58	58	58
R-squared	0.58	0.58	0.62	0.64
Adjusted R-squared	0.47	0.45	0.48	0.46
F statistic	5.21	4.33	4.26	3.5

Note; $^*p < 0.1$; $^{**}p < 0.05$; $^{***}p < 0.01$

Table 9.3 exhibits the primary results with six different model specifications. The dependent variable is the county-level percentage of the votes in favor of Proposition 8. Each model reports standard errors with HAC correction. Columns (1) and (2) present generic Lasso selection. Columns (3) and (4) show estimates from Lasso but imposing restricting on DaVita's presence as the variable of interest. Columns (5)

---

variable on the treatment variable and the union of the variables selected by LASSO in the first and second steps with heteroskedasticity robust standard errors.

Table 9.3 Double-selection post-LASSO, DaVita as variable of interest

	Percentage of voting in favor					
	(1)	(2)	(3)	(4)	(5)	(6)
DaVita			−3.764*	−3.299*	−5.614**	−5.467**
			(1.894)	(1.752)	(2.228)	(2.368)
Household income	−0.252		1.938			
	(4.980)		(4.973)			
% Asian	0.289**		0.374***		0.334***	
	(0.127)		(0.131)		(0.118)	
% Rural					−0.063	
					(0.040)	
% Adult obese	−0.742**		−0.561*		−0.654***	1.072
	(0.292)		(0.299)		(0.226)	(0.667)
% Asian × % Excess drinking		0.018***		0.020***		
		(0.004)		(0.006)		
% Adult obese × % High school degree		−0.006***		−0.005***		
		(0.002)		(0.002)		
Constant	55.605	47.227***	28.853	28.250	55.659***	43.672***
	(58.718)	(3.315)	(58.741)	(20.976)	(6.228)	(7.763)
Observations	58	58	58	58	58	58
Variables	L1	L2	L1	L2	L1	L2
R^2	0.337	0.428	0.383	0.468	0.410	0.560
Adjusted R^2	0.300	0.407	0.336	0.427	0.353	0.430
F statistic	9.145***	20.596***	8.220***	11.640***	7.214***	4.303***

Note; *$p < 0.1$; **$p < 0.05$; ***$p < 0.01$. L1 represents a set of the original 19 variables in which the LASSO is performed. L2 comprises 209 variables which includes the original variables in L1, their quadratic terms, and all the feasible interactions. Estimates presented in columns (1) and (2) are unconstrained Post LASSO performed using L1 and L2 variable sets, respectively. Estimates presented in (3) and (4) are constrained Post-LASSO (always contains DaVita) performed using L1 and L2 variable sets, respectively. Estimates presented in column (5) and column (6) are Double-Selection Post-LASSO performed using L1 and L2 variable sets

and (6) show estimates implementing double-selection post-Lasso, where DaVita's presence is the independent variable of interest.

Column (1) selects variables implementing generic Lasso from a 19-variable dictionary. The estimates show that counties with higher shares of Asian are more likely to vote in favor of Proposition 8.

Column (2) selects variables implementing generic Lasso from a 209-variable dictionary. This dictionary variable comprises 19 contemporaneous variables, their squared polynomials (19 more variables), and all the first-level interactions (19*18/2 = 171). Column (2) shows that counties with more Asian people and higher percentage of people with excess drinking behaviors are more likely to vote in favor, while counties with higher obesity rate and higher percentage of population with high school degrees are less likely to vote in favor of the proposition.

The estimates in columns (1) and (2) are explanatory only and cannot test the channel for affecting voting behavior. We hypothesize that DaVita's presence in a county explains voting behavior. Since we want to capture the effect of DaVita's presence in a county on voting behavior, we then always restrict DaVita as the variable of interest, columns (3) and (4). In the robustness checks, we argue that this seemingly obvious procedure produces biases in the estimate.

Columns (3) and (4) show that DaVita's presence in a county predicts about 3.76 and 3.3% fewer votes in favor of Proposition 8, respectively. Columns (3) and (4) select variables from 19- and 209-variable-selection dictionaries. The results from columns (3) and (4) also show that counties with higher prevalence to obesity are less likely to vote "Yes."

Columns (5) and (6) select variables based on the double-selection post-Lasso from 19- and 209-variable-selection dictionaries. The variable selections are identical to each other. The results from double-selection post-Lasso show that DaVita's presence in a county predicts about 5.46–5.61% fewer yes votes.

Table 9.4 exhibits the primary results with four different model specifications. The dependent variable is the county-level percentage of the population that voted in favor of Proposition 8. Each model reports standard errors with HAC correction. Columns (1) and (2) present generic Lasso selection with FMC's presence as the variable of interest. Columns (3) and (4) show estimates implementing double-selection post-Lasso, where FMC's presence is the independent variable of interest. Table 9.4 shows that the presence of FMC clinics in a county does not affect its voting behavior.

9.6 Conclusion

The results from our two methods are consistent with each other. They show that the presence of DaVita clinics in a county predicts 5% fewer yes votes on Proposition 8. They support the conceptual framework that the presence of DaVita clinics raises voters' risk of losing access to dialysis treatment. Since Proposition 8 was meant to reduce the price of dialysis treatments, which are paid by Medicare, and the benefit of having better treatments is much lower than the cost of losing access to care, voters in counties with DaVita clinics tended to vote to reject the cap on dialysis clinics' revenues. Using the case study of Proposition 8 in California in 2018, we contribute to the literature that campaigns and advertisement can influence voters' behavior.

Table 9.4 Double-selection post-LASSO, FMC as variable of interest

	Percentage of voting in favor			
	(1)	(2)	(3)	(4)
FMC	−0.800	2.762	0.478	−1.922
	(2.398)	(2.087)	(4.252)	(5.192)
Household income	−1.959			
	(4.642)			
% Under 18	−1.284***			
	(0.333)			
% African American	0.258			
	(0.291)			
% Native	1.089***			
	(0.308)			
% Asian	0.051		0.265*	
	(0.132)		(0.143)	
% Non-English	0.744***			
	(0.225)			
% Rural	−0.120*		−0.024	
	(0.062)		(0.051)	
% Diabetes	−0.206			
	(0.753)			
% Adult obese	−0.026		−0.428	
	(0.326)		(0.315)	
High school rate	−0.001			
	(0.058)			
% College	0.207*		0.163	
	(0.123)		(0.125)	
% Uninsured			1.557	
			(1.042)	
Constant	71.561	35.036***	29.761**	51.235***
	(54.410)	(1.797)	(14.654)	(6.650)
Observations	58	58	58	58
Variables	L1	L2	L1	L2
R^2	0.655	0.030	0.384	0.457
Adjusted R^2	0.562	0.013	0.297	0.297
F statistic	7.107***	1.751	4.444***	2.852***

Note: *$p < 0.1$; **$p < 0.05$; ***$p < 0.01$. L1 represents a set of the original 19 variables in which the LASSO is performed. L2 comprises 209 variables which includes the original variables in L1, their quadratic terms, and all the feasible interactions. Estimates presented in (3) and (4) are constrained Post-LASSO (always contains FMC) performed using L1 and L2 variable sets, respectively. Estimates presented in column (5) and column (6) are Double-Selection Post-LASSO performed using L1 and L2 variable sets

References

American Kidney Fund (2022) What are the main types of health insurance? American Kidney Fund, Rockville
Baron DP (1994) Electoral competition with informed and uniformed voters. Am Polit Sci Rev 88:33–47
Belloni A, Chernozhukov V, Hansen C (2014) High-dimensional methods and inference on structural and treatment effects. J Econ Perspect 28(2):29–50
Berelson BR, Lazarsfeld PF, McPhee WN (1986) Voting: A Study of Opinion Formation in a Presidential Campaign. University of Chicago Press, Chicago
California Secretary of State (2018) General Election – Statement of Vote, November 6, 2018. California Secretary of State, Sacramento
Chiang CF, Knight B (2011) Media bias and influence: Evidence from newspaper endorsements. Rev Econ Stud 78(3):795–820
Coppock A, Hill SJ, Vavreck L (2020) The small effects of political advertising are small regardless of context, message, sender, or receiver: Evidence from 59 real-time randomized experiments. Sci Adv 6(36):eabc4046
Ferraz C, Finan F (2008) Exposing corrupt politicians: The effects of Brazil's publicly released audits on electoral outcomes. Q J Econ 123(2):703–745
Firozi P (2018) The health 202: The dialysis industry spent more than $100 million to beat a California ballot measure. Washington Post 12 November
Givens M, Gennuso K, Jovaag A, Van Dijk JW (2018) County Health Rankings & Roadmaps 2018. University of Wisconsin Population Health Institute, Madison
Hiltzik M (2018) Dialysis firms' profits are obscene: What will happen if California tries to cap them?
Lazarsfeld PF, Berelson B, Gaudet H (1944) The People's Choice. Duell, Sloan & Pearce, New York
Motta MP, Fowler EF (2016) The content and effect of political advertising in US campaigns. In: Thompson WR (ed) Oxford Research Encyclopedia of Politics. Oxford University Press, Oxford
National Kidney Foundation (2018) National Kidney Foundation. National Kidney Foundation, Pittsburgh
Roberts MS (1992) Predicting voting behavior via the agenda-setting tradition. J. Quarterly 69(4):878–892
Strömberg D (2001) Mass media and public policy. Eur Econ Rev 45(4–6):652–663
Strömberg D (2015) Media and politics. Ann Rev Econ 7(1):173–205
Sullivan JD, Stern L (2018) The state of kidney failure in the United States in 2018. Urol Nephrol 5(1):1–2
The Centers for Medicare & Medicaid Services (2018) Dialysis Facility - Listing by Facility. The Centers for Medicare & Medicaid Services, Baltimore
Thompson D (2021) Medicare's penalties for poor-quality dialysis centers aren't helping: Study. US News & World Report 9 June
Tibshirani R (1996) Regression selection and shrinkage via the lasso. J R Stat Soc Ser B 58(1):267–288
USRDS (2018) United States Renal Data System. Bethesda
Zhang Y, Cotter DJ, Thamer M (2010) The effect of dialysis chains on mortality among patients receiving hemodialysis. Health Serv Res 46(3):747–767

Printed in the United States
by Baker & Taylor Publisher Services